What a Girl Wants?

Fantasizing the reclamation of
self in postfeminism

Diane Negra

Routledge
Taylor & Francis Group

LONDON AND NEW YORK

First published 2009
by Routledge
2 Park Square, Milton Park, Abingdon, Oxon, OX14 4RN

Simultaneously published in the USA and Canada
by Routledge
270 Madison Ave, New York, NY 10016

Transferred to Digital Printing 2010

Routledge is an imprint of the Taylor & Francis Group, an informa business

© 2009 Diane Negra

Typeset in Galliard by
The Running Head Limited, Cambridge, www.therunninghead.com
Printed and bound in Great Britain by
TJI Digital, Padstow, Cornwall

British Library Cataloguing in Publication Data
A catalogue record for this book is available from the British Library

Library of Congress Cataloging in Publication Data
Negra, Diane, 1966–
    What a girl wants: fantasizing the reclamation of self in postfeminism/
Diane Negra.
       p.   cm.
    1. Feminist theory.   2. Popular culture.   3. Sex role.   4. Mass
media and women.   I. Title.
    HQ1190.N44 2008
    305.4201—dc22

                                                                2008010043

ISBN10: 0–415–45227–9 (hbk)
ISBN10: 0–415–45228–7 (pbk)

ISBN13: 978–0–415–45227–4 (hbk)
ISBN13: 978–0–415–45228–1 (pbk)

Contents

Figures

Acknowledgments

I deeply appreciate the hospitality that was extended to me at Brown University in 2005–2006 and I'd like to thank Ellen Rooney, Lynne Joyrich, Carolyn Dean, Phil Rosen, Liza Hebert, and Susan McNeil in the Department of Modern Culture and Media, as well as Keith Brown and Michael Steinberg in the Cogut Center for the Humanities, and Liz Barbosa in the Pembroke Center for Scholarship on Women. I would also like to acknowledge the gracious assistance of the staff (particularly Bart Hollingsworth) of Brown's John D. Rockefeller Library and of the Providence Public Library in various research endeavors related to this book.

I was a most grateful recipient of assistance from the Stanley Frank Fund at Brown which enabled me to purchase materials and present a conference paper based on research in this book, and would like to thank Kaelyn McGregor in the Office of the Vice President for Research in this regard. The University of East Anglia and the Arts and Humanities Research Council provided me with the opportunity for a sabbatical which was crucial to the completion of this book and I would be highly remiss if I did not acknowledge the generous support of both.

I am grateful to those who extended invitations for me to present this research as I developed it, including Susan Pearce and the Department of Sociology at West Virginia University, Philip Drake and Andy Miah at the University of Paisley, Vicki Mayer and the Department of Communications at Tulane University, Georgina Born at Cambridge University, Mel Kohlke at the University of Wales at Swansea, Ginette Vincendeau and Richard Dyer at King's College, London, Jennifer Smyth at the University of Warwick, Estella Tinknell and Michelle Henning in the School of Cultural Studies at the University of the West of England, Vicki Mahaffey and Erica Sheen in the Modern School at the University of York, Stephanie Rains at the National University of Ireland, Maynooth, Claire Thomson at University College London, and the organizers of the Second Global Conference on Issues of Sex and Sexuality held in 2005 in Vienna.

Yvonne Tasker is an exemplary colleague and our work together on a conference, an academic collection, and a book series has informed this project in myriad ways. Many others gave me advice, feedback, and the general benefit of their thoughtful views on material in this book or topics related to it including Martha Nochimson, Cindy Lucia, Antje Ascheid, Su Holmes, Suzanne Leonard, Christine Negra, Deborah Pelton, Mandy Merck, Vicki Callahan, Sean Griffin, Sadie Wearing, Hannah Hamad, Lawrence Napper, Sarah Churchwell, Brenda Weber and Ken Wissoker, and Courtney Berger at Duke University Press. I am fortunate as well to work at a university with a group of PhD students whose energetic enthusiasm and commitment to their work enriches my experiences as a teacher.

Rowena Burgess and Sarah Burbidge in the University of East Anglia Research Office are always of great help in preparing research grant applications, two of which supported the research and writing of this book. Julia Crook, Mary Waters, John Pullinger and Shaun Brown in the Faculty of Humanities assisted me with illustrations and text-reformatting. Shelley Cobb was a most helpful research assistant at an early stage of the work on this book and continued to bring pertinent news articles to my attention long after the end of her contract. Natalie Foster and Charlotte Wood at Routledge have been strong proponents of this book and helpful guides during the production process. Carole Drummond has been an expert facilitator of the process at The Running Head Limited.

I thank Stanka Luna at CBS Television and Chiara McGee at the Hallmark Channel in London for their help in locating particular episodes of *Judging Amy*. I also want to acknowledge the help I received from Karla Kirby at Stick Figure Productions, Nick James at E Television, David Rowley at Corbis, Jennifer DeGuzman at MTV Networks, and Luke Fontneau in Warner Bros. Publicity.

Portions of this book were previously published as follows: some sections of Chapter 2 appeared in "Quality Postfeminism?: Sex and the Single Girl on HBO" in *Genders* 39 (2004); some of the concluding material from Chapter 3 appeared in "Eroticism and the Postfeminist Melancholic," in *The Sexual Politics of Desire and Belonging: Interdisciplinary Readings on Sex and Sexuality* edited by Alejandro Cervantes-Carson and Nick Rumens, and published by Rodopi in 2007; a very small amount of material from Chapter 1 appeared in a piece of commentary I wrote on postfeminism and university culture for *The Times Higher Education Supplement* which was published on December 7, 2007. The concept of postfeminist "miswanting" used in Chapter 4 is elaborated further in "Structural Integrity, Historical Reversion and the Post-9/11 Chick Flick," published in the journal *Feminist Media Studies* 8(1) (March 2008).

Chapter 1

Introduction

While individual popular press articles are imperfect indices of the complexities and contradictions of a broad and diverse culture, they can be important and resonant snapshots of the state of play on key issues such as gender and class. In this context, I want to reference two headline pieces published in late 2006 as I worked on this book. These articles appeared in two of the top three most well-read American daily newspapers: *USA Today* and *The New York Times* (and in the case of the latter on the front page on Christmas Eve). The first reported on the growing number of American Christian women (of various denominations) choosing to cover their hair and don "modest dress." In "Traditional Living Takes Modern Spin," Elizabeth Weise noted that the Internet had been adopted by many such women to shop for conservative clothing and head coverings and to affiliate with like-minded women via discussion groups. Weise observes in passing that most of her interview subjects for the piece sought the permission of their husbands before talking to her.

The second article, "Scant Progress on Closing Gap in Women's Pay," summarizes a recent set of economic data and opens with a startling observation about gender-based income equity regression:

> Throughout the 1980s and early 1990s, women of all economic levels—poor, middle class and rich—were steadily gaining ground on their male counterparts in the work force. By the mid-1990s, women earned more than 75 cents for every dollar in hourly pay that men did, up from 65 cents just 15 years earlier.
>
> Largely without notice, however, one big group of women has stopped making progress: those with a four-year college degree. The gap between their pay and the pay of male college graduates has actually widened slightly since the mid-1990s.[1]

Holding these two articles in mind as anchor points for some of the pleasures and problems currently associated with contemporary American middle-class femininity, I want to underscore the necessity of probing the links between media representation and social behavior and start to build the case that any significant engagement with the popular culture landscape of the last 15 years requires wrestling with the concept of postfeminism.

What a Girl Wants? is about a popular culture that has just about forgotten feminism despite constant, generally negative invocations of (often anonymous) feminists. To the extent that she is visible at all, the contemporary feminist appears as a narcissistic minority group member whose interests and actions threaten the family and a social consensus that underwrites powerful romanticizations of American "community."[2] By caricaturing, distorting, and (often willfully) misunderstanding the political and social goals of feminism, postfeminism trades on a notion of feminism as rigid, serious, anti-sex and romance, difficult and extremist. In contrast, postfeminism offers the pleasure and comfort of (re)claiming an identity uncomplicated by gender politics, postmodernism, or institutional critique. This widely-applied and highly contradictory term performs as if it is commonsensical and presents itself as pleasingly moderated in contrast to a "shrill" feminism. Crucially, postfeminism often functions as a means of registering and superficially resolving the persistence of "choice" dilemmas for American women. From the late 1990s renaissance in female-centered television series to the prolific pipeline of Hollywood "chick flicks," to the heightened emphasis on celebrity consumerism, and the emergence of a new wave of female advice gurus/lifestyle icons, the popular culture landscape has seldom been as dominated as it is today by fantasies and fears about women's "life choices."

Emblematic of the kinds of stories about women's lives that currently predominate in popular culture was the controversial case of Elizabeth Vargas, the first woman to anchor an American evening newscast since Connie Chung. Vargas, who in fact initially shared the role as anchor of ABC's *World News Tonight* with Bob Woodruff, found herself a solo anchor when Woodruff was seriously injured covering the war in Iraq. In May 2006 Vargas suddenly resigned from her post, citing the demands of the job and their impact on her family and in particular her pregnancy. "For now, for this year, I need to be a good mother," Vargas was quoted in a *Washington Post* article exploring the reasons for her departure and its significance for public views of women in the workforce.[3] However, a number of commentators (including National Organization of Women President Kim Gandy) expressed skepticism about Vargas' account, deeming it a face-saving "cover story" for the reality that Vargas had lost out in a power play by Charles Gibson, the longtime ABC journalist who reportedly said he would quit the network if he was not named sole and permanent anchor. Such commentators questioned the timing of Vargas' decision, observing that her personal circumstances had not previously kept her from taking on high-profile and demanding journalistic roles, and questioning why it appeared automatically to be necessary to rethink Vargas' role once she held a sole rather than shared position. Whatever the truth of the story, what is indisputable is that ABC and Vargas subsequently sought to use public interest in her case as a selling point for Vargas' relaunch as a co-anchor of the magazine pro-

Figure 1.1 In 2006 the professional and personal situation of ABC News anchor, Elizabeth Vargas, was framed as an exemplary postfeminist narrative.

gram *20/20* in which she appeared as the focus of a segment ostensibly exploring the difficulties of the "work/life balance" for women.

Among other things, this book seeks to move the issues so often posed in the simplistic terms of a feminized "work/life balance" dilemma toward fuller scrutiny, and much of the analysis here considers the distorted renditions of choice that permeate postfeminist fiction. By pinpointing the pervasiveness of postfeminist shibboleths about life, work, marriage, and motherhood, I hope to identify the kinds of identities and experiences that are withheld from post-feminist display practices and to argue for a more capacious view of women's lives, interests, and talents than is generally fostered by the current culture. One of the signature features of postfeminist culture is the way in which it extends and elaborates "backlash" rhetoric, producing discursive formulations that would often seem resistant to feminist critique. Nevertheless, I hope to show that feminist tools of analysis are effective in reading postfeminist texts, thereby countering the postfeminist presumption that feminism is dated, irrelevant, and inapplicable to current culture.

It is important to acknowledge that the analyses undertaken here are in no way exhaustive and the chapters that follow are offered in some respects as "soundings" of a postfeminist culture. What I do not do in this book is provide an account of the ways in which individual consumers negotiate the content of postfeminist representations (as many surely do) nor do I investigate the potential "open spaces" that may be available in some postfeminist texts to facilitate spec-tatorial negotiation. The reason for this is that I believe that the overwhelming ideological impact that is made by an accumulation of postfeminist cultural mat-erial is the reinforcement of conservative norms as the ultimate "best choices" in women's lives. In media studies scholarship irony and self-reflexivity are conven-tionally attributed with the power to neutralize conservative ideological represen-tations, but the political efficacy of postfeminism may necessitate reconsideration of such precepts. Recognizing the polysemic nature of all texts, I would empha-size that the readings here follow a particular path that reflects a feminist ana-lytical commitment. I do not believe that postfeminism inevitably or exclusively correlates to the re-energizing of patriarchal agendas and standards of value. However, while I fully acknowledge that there are many kinds of postfeminism (as Sarah Projansky among others has argued) some kinds are more predominant, perhaps especially in a culture in which critical literacy is so devalued.[4] While post-feminism may be politically ambidextrous in some contexts, the majority of its fictions seem to operate in support of a larger political trend toward the undoing of US democracy and the suppression of the kind of vibrant, full, and questing subjectivities that a healthy democracy both fosters and draws upon.

Postfeminism attaches considerable importance to the formulation of an expressive personal lifestyle and the ability to select the right commodities to attain it. In this book I seek to challenge cultural bromides that reinforce the importance and value of consumerist notions of taste, glamour, and serenity and to analyze the nature of a platitudinous postfeminist culture that continually cel-ebrates reductions and essentialisms as explanatory keys for women's psychologi-cal and social health. As I will show, postfeminism fetishizes female power and desire while consistently placing these within firm limits. One of the ways I will pinpoint this dynamic is by drawing upon the work of commentators like Ariel Levy who have shown how the female sexual desire which seems so unbounded and expressive everywhere in the popular culture landscape, often operates merely in mimicry of sexist codes of exploitation.[5] Postfeminism withdraws from the contemplation of structural inequities fostered by feminism, putting forward diagnostics of femininity that take the place of analyses of political or economic culture. It achieves this, in part, by relentlessly stressing matrimonial and maternalist models of female subjectivity.

Any attempt to precisely pinpoint the onset of a postfeminist era will lead to a receding historical horizon. As Lois W. Banner has observed, "Women have consistently protested against their situation, and this rebellion has led contemporaries in every decade since the 1920s to proclaim that women have attained equality and that feminist goals have been achieved."[6] If feminist interventions have long tended to be declared successful *and* unnecessary on arrival, it is nevertheless the case that popular culture in the 1990s and 2000s has been particularly dominated by postfeminist themes and debates. This book holds up a mirror (inevitably one with a somewhat refracted view) to the contemporary female subject who finds herself the recurrent target of advertisers, centralized in commodity culture to a largely unprecedented degree at a time when Hollywood romantic comedies, chick-lit, and female-centered primetime TV dramas compete for her attention and spending power. Across the range of the female lifecycle, girls and women of every age are now invited to celebrate their empowerment in a culture that sometimes seems dedicated to gratifying their every desire. This book asks why, at a moment of widespread and intense hype about the spectrum of female options, choices, and pleasures available, so few women actually seem to find cause for celebration. Why does this period feel so punishing and anxious for so many?

One of the ways in which I explain the omnipresence of postfeminist identity paradigms in the current popular culture environment is by emphasizing how such paradigms frame the search for self with an attendant assumption that feminism has disturbed contemporary female subjectivity. Over and over again the postfeminist subject is represented as having lost herself but then (re)achieving stability through romance, de-aging, a makeover, by giving up paid work, or by "coming home." (Indeed, one of postfeminism's master narratives is that of "retreatism," which operates as a powerful device for shepherding women out of the public sphere.) Popular culture insistently asserts that if women can productively manage home, time, work, and their commodity choices, they will be rewarded with a more authentic, intact, and achieved self. Such postfeminist responses to identity crisis respond specifically to the conditions of degradation of the American self fostered by "New Economy" market fundamentalism, state-supported (and sometimes state-sponsored) assaults on the environment, intense anti-immigration rhetoric in a nation that still celebrates itself as a global beacon of hope for the downtrodden, the withering role of state care for the vulnerable, and various perversions of democracy that have flourished in recent years and that take shape (among other ways) in a strategic confusion between wars fought for economic interest and those fought for democracy, justice, or human rights.

As I will show, postfeminism retracts the egalitarian principles of feminism (even if those principles were in some ways faulty or if their egalitarianism was never quite complete), taking hold as an ideological system in a period in which democratic equity may be seen to have curdled into entitlism. At different points in this book I suggest that the ideological precepts of postfeminism mesh well with a system of political and economic extremism and that postfeminism significantly emerges in the context of powerful antidemocratic tendencies and at a time when "inequality rose in a period of increasing prosperity, with the added riches going much more to the haves than to the have-nots."[7] The United States entered the twenty-first century with the sweeping into office of a president who more or less openly championed the interests of the wealthy. Recent research shows that economic mobility (the signal feature of the American Dream) has been arrested in a number of demographic categories and the rich now enjoy strikingly disproportionate benefits of health care, lifespan longevity, and access to education in comparison to the general population.[8]

Bearing in mind, then, the increasingly open celebration of wealth and privilege in America, much of the discussion in this book is framed against a social backdrop that stresses the primacy of a personal aesthetic system and an elaborated relationship to family and home even as the economic and social pressures on family life intensify for the great majority of Americans. A significant concern is with the continuities and discontinuities between representation and lived reality and in my analyses I seek to balance my readings of fictional texts with sociological and economic data. For instance in Chapter 4, I examine the "enchantment effect" of so many contemporary romantic comedies which suggest a heroine will be unlocked/relieved from her current state (often as a working woman). But I also document the proliferation of other forms of cultural representation that have highlighted the figure of the working woman, and then move to examine how and why such images acquire cultural traction. In considering how certain female job roles have become overrepresented and fetishized even as postfeminist culture exhibits a persistent distrust of the "working woman," particularly if she is an executive, I am less concerned with producing a totalizing account than with mapping the paradoxes which so often emerge in postfeminist culture.

Postfeminism both informs and is informed by a cultural climate strongly marked by the political empowerment of fundamentalist Christianity and regnant paradigms of commercialized family values.[9] Notably, it has flourished in a period of American history in which, as Henry A. Giroux has argued, "The corporate state unabashedly began to replace the last vestiges of the democratic state as the central principles of a market fundamentalism were applied with a vengeance to every aspect of society."[10] In postfeminist representations some of the most crucial institutions of democratic culture are understood to have entered a kind of twilight and there is often an implicit engagement with the prospect of long-term downward mobility for the middle class. In various ways postfeminism stifles mobility, favoring constraint and the acquiescence to normative models of identity even while hyping aspirational consumerism. In popular film, plot devices for staging this entail the encoding of discovery, adventure, and a staunch commitment to "choice" in forms such as the resignation from work (as in *Kate & Leopold*, 2001), the discovery of an aristocratic family background that automatically confers wealth and privilege on an "average" young woman or girl (as in *The Princess Diaries*, 2001), or the formula of the ready-made family which leads a "career woman" to discover that her truest vocation is stay-at-home parenting (as in *Raising Helen*, 2004). Ideologically central to the contemporary chick flick is the concept of "destiny" which recurs in innumerable recent romances. Asserting a need for order in the face of an apparently random reality and a general desire to evade ambiguities related to identity and intimacy, the films consistently "discover" that actually fate has it all worked out. With "destiny" operating as an organizing principle and themes of true love and the propitious/serendipitous meeting predominating, a number of films have gone so far as to suggest that the ideal romantic partner in adulthood is a childhood playmate grown up (*Bridget Jones' Diary* [2001], *Sweet Home Alabama* [2002], *13 Going on 30* [2004]). Even a film such as *Serendipity* (2001), which would initially appear to be the rule-proving exception in the genre when it abruptly separates its protagonist couple after an early meeting in which both feel they are meant for each other, ultimately offers a sham refutation of the destiny principle only to reconfirm it. In television, reality series such as *Wife Swap* (ABC) stage artificial and heavily contrived forays across class lines while reinforcing the notion that women inevitably operate to secure domesticity and stability. Just as each episode of a series like this closes with the restoration of women back in their proper place, many of the forms of popular culture I analyze in this book (and particularly in Chapter 2) engage the postfeminist promise of coming back to oneself in a process of coming home.

Through the study of representation this book seeks to pin down and examine a widespread set of feelings in American life. While it emphasizes the abundant fantasies of evasion, escape, and retreat that circulate in current American popular culture it tries to do so in a spirit of awareness for why such fantasies would be attractive now. As Johanna Brenner has noted, "It is not only the pressures of everyday survival but the barrenness of politics that pushes women to seek solutions in a perfected personal life."[11] In a similar vein, Imelda Whelehan has speculated that "It may be the case that some women embrace the opportunity to feel 'needed' as an antidote to the alienating effects of the workplace."[12] The goal of this book is not to trade one set of caricatures for another; rather, the analysis is attentive to the ways postfeminism "works on" some of the most intractable problems in American life, noting that women's choices and behaviors are often presented as crucial to the resolution of such problems and that the choices postfeminism urges upon women are usually traditional ones.

Accordingly, this book is structured to address the interaction of postfeminism with other cultural problem spots such as work, time, home, and commodity culture. It analyzes postfeminism's disingenuous modes of response to some of the most resonant questions in contemporary American life, questions that include:

- Where can we feel at home?
- How can we respond to the seemingly ever more time-pressured conditions of daily life?
- Where/how do we find rewarding forms of work?
- How do we (re)establish the dominion of self in a hyper-commodified culture?

What a Girl Wants? surveys the mass-mediated social landscape of roughly the last 15 years, arguing that during this time postfeminist concepts/definitions of women's interests, desires, pleasures, and lifecycles became thoroughly pervasive and ideologically normative. Analyzing the ways postfeminism conceptualizes home, work, time, and the commodity landscape, this book examines the role of media in corroborating/fostering emergent shifts in social norms and behaviors. In particular it tries to illuminate a contemporary paradox in which the interests and pleasures of female consumers are simultaneously commercially privileged and pejoratively conceptualized.[13]

Originally this book took shape as a study of the various incarnations of the chick flick and it is still to some degree shaped around that objective. One of my goals here is to counter the idea (still surprisingly widespread in film studies) that such films offer pure entertainment sessions that have no cultural agenda. The chick flick is the major (some might say the only) contemporary film genre consistently (if often unsatisfactorily) dedicating itself to the exploration of romantic intimacy. Like Catherine L. Preston I believe that "there are periods in history in which the social environment 'favors' the production of romance films," and I look to come to grips with some of the social conditions facilitating the fantasies showcased by romance narratives in the 1990s and 2000s.[14] In previously published work I have argued that the 1990s chick flick was well positioned to articulate poor and declining female social health.[15] I still believe this to be the case and find it valuable to investigate how complicated questions of work and sexuality are so often "wished away" by the contemporary chick flick. The romantic comedy that has flourished since the 1990s has shown itself to be extraordinarily adept in pigeonholing the perceived truths of women's experiences in a "lifestyle" culture. Although the dilemmas it so precisely renders are typically occluded in the films' resolutions, in the 1990s and 2000s chick flicks spoke from and to a neoconservative cultural context that (among other things) prioritized "housewife chic," the spectacle of an affluent wedding, the allure of luxury commodities, and achievement of a sumptuous domesticity, the disappointments of the world of paid work, and the rewards of motherhood while identifying the spectre of singlehood as a fate to be avoided at all cost. The enhancement of the aberrant, frequently abject status of single women by postfeminism is a subject I explore in more detail in Chapter 3, arguing that the contemporary chick flick depends heavily on the presumptive failure and emotional disconnection of such women (given that only those emotions that bind women to children and romantic partners are deemed valid ones).

At times my analysis will be directed toward films that probably don't meet the conventional definition of a chick flick but that do illustrate how chick flicks interface with other generic forms such as the suspense thriller and the male-oriented sex comedy. On the whole, though, this book has significantly broadened its view beyond chick flick forms. Because postfeminism is such a comprehensive discursive system, my analysis ranges from films to music videos, from "breaking news" coverage on CNN to civic and corporate websites. Accordingly, this book also incorporates analysis of postfeminist commentators and tastemakers such as Martha Stewart, Nigella Lawson, and Caitlin Flanagan and a range of female media celebrities as well as popular critics of postfeminist culture including Maureen Dowd, Ariel Levy, and Judith Warner. The book is set up to investigate postfeminist lifestyle politics more broadly and, in Chapter 5, I address the current high profile of the expensively maintained female body, the turn toward conspicuous consumption of elite beauty products, and the routinization of cosmetic surgery and implants.

In a synergistic media environment, analysis of a single medium holds less explanatory power for any account that seeks to explain the complex relations between social life and media representation. Therefore, this book seeks out contemporaneous developments in film, television, print culture, and journalism. It does not compartmentalize media forms but rather takes a wholistic view— the compartmentalization that is still reflexive in some parts of the discipline of media studies would particularly ill serve this project. The necessity for this sort of composite approach stems from my belief that a potent combination of cinematic, televisual, journalistic, and other discourses cumulatively articulate the character and content of female experience and I wanted to adopt a perspective that approximates as closely as possible the synergistic experience of media consumers. Isolating one medium or form may make for organizational tidiness but it conceals the way in which these forms currently comprise in effect an "echo chamber" of repetition and reinforcement. This book works off the principle of intermediality and is therefore always keen to explore adjacent cultural forms rather than a single form in isolation.[16]

Another goal of this book is to analyze postfeminism's role in the naturalization of class warfare in America since the vast majority of postfeminist texts (and by texts I refer to popular cultural material including films, television programs, advertisements, and popular music) present the habits, interests, and desires of the wealthy as universal. The options, opportunities, and rewards experienced by women in postfeminist media are consistently those that accrue to an elite minority in possession of considerable educational, social, and financial capital. Accordingly, postfeminist conceits such as "retreatism" (the pull back by affluent women to a perfected domesticity) take distinct shape as class and race fantasies. In this book I explore the compatibility of postfeminism with the emergence of "winner take all" markets, and by implication invite readers to consider those women who are all the more marginalized when a narrow percentage of the population is presented as the only constituency that matters.[17] Postfeminist culture has endowed some white female demographic groups with greater visibility but it has tended to reinforce racist and classist exclusions.[18] (Marginalization, it should be noted, does not always take the form of representational neglect. As I have suggested above for example, postfeminism might be seen as particularly punishing in its relation to single women, having raised their cultural profile though without any corresponding enlargement of their status/options.) In each of the chapters, attention is paid to the "lesser" femininities positioned outside of postfeminist categories of value.

Postfeminism entails an aggressive (re)codification of female types. In gestures that often tout the "freedom" from political correctness, postfeminist culture revives the "truths" about femininity that circulated in earlier eras—women are bitches, golddiggers, "dumb blondes," spinsters, shrews, and sluts. The postfeminist twist here is that women are to apply these characterizations to others and sometimes to themselves in a display of their political and rhetorical "freedom." Frequently the application of such terms correlates with a sense of glee about "getting one over" on censorious feminists, but of course most feminists never maintained that there weren't individuals to whom such terms might apply, they just objected to these being the default categories into which women were sorted. In this way, we can begin to see how reliant postfeminist culture is on the "imaginary feminist."

A glimpse of the mainstream acceptability of a renewed typological mindset as well as some of the ways that postfeminism gives cover to a set of divisive and oppressive social and economic conditions is provided in a pivotal incident in the last season of the television series *Sex and the City* (HBO). This incident starkly illustrates the limits of putative postfeminist female empowerment and autonomy. While often cited as an example of the kind of female-oriented lifestyle fiction that has flourished over the last 15 years in a variety of media forms, the much-celebrated/much-debated *Sex and the City* nevertheless came to closure in a strikingly ideologically conservative fashion with the safe settlement of its four ensemble members into commitment and motherhood. In order to highlight the dangers of a life lived counter to the postfeminist script, the series employed a guest character/cautionary figure named Lexi Fetherston (Kristen Johnston) in the bluntly titled episode "Splat" (broadcast February 8, 2004). In this key episode broadcast close to the series' conclusion, Carrie (Sarah Jessica Parker) is weighing her decision about moving to Paris with her boyfriend Aleksandr Petrovsky (Mikhail Baryshnikov) when the two attend a party together thrown by *Vogue* editor Enid Mead (Candice Bergen) at her high-rise apartment. This sequence will prove formative to Carrie's decision-making and to her sense of self, as a brutal drama of female obsolescence unfolds. Enid is obviously interested in Petrovsky and chides Carrie for dating a man who is Enid's age and thereby "swimming in my pool." Meanwhile an unattractive (but

Figure 1.2 Postfeminist age anxiety is invoked to advertise a wide variety of goods and services targeted at female consumers. (Catherine Zeta-Jones "Girl vs. Woman" advertisement for Elizabeth Arden)

age-appropriate) man whom Carrie has brought for Enid to meet is rejected by her as "a hobbit." Also at the party is Lexi, a 40-year-old cocaine-sniffing anachronism, a "legendary party girl" who has wangled an invitation to an event where she clearly doesn't fit in. When Lexi tells Carrie that they are "the only two single girls here," Carrie tells her "well, actually I'm with someone." Opening a window for a smoke against her host's wishes and disrupting the party, Lexi delivers a diatribe about how New York isn't fun anymore, then suddenly trips over her Manolo Blahniks and topples out the window to her death. In voiceover Carrie observes dryly that "it was the first time Lexi had ever left a party early." In effect this episode stages two cautionary tales for Carrie: the spectre of the aging 50-something who finds men her own age dating women of Carrie's and the obsolescent 40-year-old "single girl" who is brutally dispatched by the series as a function of her socially expendable status. Needless to say, after this sequence, Carrie resolves to go with Aleksandr to Paris.

Postfeminism thrives on anxiety about aging and redistributes this anxiety among a variety of generational clusters while also always extending the promise/possibility of age evasion. The distaste accorded to any evidence of aging femininity has left midlife women under intensified pressure to preserve the appearance of youth even as too transparent efforts to do so may leave them open to critical allegations of age-passing, of in essence, attempting to appear as "mutton dressed as lamb" (another byproduct of postfeminist culture is that it makes demeaning formulations like this acceptable again to large numbers of social constituencies).

Such contradictions are often resolved in postfeminist media through an appeal to banal concepts of power and fantasies of age transcendence (as in the Catherine Zeta-Jones cosmetics ad in which the Hollywood star is posited as both proactive and purposeful ["enjoying a good fight"] in attempting to retain the perpetual girlhood that is frequently now presented as being available to women in a range of age cohorts). In Chapter 3, I examine in more detail the zealous timekeeping functions of postfeminist popular culture, but for the moment I'd like to emphasize the significance of the ways that postfeminism codifies and essentializes femininity, relentlessly insisting that all women are bound together by a common set of innate desires, fears, and concerns. By asserting this untruth as not only true but commonsensically true, the culture industries have mimicked the broader habits of a right-wing political culture, recycling and reflecting a gambit that has proved remarkably effective at suppressing dissent. (After all, only contrarians and iconoclasts can disagree with common sense.) As I have suggested above, postfeminism concentrates a great deal of representational attention on home, time, work, and consumer culture and tends to produce narratives and images that represent female anxiety and fantasize female empowerment in these realms. The title of this book is meant to call to mind not only postfeminism's strong connections to an affective economy that reinforces a set of "feeling rules" around gender; it is also meant to gesture in the direction of its revisions of the female lifecycle.

At a time when so many films depict female childhood as a space of epic fantasy (*Pan's Labyrinth* [2006], *The Golden Compass* [2007], the *Harry Potter* franchise [2001, 2002, 2004, 2005, 2007]), such portrayals would seem to contrast more and more forcibly with the ideologically uncertain terrain of female adulthood. Recent popular culture is equally preoccupied it seems with womanly girls and girlish women, and Hollywood hits like *13 Going on 30* (2004) and *Enchanted* (2007) with their confusion of girlhood and womanhood can thus be seen as quintessentially postfeminist. In the former film a gawky adolescent

Figure 1.3 Postfeminist media represent female adulthood as a vacillating state of pleasure and panic. (Jennifer Garner in *13 Going on 30*, 2004)

girl who wishes to be an adult finds herself transformed through "magic dust" into an instant adulthood whereupon her experience of disenchantment with the glamorous urban life she'd envisioned, the industry she is a part of and, in particular, her female co-workers make her long to return to childhood. In the latter, a blend of animation and live action that critics alternately read as sardonic and fervent, a hyperfeminine fairy tale princess is transported from the magical land of Andalasia to present-day New York. Among the various functions she serves, Princess Giselle appears to provide a role model for Morgan, the young daughter of Robert, a wealthy single father who at the start of the film seeks to inspire the six-year-old by buying her a book about great women in history. The girl's disinterest is plain and is implicitly matched with Robert's diligent but contrived attempts to elicit enthusiasm for women like Rosa Parks and Marie Curie. When the father ruefully acknowledges that Curie died of radium poisoning, this small detail resonates in a film obsessed with happily-ever-after prospects and management of the kind of disenchantment with achieving female adulthoods showcased in *13 Going on 30*. Morgan is equally indifferent to Nancy, Robert's long-term girlfriend, who her father will later tell her "is a lot like the women in your book." The "real world" Nancy, suspicious, overscheduled, and utterly typical of the "burdened" female professionals of contemporary romance, contrasts forcibly with Giselle whose restorative, refreshing ingenuousness enlivens everyone she meets including the large crowd of strangers who join her in an exuberant musical number in Central Park. When the book about "great women" is set aside as Robert and Morgan have their first encounter with Giselle, the film emphasizes the viability of princesshood as an alternative to the troubled terms of "real world" female achievement. In its title, *Enchanted* names the effect contemporary romances strive to achieve for their audiences, and the terms of this "enchantment effect" are decidedly ideologically evasive. This is fully in keeping with the ways that postfeminism often seems to be fundamentally uncomfortable with female adulthood itself, casting all women as girls to some extent. This book sets out to explore the implications of this, the strong and decisive role that postfeminism plays in organizing the working, domestic, and intimate lives of women in contemporary culture, and the deep uncertainty postfeminism implies about what it really means to live as an adult woman in early twenty-first-century America.

Chapter 2

Postfeminism, family values, and the social fantasy of the hometown

This chapter argues that a number of recent romantic comedies and female-centered dramas are working to manage a pervasive cultural contradiction in which claims of feminist victories need to be squared with abundant evidence of feminism's losses. A highly serviceable narrative scenario used to reconcile this contradiction is that of the professional, urban woman who returns to her hometown; this scenario has been remarkably recurrent in contemporary media. While the rediscovery of hometown via romance (and vice versa) is also a regular feature of popular print fiction of the chick-lit variety as in Lauren Weisberger's 2005 novel *Everyone Worth Knowing* or Lucinda Rosenfeld's 2004 *Why She Went Home*, journalistic accounts and pop sociology regularly document a variety of forms of female retreatism from the "mommy track" (in which women leave their careers to raise their children) to the "daughter track" (giving up paid work to care for elderly parents). A 2005 front-page article in *The New York Times* exploring the latter phenomenon typified the latent hostility of some such coverage in which professional women are cast as modulating their ambition and reduced/restored to care-giving roles. The article profiles Mary Ellen Geist, a successful radio news anchor in large urban markets who quit her job to return to her parents' Midwestern home when her father became ill with Alzheimer's, noting rather gratuitously but tellingly that "Ms. Geist sleeps in the dormered bedroom of her childhood and survives without urban amenities like white balsamic vinegar."[1]

Of primary interest to me in this chapter is the (re)gendering of retreatism and the emergence of this dynamic in a turbulent and highly unsettled economic and social moment. Retreatism is one manifestation of what Kathleen Stewart calls "trauma time," in which

> There is a search for new forms of sentimentality and a longing for interiority. We find ourselves in the midst of the self-help movement, privatization, cocooning, family values, utopia walled up in theme parks and franchise culture, feel-good movies and colorful décor . . . But there is trauma, too, in the anesthetized distraction of an OK middle ground defending a womb against the world. Here, fear of falling meets a more profound fear of burst bubbles.[2]

As David Morley has pointed out, concepts of home acquire greater meaning in a hostile social environment.[3] Some of the features of the current environment are effectively sketched by Ghassan Hage as follows:

> Increasingly, there is a sense of society's shrinking capacity to provide a good life to everyone. As a result, a defensive attitude of guarding whatever good life is left supplants the enjoyment of that good life. In this phobic culture where everything is viewed as either threatening and in need of extermination or threatened and in need of protection, there is an invasion of the order of the border. From the borders of the self to the borders of the family, friendship, neighborhood, nation, and all the way to the borders of Western civilization, everything and everywhere is perceived as a border from which a potentially threatening other can leap.[4]

Idealized hometowns, I would suggest, allow us to believe this isn't so. Hometown fantasies specifically compensate for a set of social/economic conditions that actually make generational continuity and financial stability in a clearly-demarcated "town" space unlikely. In fact, we celebrate and romanticize hometowns in inverse correlation to the conditions of their viability in the age of sprawl. Just as the term "homeland" operates as political cover and justification for uncertainty about the nation's security and coherence, "hometown" is now a fundamentally defensive term that works to manage a creeping uncertainty about the sustainability of the American way of life.[5]

It is also likely that patriarchal culture exhibits a greater need to fantasize homebound women as global capital becomes ever more peripatetic. Redomesticated women are matched in current popular culture with a set of images of globally itinerant, transnational men.[6] These images range in their emotional tone from an emphasis on the exhilarations of the new global economy to a stress on the need of such diligent road warriors for emotional succor at home. In an essay on the new business class, Pico Iyer cites the phenomenon of the emergence of "resident expatriates," a transnational professional class that lives like they are elsewhere even when they are at home.[7] In a similar vein, Susan Jeffords (in part drawing on Iyer's profile of this class) offers a reading of the film *Breakdown* (1997) in which she observes that "While gender equity may be the rhetorical façade of the modern corporate economy, *Breakdown*'s narrative suggests that beneath that façade lies a continuing need for gender distinctions and gendered roles, if the corporate urban class is to keep apace of its own obsolescence."[8] For Jeffords the "new global man" transcends local, regional, and national affiliations. By contrast, women are regularly exhorted to re-secure local, communal, regional, and in some cases even national meanings through their rejection of global cosmopolitanism. They must do this not only to enrich family life, but to play a (gendered) part in staving off class and economic others.

Against this broad backdrop of postfeminist retreatism, I begin here with a brief identification of the retreatist formulae of contemporary chick flicks including *Practical Magic* (1998), *Hope Floats* (1998), *One True Thing* (1998), *Kate & Leopold* (2001), and *Sweet Home Alabama* (2002) where a female protagonist leaves the city to take up again the role of daughter, sister, and/or sweetheart in a hometown setting.[9] I will then move to consider how such retreatism is echoed and elaborated in a number of female-oriented television series of recent years, notably *Gilmore Girls* (WB), *Judging Amy* (CBS), and *Providence* (NBC).[10] Actively refuting the truism that "you can't go home again," all three series are strikingly unified by the following shared features:

- Reliance on a girlish 30-something protagonist who is either resettled within her family of origin or forced to reconcile with it.[11]
- A protagonist whose paid professional work never drifts too far from the skillset associated with familial domesticity.
- A postfeminist preoccupation with the losses attached to professionalization and maturation and a dominant tone of whimsy or wistfulness in measuring the distance between youth and maturity.
- A romanticization of New England (all three series are set in idyllic "old money" locales in Connecticut and Rhode Island). These settings speak in complex ways from/to a culture whose recent population shifts have been to the south and west.

In examining these media forms I hope to shed light on the social fantasy of the ideal hometown, offering precise social historical explanations for its centralization in a variety of media narratives, ranging from romantic comedies to prime-time television dramas to cable news mediathons centering on lost "hometown girls." As part of my effort across this book to examine the subject positions that postfeminist culture makes available to women, I will turn here to a range of texts that site femininity within a particular and defining locale. The hometown girl as she is rendered in contemporary popular culture acts to hold in place a precarious imaginary geography of smooth generational continuity, contained cost of living increases, and small-scale social intimacies.[12] When women's experience is focalized in recent media texts, the likelihood that some version of a hometown will be engaged appears great. However, all hometowns are not necessarily equally valued; I will draw here upon concepts and terminology developed in critical regional studies to address the ways that current media's hometown fixations are almost without exception situated in the northeast or the south.

In this context it is worth adding that NBC's high-profile morning show *Today* has, for the last several years, planned in minute detail and then subsequently broadcast the wedding of a selected couple. This annual feature which runs through late summer and early autumn is now a familiar enough format that NBC has seen fit to start tweaking it a little and in 2005 the original "Today Throws a Wedding" concept was modified to become "Today Throws a *Hometown* Wedding." A social theatrical event of this kind certifies the imaginary power of the hometown for an audience of millions of viewers, even while perversely celebrating the values of local intimacy in an event broadcast from midtown Manhattan's Rockefeller Plaza. It is clear that the "going home" fantasy is rooted in a powerful valorization of female geographical monogamy and is surely part of a broader matrix of behaviors in which women are seen to "unlearn" feminism. It is essential that we move beyond surprise and dismay at postfeminism's representational recidivism without going so far in the other direction as to fall prey to its disingenuous rhetorics of empowerment and achievement.

While the romantic comedy has long grappled with its particular obligation to reconcile individuality and destiny, it has become common practice for the female protagonist of the contemporary romantic comedy to abjure an urban environment, "downshifting" her career or ambitions in order to re-prioritize family commitments and roles. Films such as *One True Thing* (1998) and *Sweet Home Alabama* do this more or less straightforwardly, while time-traveling romances like *13 Going on 30* and *Kate & Leopold* tweak the formula by expanding its temporal parameters.[13] As Yvonne Tasker and I have noted, postfeminist culture often combines "a deep uncertainty about existing options for women with an idealized, essentialized femininity that symbolically evades or transcends institutional and social problem spots."[14] One of the most functional formulas for resolving this contradiction over the last decade has been the story of an adult woman's hometown re-dedication. Thus, many contemporary female-centered genres whether in cinema or television have adopted what I call a retreatist posture as they feature the narrative of a migratory, transplanted, and/or urban heroine re-situating herself in her hometown. To take just a few examples, in the 1998 chick flick *Hope Floats*, Sandra Bullock's Birdee Pruitt leaves behind an unfaithful husband in Chicago when his infidelity with her best friend is humiliatingly revealed to her on national television. Her character's return to her Texas hometown is depicted as a healthy re-connection with her family, the social intimacies and rituals of small-town life, and the honesty and integrity incarnated by Justin, a man whom she grew up with. In *Sweet Home Alabama* Melanie Carmichael (Reese Witherspoon), a "small-town girl" who has established herself as a successful fashion designer in New York and is engaged to the mayor's son there, is obliged to return to Alabama to finalize her divorce from her childhood sweetheart. Her (predictable) return to that earlier relationship is matched in thematic importance by her re-dedication to the values of family, hometown, and region. (This process is signaled in part by Melanie/Witherspoon's use of an intensified Southern accent and idiom in the film's closing scenes.) Significantly, Melanie's discovery of her husband's success as an entrepreneur and craftsman (he is the owner of a company called "Deep South Glass") leads the film largely to "forget" Melanie's own successful career and in a closing montage the couple and their daughter are seen opening a branch of his company in New York. Similarly, in *Providence* (1999–2002), a hit NBC television program of the late 1990s and early 2000s (broadcast in the UK on the Hallmark Channel and ITV3), Sydney Hansen, a successful Los Angeles plastic surgeon, disavows what the series portrays as the venal, sexually unstable culture of Southern California to live again in the New England home she grew up in, a step the series suggests is necessary for her to truly know who she is. I mention these examples because they help me to illustrate the depth and reach of a popular culture that repeatedly locates the defining site of female identity formation in an idealized American hometown. Later in the chapter this will in turn help to explain the ideological breach 2005 headline-maker Jennifer Wilbanks (known as the Runaway Bride) was seen to be committing when she apparently fled from hers.

As I have argued elsewhere, in contrast to high-profile female-centered 1980s films that frequently staged urban female rejuvenation (*Desperately Seeking Susan* [1985], *Moonstruck* [1987], *Working Girl* [1988], *Suspect* [1987]), 1990s and early 2000s films frequently conjoin self-discovery with the rejection of the city.[15] Recent chick flicks routinely depict urban professional women whose crises of identity are linked to a dawning realization that they cannot truly be at home in an urban milieu. The focal females of the texts I discuss here represent an inversion of that same conservative, place-based formulation of femininity; rather than casting ambition into doubt through emphasis on urban misplacement, they implicate femininity in the hometown's recovery of self and society. Throughout its history, Hollywood cinema has regularly incorporated stringent critique of the idyllic hometown (in films ranging from *The Wizard of Oz* [1939] and *The Miracle of Morgan's Creek* [1944] to *The Witches of Eastwick* [1987]) yet recent hometown fictions seem less likely to tolerate such criticism. While the late 1990s saw the emergence of a cluster of anti-suburban films (*The Ice Storm* [1997], *Happiness* [1998], *The Truman Show* [1998], and *American Beauty* [1999]), more recent cinematic portrayals of hometown experience as surreal and ersatz have tended to falter narratively and commercially (*State and Main* [2000] and *The Stepford Wives* [2004]).

Taking up one example of the kind of equation made in recent popular culture between idealized femininity and the hometown, I want to briefly discuss *Win a Date with Tad Hamilton* (2004), a film whose self-consciousness about hometown rhetoric and nostalgia makes it a useful case study. *Win a Date* sets up a contrast between Hollywood bad boy Tad Hamilton and small-town girl Rosalee ("Rosie") Futch, a Piggly Wiggly grocery store checkout clerk in Frazier's Bottom, West Virginia. While Rosie and her best friend Cathy swoon over Tad Hamilton's movies at their local cinema, Pete (the store manager) pines for Rosie. Concerned about the damage Tad is doing to his career when he starts to make tabloid headlines for carousing and drinking, his manager and agent (both named Richard Levy) arrange a national date contest and Rosie is the winner.[16]

Pete sees Rosie off for Los Angeles with great trepidation about her sexual and moral welfare, warning her that Tad "has probably slept with at least 15 to 20 women," to which the chaste Rosie replies "that's not even possible." On their date, Tad is utterly charmed by Rosie's combination of integrity and gaucherie—the complicated moral dilemmas he confides about his career appear straightforwardly resolvable to her and Tad is entranced by Rosie's moral clarity. When she returns to her hometown, Tad shows up there, telling her "I need someone with solid and substantial qualities. Someone who seems to understand life and how to live it in a good and happy way like you." Local residents are starstruck by Tad's appearance and deeply impressed by Rosie's attractiveness to him. When she returns to Piggly Wiggly after seeing him, the store customers and workers (save Pete) applaud her and a black checkout clerk yells "You go girl. You get your man!"[17]

While Pete continues to pine for Rosie without her knowing it, Tad buys a local farm and appears to be planning to settle down in Frazier's Bottom. Pete interrogates Tad about how well he really knows Rosie and exhibits his superior knowledge of her when he details to Tad the six different smiles she gives through which he can read her emotions. Shortly after, Tad's agent and manager appear in town to let him know that he's gotten a plum part; Tad tells Rosie he loves her and asks her to come back to Los Angeles with him. She is suspicious about his sincerity (he has regularly exhibited a habit of recycling his film dialogue to convey deep emotion) but Tad wins her over by appropriating Pete's concept of her six different smiles and thereby convincing Rosie that he really does know who she is. Heartbroken, Pete finally tells Rosie he loves her, but she is too surprised and confused to call off her plans. On the flight to California however, she becomes ill at ease and when Tad can't reproduce the typologization of her smiles, she asks that the plane be turned around. Returning to Frazier's Bottom she chases Pete down, reveals her intimate knowledge of him by delineating his five different smiles, and they dance in the street together, reproducing the concluding tableau of a World War II-era Tad Hamilton movie that Pete, Rosie, and Cathy had watched together in *Win a Date*'s first scene.

While I realize the above description might seem to indicate little other than the general structural frame of a rather insipid Hollywood romance, there are features of *Win a Date with Tad Hamilton* that complicate that structure and deserve scrutiny. What is most important about the film is its status as a pseudo-critique of Hollywood simulations of small-town intimacy. While critically narrativizing Hollywood's desire to co-opt and market hometown integrity, nevertheless the film insists upon *its* ability to deliver an ideal and morally pristine hometown.

There are two further complications at work in the film as well. The specific use of the real-world Southern grocery store chain Piggly Wiggly as the workplace for major characters and key scenes matches a pre-existing corporate hometown rhetoric with the broader claims of the film. The chain (whose slogan "Down home, down the street" is displayed prominently on a banner in the employee break room) is associated with smaller towns, traditional services, and neighborliness. In addition, despite the nostalgic warmth of its last scene, *Win a Date* develops a contradiction in the way it repudiates Hollywood superficiality yet internally restages its own non-existent Hollywood movie to come to closure. Moreover, while Rosie and Cathy had been moved to tears by the Tad Hamilton film that opens *Win a Date*, Pete had asked in disgust "What kind of pathetic and desperate emotional cripple would actually buy that as an ending?" Since this proves to be the very ending *we* are meant to "buy" at the close of the film, certain questions persist. Is the conclusion a contemptuous swipe at the emotional gullibility of the chick flick audience? Or does it lay bare the film's own status as a complicitous critique of the nostalgic Hollywood hometown fantasy? Ultimately, *Win a Date* offers evidence of Elisabeth Bronfen's contention that "cinematic narratives, particularly when they are concerned with concepts of home, are inscribed by a nostalgia for an untainted sense of belonging, and the impossibility of achieving that is also the catalyst for fantasies about recuperation."[18]

You can go home again: femininity, feminism, and the retreatist scenario

In exploring the repressive and expressive functions of a set of recent media fictions, I want to highlight that such fictions fed (and fed *from*) a popular cultural preoccupation in the late 1990s and early 2000s with the dilemmas of work, family, and female identity in the age of postfeminism. Most often cast in term of the prominent cultural cliché of the work/life balance, that preoccupation played out in advertising, print bestsellers, the self-help culture and, at times, even popular music.[19] As argued above, cinematic romances regularly include a retreatist epiphany in which the professional woman comes to realize that the self she has cultivated through education and professionalization is in some way deficient unless she can rebuild a family base.[20] Conservative maneuvers to scale back the power and agency of the professional woman have, of course, hardly been confined to the chick flick genre. As Joel W. Martin has argued, even a genre as far removed from romantic comedy as the disaster film made a habit in the 1990s of depicting an "odd mix of initiative and passivity" in its female protagonists, often functioning "to return a single, professional and . . . romance resistant woman to a traditional role."[21] Yet it has been television that has proven itself perhaps most adept in codifying a broad set of ideological concerns about femininity, agency, domesticity, and work through narrative formulae.[22] As Amanda Lotz has pointed out, "the protagonist-centered family drama" took cultural center stage in the late 1990s, with a number specifically inverting the establishing premise of a set of earlier female-centered programs (including *That Girl* and *The Mary Tyler Moore Show*) that originated with the protagonist's departure *from* home—in these series she returns to it.[23] From the late 1990s, major networks built some of primetime's most important hits (and misses) around the creative concept of a lead character who flees life in a big city and a career that has become unrewarding to move back to the town in which they grew up. In addition to the series that concern me here, we can point to examples such as *Maggie Winters*, *Ed*, *Normal, Ohio*, and *Any Day Now*.[24] In these kinds of series,

Figure 2.1 In the late 1990s, American television debuted a set of primetime
dramas in which a professional woman returned to her hometown.
(*TV Guide*, October 14–20, 2000)

the general rule is that no important changes have taken place in the time since
the protagonist's departure except for those that help underscore the appropri-
ateness of their return. For instance, in *Providence*, Sydney Hansen's mother has
died, making a place for her as the symbolic new mother of the family.[25]

We might speculate that such series differentiated themselves by providing a counterpoint realism to the fantasy of such female-centered 1990s franchises as *Buffy the Vampire Slayer*, *Xena: Warrior Princess*, and even the semi-fantastical *Ally McBeal*. Still, it is interesting that (more or less) the same cultural moment gave rise to such different versions of the female-centered primetime series. On the one hand we have the professional woman returned to her hometown, but on the other we have the globally itinerant professional female of *Alias*, a series whose core ideological problematic might be characterized as the notion of placelessness and the impossibility of familial stability.[26] In the hometown dramas, fears about the potentially migratory professional female loom large and the greatest character flaw is a failure to appreciate the values of home and hometown. In a revealing sequence near the end of *Providence*'s series life, Syd finds herself intimidated by her fiancé Owen's multilingual international spy family, and is romantically tempted by a new colleague at work. With uncharacteristic sarcasm Syd asks him "Where's your home? Or are you one of those citizen of the planet types?" The "wrong man" for Syd (David Baylor) is thus defined in terms that are specific and integral to the series' concerns. While David is rootless, Owen will mediate global cosmopolitanism for Syd—though his relatives are exactly the kind of dangerous "citizens of the planet" Syd alludes to, Owen shows himself to be a stabilizing figure and one who represents home.[27] While the series maintains its primary focus on hometown rewards for its regular ensemble, female guest characters from time to time echo the necessity of retreatism. In the episode "The Third Thing," Syd gets a job as director of St. Clare's Family Clinic when Helen, the young black woman who holds the post, accepts a job offer in her hometown in Georgia. Helen almost immediately reconsiders, saying that she has decided she is just not ready for small-town life. Shortly after this Helen is shot at the clinic by a deranged woman who believes her baby has been taken from her. This trauma Helen interprets as a "sign from above" and she conveys her intentions saying "It's time for me to go home, Syd. I can't wait another ten years. We tend to think life goes on forever, until we get a reminder, otherwise."[28] In *Gilmore Girls* Lorelai's dedication to her adopted hometown of Stars Hollow is reinforced again and again and the theme of rootedness plays through her romantic dilemmas. The two men with whom she was most regularly paired in the series, Luke and Max, both had failed relationships with career-minded women who wanted to see the world, in one case a photographer and in the other a Bank of America employee who moved to Thailand. In this way the series works to foil Lorelai's warm, situated maternity with transient, globally-cosmopolitan femininity.

Nostalgic impulses to retrieve a pure hometown uncontaminated by the difficulties and ambiguities of contemporary life play through a variety of media.[29] While it is beyond the scope of my analysis to sketch the multitude of formats through which the retreatist fantasy is staged, I do want to establish two key concerns that structure my arguments. I proceed here mindful of Joanne Hollow's apt caution that "We can't simply dismiss the appeals of going home as evidence of false consciousness but need to take seriously, and analyze, the cultural significance

Figure 2.2 A key strand of postfeminist discourse in the early 2000s celebrated the choice of leaving the workforce in favor of stay-at-home mothering. (*Time* magazine, March 22, 2004)

of wanting to go home. It seems that feminist cultural studies is caught in some kind of refusal to take on these issues."[30] Secondly, although a stridently antifeminist postfeminism colors many of the debates about female retreatism, we need to acknowledge that "some justifications of downshifting draw on a feminist critique of the masculine-centred nature of work and masculine-centred definitions of success."[31] Among the precipitating factors for female retreatism are clearly some of the very concerns about gender and the workplace that have been central to feminism, and on this basis it is increasingly classed as an expression of personal empowerment. In "The Opt-Out Revolution," the 2003 front-page *New York Times Magazine* article that drew record reader mail and caused a stir by naming a phenomenon many seemed to relate to, Lisa Belkin chronicles the trend of well-educated, affluent (largely white) professional women leaving paid work to care for their children at home. The piece closes in a tone of guarded optimism, asserting that by their actions such women are contesting the terms of workplace control in the era of the "white-collar sweatshop" and fomenting a revolution in which their male counterparts will come to join them through more regularized family leave. This characterization of quasi-feminist empowerment as the ability to stay at home typifies a broader cultural tendency to represent feminism in terms antithetical to its actual political agenda. Postfeminism manifests a habit of "solving" broad economic and cultural problems with gender solutions; such solutions are attractive less because women want to lead limited lives and more because the promise of resolving these dilemmas (which seem to defy political redress) is immensely attractive. One of my suppositions in this book is that "relentlessly focusing popular investments within the private family makes it exceedingly difficult for people to invest in more public forms of social connection."[32] Romanticization of female withdrawal from the working world has clear ideological, financial, and broadly social ramifications. Retreatism is emerging as one of the key social practices of postfeminist culture; it presents itself as both ambiguous and politically indeterminate. Yet there is a political code to many of its manifestations and that code necessitates analysis.

All three of the television series I analyze here engage in a certain positively-coded feminization of the workplace that would appear to reflect the kind of critique of masculinist norms Hollows identifies. *Gilmore Girls'* Lorelai manages an inn, while *Providence*'s Syd is a physician at St. Clare's Family Clinic and the eponymous heroine of *Judging Amy* presides in family court. We are given to understand that in the feminized space of Judge Amy Gray's courtroom, decisions are rendered with particular empathy and compassion.[33] In *Gilmore Girls* work is largely a manifestation of female friendship, highlighting the bonds between Lorelai and Sookie, who run an inn together keeping work strongly tied to cooking, decorating, and hospitality.

There are also important similarities across the three series with respect to career motivation and inspiration. The emphasis in *Judging Amy* is on Amy as a fallible family member and an authoritative public official. Her career extends a commitment to social welfare exhibited by her mother while expanding her authority and power. This theme of maternal inspiration is dimensionalized even further in *Judging Amy* by the fact that series star Amy Brenneman's mother is a Hartford judge and the actress has identified her performance (especially in courtroom scenes) as in many ways an impersonation of her.[34] Relatively frequent conversations take place in the series between Amy and her mother Maxine about how to handle particularly thorny cases, but often with Maxine emphasizing her daughter's higher degree of authority. Similarly in *Providence* there is a connection suggested between Syd's career and her father's—again

Figure 2.3 Advertisements such as this one work to plot a course from Gen X coffeehouse sociality to domestic retreatism. (© Nescafé)

with the daughter's work carrying higher cultural status. (Indeed, the series regularly explains Jim Hansen's emotional limitations through reference to his veterinary work treating animals.) In the voiceover sequence that launches the series Syd not only recalls the pleasures of restoring families through medical interventions that she participated in as a child, but also links the best moments of her work to being her "father's daughter again." In *Gilmore Girls*, Lorelai has purchased an inn from its original owner, a woman who acted as a symbolic mother to Lorelai when she left her own home as a teenager. Work thus has a familial (or quasi-familial) point of origin in all three series and this both naturalizes the hometown return and explains female authority (particularly in *Judging Amy* and *Providence*) in such a way as to diminish its ideological threat.

All three series proceed from a retreatist impulse, but they inflect this impulse differently. An important twist in *Gilmore Girls* is that Lorelai invents a hometown for herself (one that is crucially not the economically sluggish and racially bifurcated Hartford) yet the series compels her to forge a relationship with her parents through a plot device in which she exchanges weekly dinners with them for money to defray the costs of her daughter's private school tuition. Scenic New England factors heavily in the credit sequences of all three series and, despite the fact that both *Judging Amy* and *Providence* play out in urban locales, as Amanda Lotz has noted, "visual composition ignores the status of Hartford and Providence as large cities."[35]

In *Gilmore Girls* the picture postcard aesthetics of Stars Hollow constitute the proof that Lorelai has given her daughter a better upbringing than her own parents gave her.[36] Clearly "the settings in these stories operate as fantasy locations in response to late twentieth century concerns about the status of suburban life (especially in the wake of the Columbine school massacre), while negative perceptions about the quality of city life for families still abound."[37] Yet I think this characterization only strikes at the surface in fully accounting for the ideological reassurance these series seek to provide. After all, the protagonists of these series are all women from Generation X, a demographic that according to Jonathon Oake is more usefully defined as a spectatorship rather than a group of individuals with common practices and rituals.[38] Generation X is that cohort of people (many college educated and highly aspirational) who got a glimpse of downward mobility in the recession years of the early 1990s. Characterizations of Generation X generally ascribe its members with a set of attributes that are fundamentally retreatist. Typical in this regard is Meredith Bagby who writes as both critic and member of Generation X: "Our role in American history seems clear. If our parents' generation was about dismantling the status quo, our generation will be about building new institutions, moral codes, families, churches, corporations . . . Our job is to make order out of the chaos."[39] For this generation most particularly, the work/life balance and reward expectations of earlier eras tend to be idealistically interpreted. In the retreatist dramas "everyone's childhood house is traditional, tasteful, and lovely, making it the perfect escape from an era of overwork, time anxiety and trophy stress."[40]

These series respond to the destabilization of social, familial, and national identities at a level that far exceeds the moral panics about suburbia. They are, I would contend, deeply invested in mapping the struggles of women to cope with a radically revised set of social/economic conditions even if those conditions are seldom named outright. Their postfeminism is in part attributable to a rather regular tendency to scapegoat feminism for changes much more directly attributable to the power of new economies to chip away at social health and family life. As Kathleen Karlyn puts it, "Feminism has become an easy target for women who do not feel that they have benefited from the highly-touted booming economy of the late 1990s, and who in fact are working harder than ever to get by, with less time to enjoy the rewards of family life and domesticity."[41]

Cindi Katz has pointed out that "A hallmark of the globalization of capitalist production has been a retreat by capital from its prior commitments to place. Reproducing a labor force and the conditions of production in any particular locale is less germane to enduring economic growth than it was in the past."[42] The hometown drama redresses exactly this state of affairs through its insistence that local economies are still self-sustaining and its careful avoidance of the impact of newly globalized production and consumption circumstances.

I do not propose that each of these series works in exactly the same way, rather they each occupy a point on a continuum. John Masius, the creator of *Providence*, has offered a blunt description of his series' ideological formula for character development, sketching his heroine Sydney Hansen as "someone who has made what look like all the right choices but is unhappy in her life."[43] The extraordinary pilot assembles all of the series' deepest fears (geographical migration, sexuality that doesn't further the family, and work without redeeming social value) and situates them in relation to the "depraved" culture of Southern California. Our skepticism and concern about the content of Syd's pre-retreat life are immediately triggered. We see that her work as a plastic surgeon has become detached from her goal to help disfigured children, her skills now at the service of vacuous, image-conscious Southern Californians; moreover, Syd operates in a zone of disturbingly unregulated sexuality. When she comes home from her mother's funeral to find her boyfriend in the shower with another man, this single moment of shock and horror precipitates her immediate return to Rhode Island and specifically to a reassuringly stable familial/ideological geography. Linked to its regionalization of morality is *Providence*'s hyper-retreatist conceptualization of the family home and rendering of it as physically, financially, and emotionally expansive. In its early seasons the Hansen house contains a father (Jim) for whom home is also a workplace with his veterinary practice in the basement; two adult daughters (Syd and Joanie); a granddaughter; and an adult son (Robbie), though he is relegated to the attic.[44] In the pilot Syd testifies that "the outside world is overrated," and she helps prepare for her sister's wedding, hosts her mother's funeral, and delivers Joanie's child all in the family home. One of the thematic threads of the pilot deals with the regionalized imbalance sketched by the series between East Coast hometowns, in which professional skills are valued only insofar as they can help the family, as opposed to a West Coast environment in which professional priorities are represented as dictating conditions of intimacy. When Syd finds Jerry, her cheating boyfriend, in the shower he tellingly tries to rationalize his behavior by telling her that the man he is with "is a new client." Syd's very relationship with Jerry is dangerously professionalized— as an agent in the entertainment industry he has been referring many clients to her. By contrast, in Providence Syd is immediately confronted with two family medical emergencies that require her skills—her mother's heart attack and her niece's birth. The pilot suggests that Syd makes up for the fact that she is unable to save her mother by bringing a new life into the world.

Providence also relies on fantasies of small business ownership that help to create the kinds of local encounters it relies on.[45] Not only is Jim Hansen's practice located in the basement, Joanie runs a spinoff petfood store called The Barkery and Robbie co-owns a local bar. Syd's work in a deconsecrated church, transformed into St. Clare's Family Clinic, serves much the same function. *Providence*'s intense idealization of family and local community marks one end of the ideological spectrum of these three series.

Judging Amy might perhaps mark the other. The series carries great subversive potential, treating as it does the lives of two generations of single mothers—the divorced Amy and the widowed Maxine—and is, for instance, much less sentimentalizing of parenthood than the other two. (Karle Warren, the actress cast as Amy's young daughter Lauren, did not generally "play cute" and was particularly adept at conveying whininess and filial disappointment.) *Judging Amy* distinguished itself from the other female-centered series in its directness and its ability to convey ambiguity and contingency. Maxine is far more likely to affirm dilemmas for her daughter than to magically resolve them, and as a result the mother–daughter relationship of this series is one of the most full-bodied, rich, and rewarding that we have seen on television. At the conclusion of "The Wee Hours" an overworked and exhausted Amy discusses with Maxine how much she misses the lack of sex and intimacy in her life and, as they joke about this, Amy's laughter suddenly transforms into tears. Sadness in this series isn't a stylized melancholy but something tougher, more emotionally candid. In the episode "Ye Olde Freedom Inn" Maxine sobs to Amy that she "wants it all," to travel the world, do her job, marry, and live with the man that she loves but also to go on enjoying shared domesticity with her daughter. This depiction of the "having it all" dilemma so characteristic of postfeminism is remarkably recast here from the perspective of a woman in her 60s. In its last season *Judging Amy* complicated and expanded its original premise by having Amy joined in adult life at home by her two brothers. By this time, Amy had purchased the family home from her mother and the series did not shy away from posing awkward questions about the new inversion of domestic and economic roles in the household. In its series finale, *Judging Amy* specifically repudiates retreatism, with Amy in despair over the limitations of the judicial system and intent on giving up her career, then finding an alternate and higher professional pathway through which to concentrate her efforts. In its closing scene Amy is shown proudly giving testimony before Congress with the suggestion that this is the beginning of her new political career.[46]

Gilmore Girls is less willing to take such feminist chances. Instead, it comes worryingly close to participating in the representational trend that posits motherhood as salvation.[47] In the episode "Rory's Birthday Parties" Lorelai toasts her daughter "without whom I would have no reason to get up in the morning." A roomful of assembled friends and townspeople respond to the toast by saying "aw" in unison, apparently deeply touched by this profession of sentiment. Typical of the series' casual denigration of any meaningful feminist-inflected decision is Rory's explanation of her name in the series pilot: "It's my mother's name too. She named me after herself. She was lying in the hospital thinking about how men name boys after themselves all the time, you know, so why couldn't women? She says her feminism just kind of took over. Though personally I think a lot of Demerol went into that decision." Thus, from the pilot forward, irony is often overlaid upon very conservative gender rhetorics in *Gilmore Girls* in ways that help us to understand why the series garnered strong support from the conservative Family Friendly Programming Forum, a coalition of powerful advertisers.[48] In the same opening episode Lorelai chastises her daughter for wearing a bulky (and presumably unfashionable) piece of clothing, telling her "Men don't make passes at girls who wear that sweater."

In many respects *Gilmore Girls* can be seen to typify the economic and class blindness of postfeminism. It suggests that those who don't have the cultural or economic capital to stylize their lives are merely ridiculous—on the few occasions when it looks beyond white hometown affluence the series exhibits a contempt strikingly at odds with the fond indulgence it demonstrates toward the idiosyncratic residents of Stars Hollow. The episode "A Tale of Poes and Fire" for instance includes peripheral caricatures of Southerners and of the kind of people who work at Wal-Mart. There is, however, a rich and engaging question set in place in the pilot in which Lorelai agrees that she and her daughter will have dinner with Lorelai's estranged parents each Friday night in exchange for their payment of Rory's private school tuition. This plot point carries the potential to break through the series' regular repression of economic and class concerns: now that Lorelai has made a bargain of money for "quality time" with her parents, how is this family to recover from the crude economic exchange that centers their current relationship?

Mother and daughter relations in the postfeminist drama

Single motherhood is an important feature of all three of these series. Both *Gilmore Girls* and *Judging Amy* center upon 30-something single mothers, while *Providence* includes Syd's sister Joanie, a woman in her early 20s raising a young daughter. An older generation of mothers generally prove problematic across these series texts. In *Providence* Syd's mother dies in the pilot, yet lives on (perpetually in her mother-of-the-bride suit and corsage) through the series, dispensing commentary and sometimes advice from beyond the grave; in *Gilmore Girls* Emily Gilmore's severity and coldness distinguish her as Lorelai's anti-role model; *Judging Amy*'s Maxine Gray is the warmest of the three but occasionally highly problematic. Another way in which *Judging Amy* differs from the other two series is in its refusal to stigmatize the "bad mothering" of an earlier generation. Indeed, the series celebrates Maxine as a maternal and professional role model to her daughter and centralizes their close bond, as I have indicated above. It is typical of *Providence*'s broad conservatism that it employs the postfeminist representational habit of showcasing the identity dilemmas of a young woman whose mother is dead or absent.[49] Lydia Hansen is excluded from the warm supportiveness that typifies relations in the Hansen household, despite the fact that she undertakes a great deal of emotional work in the family. Casting her as a ghost, the series manages to shunt her off in a novel way so that she is participative yet invisible (to all but Syd).

Celebrations of the maternal in all three series work in tandem with a shift to the "New Momism" delineated by Susan Douglas and Meredith W. Michaels. This shift has entailed a broad intensification of idealized motherhood in the form of "a set of ideals, norms, and practices, most frequently and powerfully represented in the media, that seem on the surface to celebrate motherhood, but which in reality promulgate standards of perfection"[50] beyond reach. According to Douglas and Michaels, "the new momism has become the central justifying ideology of what has come to be called 'postfeminism.'"[51] The struggle to mother fully and generously comes across in all three series, but these celebrations often take place at the expense of bad mothers who appear as patients in *Providence* and as courtroom plaintiffs and defendants in *Judging Amy*. The latter series is sprinkled with failures who emphasize Amy's exceptionalism, beginning in the pilot when an angry defendant who has been compelled to take a parenting course after leaving her eight-year-old alone for five days tells her "You clearly have no concept of what it's like to be a single working mother." In the episode "You Can't Hurry Love" of *Providence*, Syd counsels an alcoholic patient who is also the mother of Megan, one of her former school classmates, taking a hard line with the woman but deploying a troubling logic of maternal obligation, saying "You have every right to drink yourself to death. But you have no right to do this to Megan. If you're hellbent on killing yourself, you could at least wait until after she gets married."

One of the most distinctive shared features of these series is their reflection of a turn toward heightened cultural profiles of mothering and daughtering. All three came to television in what David Denby (in a review of Catherine Hardwick's film *Thirteen*) refers to as a "defining moment," marked by "the first generation of women in which mothers and daughters have worn the same clothes."[52] The necessity and integrity of mother–daughter bonding in these female-centered television dramas might be seen to reverse a 1990s cultural prioritization of father–son narratives as well as a general erasure of midlife women in adult dramas (in everything from the dying woman melodrama [*One True Thing*, *Stepmom*] to many of the films of Mel Gibson) that accompanied a hypervisibility of female teens. In the late 1990s, partly, I believe, in reaction to a wave of cultural concern about the psyches and behavior of teen girls (a concern which has not yet abated as we can see in the success of 2004 box office hit *Mean Girls*), creative formulas in which mothers and daughters were co-profiled seemed to take center stage. The 2003 releases of an intense mother–daughter psychological drama (*Thirteen*) and an age-reversal comedy (*Freaky Friday*) seemed to highlight the trend.

A number of high-profile early millennial advertising campaigns such as those by GAP and Bulova brought mothers and daughters together as co-consumers.

GAP's broadcast and print campaign in particular focused on celebrity mothers (including Glenn Close and Carole King) and their daughters. The Carole King television ad featured the singer and her daughter Louise Goffin harmonizing on King's hit "So Far Away" adapted in this context to implicitly celebrate the value of familial and geographical stability—one of the song's lyric lines asks wistfully "Doesn't anybody stay in one place anymore?"—and in effect the song is performed so as to convey the broader cultural rapprochement between mothers and daughters. At the close of the ad Goffin professes to the camera "My first love, my Mom."

Recent accommodation between the intense cultural focus on teen girls and the desire to bring the mother back entails narrowing the ideological gap between mothers and daughters and emphasizing their co-consuming status. *Gilmore Girls* with its intense focus on a mid-30s single mother and her teenage daughter stands out particularly in this regard. In this series, Lorelai and Rory speak essentially a private language larded with in-jokes and popular culture references; in many ways they typify the new mother/daughter pairs in which both figures recognize themselves in the other and in which their sense of self is heavily reliant on a consuming bond. *Gilmore Girls'* innovation has been to bring together two of postfeminism's favorite archetypes, the precocious teen girl and the girlish 30-something woman. This series suggests that the return of the mother not only stabilizes official fears about the psychological wellbeing of girls and unofficial fears about their cultural power, but it provides a "safe" route for mothers to return to the field of popular culture newly authorized and individualized in their own right. In *Gilmore Girls* the quirky, cute Lorelai gets to retain the freedoms of girlhood through her daughter. Moreover, the series demonstrates that it can tolerate Lorelai's iconoclasm, couched as it is in discourses of class privilege, style-conscious femininity, and family values.

Retreatism and northeastern exceptionalism

Arguably, American television has intensified its sense of regional identity in recent years. Both network primetime and some of the biggest cable hits over the last ten years have demonstrated an acute sense of regionalism whether in sitcoms like *Seinfeld* and *Will & Grace*, dramas like *Everwood* (whose Colorado setting is vital), or the original and spinoffs of *CSI*. The series that concern me here take part in this trend. *Gilmore Girls*, *Judging Amy*, and *Providence* were all conceptualized and first broadcast in the late 1990s and share strikingly similar settings.[53] It is important to ask how these series' intense romanticizations of family and community life in New England speak to a culture that is rapidly resettling in the south and west, for by the end of the twentieth century it was becoming evident that the northeast, long the seat for political, economic, and cultural power in the nation, was seeing those powers migrate away. Sociologist David Brooks straightforwardly acknowledged the decline of northeastern regional clout in a *New York Times* editorial, pointing out that no northeastern candidate had gained the White House in 43 years and observing "We know that our region is not the future. Every year, people move out of the northeast to Scottsdale and other places . . . We know that every year the political center of gravity in this country moves further south and west."[54]

In place of regional power was an accumulating sense of northeastern exceptionalism—a growing perception of difference from the nation as a whole. That sense of difference was often founded on the notion that the northeast retained "older" customs and virtues. Increasingly, television and radio seemed to situate the northeast as the region in which old-fashioned values and skills still flourished. Regionalized home renovation programs like *This Old House* on PBS associated the northeast with the maintenance of heritage and were discursively analogous to the popular NPR advice program *Car Talk* whose hosts' thick Boston accents helped to cement an image of Yankee thrift, ingenuity, and gregariousness. These programs in large part cemented a regional image that "social capital" (to use Robert D. Putnam's term for social networks and their attendant values of trust and reciprocity) still resided in the northeast.[55] Such perceptions were apparently corroborated by a study ranking the states in terms of a set of indices for "caring." These included education, health, volunteerism, safety, protection of the natural environment, civic engagement, etc., as measured by the United Way State of Caring Index. The highest-ranking states were exclusively in the northeast and north: Minnesota, New Hampshire, Connecticut, Massachusetts, Maine, Iowa, Vermont, Wisconsin, South Dakota, and North Dakota. Meanwhile the lowest-ranked states were exclusively southern and western: Louisiana, New Mexico, Arizona, Mississippi, Arkansas, Nevada, Texas, South Carolina, Florida, and Tennessee.[56] Keeping the revised regional status of the northeast in mind then, it becomes evident that fantasies of retreatism in these series are multi-layered—the series' protagonists' recovery of family and community play out in settings that help to "explain" their actions as the northeast itself became associated with retreatism at a broad national level.

Other developments in retreatist media fiction

At a time when the hometown critique seems to have lost coherence and credibility, two of the most consistent representational paradigms for women in popular culture are the "unlearning" of feminism and the repudiation of feminist-inflected working women career models in an urban context (most consistently though not exclusively in film) and the return to a New England or southern hometown (in both film and TV). In the set of television series in which adult women return to their hometowns, work choices always fall into line with the protagonist's central identity as a maternal caregiver. In *Providence* Syd gives up her job as a Los Angeles plastic surgeon to open a family clinic in a deconsecrated church; in *Judging Amy* Amy quits a Wall Street post to become a judge in family court; and in *Gilmore Girls* Lorelai runs a local inn, emphasizing a feminized provision of hospitality.[57]

Not only did *Judging Amy*, *Providence*, and *Gilmore Girls* enjoy a high level of success, they all made various claims to the status of "quality television," and they signaled these claims in part through casting of recognizable stars from quality franchises of earlier eras. Mike Farrell (as Jim Hansen) carries the intertextual connotations of *MASH* in *Providence*, Tyne Daly (as Maxine Gray) represents an earlier era's generation of quality female dramas in the form of *Cagney & Lacey* for *Judging Amy*, and Sally Struthers (Lorelai's neighbor Babette) does the same with respect to her earlier role in *All in the Family* when she appears in *Gilmore Girls*. In the opening moments of the *Providence* pilot (as we have seen) references to *Friends* and the characterization of a life-changing surgery as taking "less time than it takes to see a movie" bespeak the series' desire to position itself above mere escapist television and the triviality of entertainment. The quality connotations at work in these series signal their desire to be seen as having something pertinent and trenchant to say about women, parenting, the work/life balance, and family culture.

It may be seen that the success of series like *Judging Amy*, *Providence*, and *Gilmore Girls* clearly laid the groundwork for a hit like *Desperate Housewives* (2004–) which in its phenomenally successful first season took the retreatist ideological agenda for granted to such an extent that it barely needed to account for its focus on the exclusively stay-at-home wives and mothers of Wisteria Lane. Indeed, the series' aggressive eroticization of retreatism registered as innovation to many viewers.

More recently, the Jerry Bruckheimer-produced CBS legal drama *Close to Home* (2005–2007) centralized Annabeth Chase whose return to her job as a prosecutor after recently giving birth to a daughter reflected an ongoing effort to merge/negotiate these contrasting roles. While in its opening episodes the series seemed to want to depict a protagonist who was uniquely perceptive about/sensitive to the dilemmas of suburban female experience because of her motherhood, *Close to Home* seemed to be moving increasingly toward a position of contrast between Annabeth and the endangered or criminal women she interacts with. The series was unsure about whether her work could operate as an extension of her maternal domesticity and accordingly began to directly contrast her situation with those of the series' misguided criminal subjects. At the end of its first season, *Close to Home* abruptly killed off Annabeth's husband as the series increasingly strained to imagine any integration of domesticity and public sphere advocacy.

The "choosing home" story so installed in contemporary popular culture resonates on several levels—it removes women from the contaminating corporate workplace in an era of widespread cynicism about the morality of the business culture and it also works to buttress the idea that our society retains strong communal features. Violations of this scenario increasingly operate as subversions of the approved social script. Within this framework of concepts of home and stability we can begin to observe a representational schism between the hometown girl (in her various guises) and her opposite. In American popular culture

Figure 2.4 A British tabloid invites female viewers of *Desperate Housewives* to typologize themselves in relation to the series' characters.

women who are geographically unsettled are likely to be represented as fearsome and unfeminine, or dead. (The urban female corpses found in transient "magnet cities" on television hits like *CSI* and *Law and Order* add a forensic gloss to this established trend.)[58] One recent film that explicitly poses the contrast between hometown girls and their opposites is *The Exorcism of Emily Rose* (2005) in which a young sheltered rural woman leaves her hometown to go to college despite her family's misgivings. The film takes shape as an elaborate punishment (one arguably coordinated by her family) as she is tormented by demons until she dies. The legal case of neglect against the priest who oversaw an exorcism attempt is managed by an ambitious female prosecutor who through the case downscales her own ambition and draws closer to religious faith (partly as a result of ominous signs that the supernatural forces that took hold of Emily Rose may be stalking her as well). In this way, the film (an unheralded release that became a moderate hit in late summer) doubles the retreatist plot so characteristic of the contemporary chick flick. The 1990s we may remember opened with a storm of controversy over the ur-female road movie *Thelma and Louise* (1991), a film that inscribes the euphoria but also the ultimate fruitlessness of female geographical mobility. While hyper-mobile action heroines from Lara Croft to Sydney Bristow (of *Alias*) are certainly to be found in the popular culture landscape, their exploits are framed in bleak, beleaguered terms in narratives that tend to emphasize familial loss. Positive assessments of female experience are now most often associated with urban renunciation and/or hometown re-dedication. Against the backdrop of these highly gendered and highly value-laden concepts of home and stability, I want to begin to consider how American overinvestment in an idealized hometown impacts news reporting of women's experiences. What happens when the postfeminist "going home" story meets its opposite?

Postfeminism lost and found: tracking the Runaway Bride

The story of a missing/murdered white woman or girl dominates American television. Although they adhere to different generic codes, forms including cable news, primetime dramas, and court television all centralize microdetailed investigations into the manner of and motive for female death. Indeed, the primary narrative energy in all of these forms is crucially linked to the prospect of "discovering" the dead woman again and again. This produces a particularly concentrated example of dynamics aptly pinpointed by Kevin Glynn who writes ". . . under current conditions distinguished by the hyperspeed of media mobilization and a hyperabundance of images and discursive output, hypers(t)imulation and overpresence produce events that verge on a necrotic form of history even before their achievement of narrative closure."[59] As comedian Chris Rock aptly observed when asked to comment on the Runaway Bride case on *Late Night with Conan O'Brien*, on May 31, 2005, "No one cares about missing men."

It is beyond my scope to generate a thoroughgoing explanation for why the missing white woman has been so zealously seized upon as a subject for the aggressive, sensationalistic overreporting that is the hallmark of cable news. Here I want to assess a recent seemingly minor mediathon that produced a distinctive celebrity for its focal figure; media events of this kind tend to engage ideological flashpoints and this one, I would suggest, is no different. In generating a close reading of this particular scandal, I am adopting the perspective advocated by Adrienne L. McLean and David Cook who contend that what scandalizes in one era versus another has often to do with the ability of a scandal to pull into focus resonant and timely cultural, moral, and ideological dilemmas.[60] The story of the Runaway Bride which consumed US media outlets for a few days at the end of April and beginning of May 2005 turned on 32-year-old Jennifer Wilbanks, a Duluth, Georgia, bride-to-be who secretly ran away via Greyhound bus a few days before her wedding. Wilbanks and her fiancé, John Mason, both came from prominent families in Duluth and had planned a wedding with 600 guests and 28 attendants. (Before she fled, Wilbanks had been the guest of honor at eight bridal showers.) In the time that Wilbanks was missing, a well-rehearsed and familiar media response swung into operation driven by the assumption that the story of the vanished white middle-class woman ends with a corpse. Wilbanks' family (particularly her father, father-in-law, and fiancé) and friends were repeatedly broadcast expressing their fears that she was the victim of foul play.[61] Meanwhile a large and costly search operation that had volunteers canvassing local rivers and woods was undertaken, with nationwide publicity stressing discourses of protective paternalism and hometown solidarity. Yet the story abruptly changed course with the revelation that Wilbanks had run away on her own, traveling first to Las Vegas and then to Albuquerque, in an effort to avoid her upcoming wedding. The unconventional ending to a familiar script was greeted, as I shall show, by public anger and scorn for a woman who had flouted the usual rules of the "missing woman" story. In tones of indignation, news anchors on CNN said things like "I couldn't believe it when I heard on Saturday morning that she'd turned up alive." People on the street interviews and newspaper opinion polls lambasted Wilbanks as selfish and cruel; a commentator for Fox News opined that "Wilbanks should be disowned by her parents, shunned by friends, and bitten by the family dog."[62] Through such forums it became evident that Wilbanks had spoiled the expectations of many more people than just her fiancé and family.

What are we to make of the vehement media response that defined the overnight celebrity of Jennifer Wilbanks? One very interesting feature of the Runaway Bride coverage was the rather transparent shift of the unreliability of the story to the unreliability of Wilbanks herself. In the "breaking news" coverage of the case by CNN on April 30, the day that Wilbanks called 911 in Albuquerque, reporters initially sought to spin the story as a "recovery" brought about by solidarity and prayer, and stressed that Wilbanks had been found on her wedding day "of all things." CNN anchor Betty Nguyen reported wrongly on air that Wilbanks "didn't call police, she called home and maybe that's a testament to how close this family truly is." The restoration story curdled however when an FBI news conference made clear that the protagonist had planned her own disappearance, manufactured a tale of abduction and assault, and had apparently been serious enough in her intention to travel unrecognized that she had cut her hair. News anchors openly expressed consternation and disapproval that the story had taken a detour into uncharted territory; at one point Nguyen abandoned the conventions of news reporting and in-studio banter to directly inform the viewer "I gotta tell you, when we saw that news conference our jaws dropped." Anchors on CNN were rather awkwardly left to fill air time when the assembled family and friends at the Mason home retreated, emerging only to issue a terse statement acknowledging that "It has been determined that Jennifer has some issues the family was not aware of," and essentially calling off the media by asking for time and space.

Clearly the revelation that Wilbanks had faked her abduction chipped away at the ideological underpinnings of her story as it had been reported up to that point. At a deeper level Wilbanks violated two of the most high-profile narratives of contemporary femininity—the wedding story and the abduction/murder story. As scholars including Elizabeth Freeman, Cele Otnes, and Elizabeth Pleck have shown, the magnitude and scope of the approximately $40 billion a year wedding industry takes up a pre-eminent place in the commodification of American femininity.[63] Less comprehensively researched but increasingly drawing attention is the fact that one of the key templates for news representations of women's experience in America is the suspicious disappearance story, a staple of programming on cable outlets from CNN and Fox to Court TV. In a postfeminist discursive climate that regularly emphasizes female choice and agency though in highly proscribed ways, Jennifer Wilbanks' flight constituted a novel representational problem. Simultaneously rejecting a number of the "approved" roles for women in a postfeminist culture—the bride, the daughter, the hometown girl—she exhibited altogether the wrong sort of desperation. Although recent popular culture has displayed a penchant for constructing femininity as romantically/sexually desperate, Wilbanks was not the neurotic romantic comedy heroine in zealous pursuit of "her man," nor was she even a "desperate housewife." Rather her spontaneous celebrity seemed to generate a challenge to the security of current postfeminist archetypes and interrupted a familiar representational dynamic in which the reasons why a middle-class woman could disappear in America are officially mystified but culturally "understood."[64]

Wilbanks' closely tracked flight from her upcoming wedding, her fiancé, and her hometown placed her, in effect, in the position of a postfeminist subversive. Her anti-retreatist behavior stood as an affront to idealized notions of community that had grounded the coverage of her as a missing person. In abandoning her home and family, Wilbanks had in essence made a bid to convert from a position of geographical monogamy to one of geographical promiscuity. These terms are employed by Agnes Heller and drawn upon by David Morley in his book *Home Territories: Media, Mobility and Identity* and are used by both (despite their implications) without prejudice. My sense, however, is that these terms work well (and very prejudicially) to describe the ideological implications of hometown rhetoric in contemporary American culture.

In this particular case, it is worth pointing out that Duluth, Georgia, had a heightened investment in presenting an image of social harmony to the nation. Just six weeks prior to the Wilbanks case, Duluth had made national headlines when (African-American) Brian Nichols killed four people including a state judge, a federal agent, a court reporter, and a sheriff's deputy then took Duluth resident Ashley Smith hostage in a drama that riveted the country.[65] Smith reported that she was able to persuade Nichols to free her by talking to him about her young daughter and faith in God and by making him pancakes and he was subsequently taken into custody.[66] Nichols' shooting rampage was reported to be psychologically devastating to the local community (which effectively, here, seemed to constitute the greater Atlanta area). For instance, a county chaplain attested that the shootings had "fractured the 'whole fellowship of the Fulton County family.'"[67] The rampage and kidnapping presented a dramatic contrast to Duluth's image of itself, which is strikingly conveyed on its website with images of children in a park, families attending outdoor concerts, and smiling police officers. The website describes Duluth as "an active, thriving community where families come together, children play and where we embrace the community with events." It also notes that "The City of Duluth prides itself on its ability to accommodate a growing, diverse population in metropolitan Atlanta while maintaining its small-town charm and sense of community. While tremendous growth in the area has presented challenges, city leadership and services have consistently met the changing demands." This slightly less rosy account of Duluth is one tipoff that for all its rhetoric of community and small-town sociality, Duluth is, in fact, less a prototypical hometown and more of an edge city, the kind of semi-suburban commercial zone where the rhetoric of community often camouflages massive development, rising property prices, and a transient population. These facts, I suggest, ought to be borne in mind when considering the story of Jennifer Wilbanks as a cherished hometown girl.

Another feature of the Wilbanks story and one particularly pertinent to the high level of national coverage it received is its status as a story set in and revealing of the south. With a dramatic southward population shift in the late twentieth century, rising political clout, the flourishing force of urban Sunbelt economies and the broad de-stigmatization of southernness, the region is now linked more firmly to the nation as a whole than at any other time in American history. Broadly speaking, the south is now imagined as less exceptional and more typical, and popular media fictions have broadly reflected this shift. While a film like *My Cousin Vinny* (1992) comedically updated the stock plot of the south as a place outsiders dare not be caught in (thereby drawing upon films from *Deliverance* [1972] to *The Texas Chainsaw Massacre* [1974] to *Mississippi Burning* [1988]), by the late 1990s and 2000s popular culture tended to render a non-problematic transit between the south and other places and sometimes highlighted the south as an identity-restoring home for white women (this is the case in the two examples I alluded to earlier, *Sweet Home Alabama* and *Hope Floats*). As Peter Applebome has noted, the south is significantly the site for the "redeemed drama of family values, roots, racial peace and national healing" in one of the most successful and high-profile Hollywood hits of the last decade, *Forrest Gump* (1994).[68] While being hesitant to extract too much meaning from the vagaries of decision-making in a national call-in contest, I would suggest nevertheless it also bears noticing that (at this writing) the phenomenally popular broadcast hit *American Idol* has seen all four of its season winners (and for that matter three of its runner-ups) come from the south.[69]

Over the last 20 years, southernness has signified most often as a positive element in commodification, with the nationalization of previously Southern brands like Dr. Pepper and Krispy Kreme and the success of magazines like *Southern Living* marking the emergence of the "not just economically vibrant but racially cleansed and thoroughly Americanized 'No South.'"[70] In this context where the south paradoxically signifies as less regionally specific than in the past but also as a positive refraction of "Americanness," the Wilbanks case acquired another disruptive narrative/ideological valence. It suggested that perhaps national myths of the harmonious, post-civil rights, family values south didn't quite hold up.

Another layer of the Wilbanks narrative connected to the archetype of the southern lady for the image of the south remains particularly tied, as Tara McPherson has shown, to notions of white female propriety. McPherson contends that "the southern lady was a key image around which the south constructed (and still constructs) its postbellum identity." Moreover, "this lady was (and is) most often situated within a particular southern landscape," frequently entailing "the inter-related trajectories of the southern lady and the plantation home."[71] Indeed, the pre-eminent fiction of southern US identity, *Gone with the Wind* (1939), produces an equation between stalwart southern femininity and home (in that instance, the female-named plantation Tara). This paradigm of idealized southern white femininity surely inflected the contrast presented between Jennifer Wilbanks and Ashley Smith, the former having abandoned home and family and the latter taken hostage in her own home yet somehow from within that space thwarting the criminal impulses of the black man who held her.

It is clear that the bright spot in the Brian Nichols story for many was Smith, whose composure, religious faith, and staunch family values were represented as powerful elements in the case and proof that stalwart femininity was a kind of civic resource.[72] In this respect, the public story of Ashley Smith was consistent with the broader discursive patterns of a postfeminist culture in which women's strength and power are often emphatically posited in family values terms. As the Jennifer Wilbanks case developed, her "wimpiness" was increasingly posited as a failure of her femininity. In an intriguing moment in the CNN coverage of April 30, one reporter likens her to the kind of "guys who go out for cigarettes and never come back." Increasingly, as I shall show, US news media dealt with the apparent "paradox" of Jennifer Wilbanks by suggesting that her femininity, her middle-classness, and her whiteness were insecure and open to question.

For example, certain assessments suggested that Wilbanks had performed a kind of subterfuge that one would associate with minority group membership. The implicit suggestion of some accounts was that this affluent white woman ought to be classed with non-white or lesser white tabloid figures such as Tawana Brawley, Susan Smith, or Tonya Harding, all of whom made headlines in the 1980s and 1990s for hoaxes or conspiracies. An article in the *Atlanta Journal-Constitution* gave this account of Wilbanks a month after the revelation that she had staged her own disappearance:

> She came home cowering under a festively-colored blanket that shielded her face. You'd think the last thing she'd want to do is bring attention to herself.
>
> Not Jenny.
>
> Our runaway bride has sold her story. A New York multimedia company is pitching a television movie about Wilbanks' life and that of her fiancé . . . *Homegirl* [emphasis mine] may see a payoff of $500,000. It's the kind of development we've come to expect. A nobody gains notoriety for breaking the law, then capitalizes on it. There's no state law against profiting from a crime,

but it speaks volumes about those who do. They're shameless and selfish . . .
Wilbanks hasn't said what, if anything, she's going to do for a community that
showered her with so much love. But I think we already know.[73]

This resentful characterization of Wilbanks as a woman who failed a community
that had so staunchly supported her is discursively typical of much of the follow-
up reporting on her story. However, the key signifying detail that stands out
here is the use of the term "Homegirl" midway through the second paragraph.
With its connotations of black/Latina identity and ironic evocation of Wilbanks
as an undeserving community member, this specific choice of wording helps to
convey the sense that a troubled woman had neglected to live up to the expectations of whiteness. The bitter racialization here also reflects the scrambled terms
of the hometown girl story the Wilbanks case had initially represented to the
mainstream press.

What new forms of celebrity are spawned in a media environment that has
dramatically expanded its definition of "breaking news?" How might current
theories of celebrity be updated/modified to account for the kind of sensational,
high-profile but often briefly-tenured fame that seems to flourish in the 24-hour
cable news cycle? Further, what ideological tendencies may be glimpsed in these
new celebrity modes? (I'm operating on the assumption that new representational
capacities deliver someone like Jennifer Wilbanks into public consciousness in a
way that's different from other headline-making women such as say Patty Hearst
or Lynette "Squeaky" Fromme in the 1970s.) Does this kind of female celebrity open a (small) wedge space for debates that postfeminism more regularly
constricts or shuts down altogether? While not discounting the possibility that
it could, in the case of Jennifer Wilbanks all signs appear to point in the other
direction. For instance, rather than inspiring debate about the kinds of pressures
that might produce "runaway" behavior, the case quickly settled into popular
consciousness on conservative commercial terms. Sales of Runaway Bride merchandise including country song CDs, action figures, and hot sauce were robust,
illustrating how the mediathon transformed into a saleable concept that could
be attached to a variety of commodities. In May 2005, a New Jersey man carved
Wilbanks' face into a piece of Wonder bread toast and listed his artwork on Ebay
fetching over $16,000 for the likeness of a woman he described as "the scam
artist of the year."[74] Especially striking was the way that the Wilbanks case was
absorbed as/adapted into a selling point for the bridal and couples travel industry. In June 2005 the *Boston Globe* reported that an upscale New Orleans hotel
was featuring a Runaway Bride accommodation package. "Uncertain guests get a
private palm reader, foot massages (to help with the fleeing), diamond resetting
recommendations from the recovery concierge, an in-room DVD of *Runaway
Bride*, a look-changing haircut and a Mardi Gras mask for purposes of disguise."[75]
When celebrity news anchor Katie Couric interviewed Wilbanks and fiancé John
Mason in a heavily promoted primetime television broadcast, remarkably their
story was recuperated into matrimonial commodification with fetishistic attention

paid to the choices that had been made for the couple's wedding china, brides-
maid dresses, and other details. It is clear that Wilbanks also entered into popular discourse as a comparative reference point of "failed" femininity that could
be used to evaluate other women's public behavior. Profiling the female race-
car driver Danica Patrick for *The New York Times*, sportswriter Selena Roberts
reported that Patrick "refused to play the runaway bride as she withstood the
pressure to take a remarkable fourth-place finish."[76]

In short, while Wilbanks became a lightning rod for discussion, her motivation, her desperation and her deception were all thoroughly taken for granted.
Her emergence in popular understanding as a weak and foolish woman illustrates in my view the greater license postfeminist culture gives to the expression of contempt for issues of women's emotional and social health, particularly
in contexts where a woman's "life script" appears aberrant. Interestingly, as
Wilbanks was positioned in this role, the photos used to accompany the reporting of her story became less and less flattering. In August 2005, the New York
tabloid *Daily News* published a front page photo of Wilbanks serving her community service sentence by mowing lawns while wearing a "Life is Good" baseball cap in a strange spectacle of contrition. Mobilizing a variety of clichés to
suggest that punishment was justly deserved, the piece tags Wilbanks as a "jail-
dodging jilter," a "mow-dern bride," and a "pain in the grass."

There are other aspects of this case that inform on the habits of a postfeminist culture when it acts to discipline subversive femininity. For instance,
the fervent denunciations of Jennifer Wilbanks rang oddly in the context of the
story's seemingly lighthearted Runaway Bride promotional tag. The phrase itself
is doubly associative, calling to mind both the classical screwball comedies of
the 1930s as well as the 1999 Julia Roberts romance. Scholarship on screwball consistently reads the runaway bride as a liberating, empowered image.
Famously, of course, in *It Happened One Night* (1934) Ellie Andrews' flight
is away from what is expected of her and toward her desire. By contrast, the
Jennifer Wilbanks story is marked by a decisive momentum *from* but there is
no corresponding *to* and Wilbanks' haphazard progress was rather a narrative
letdown.[77] What happened in this mediathon may thus constitute an instance
in which the conventions of screwball comedy are "re-purposed" but without
their original egalitarianism. This, I would suggest, is very much in keeping with
a postfeminist media culture that tends to recycle classical representational codes
but strip them of their progressive and/or ambivalent features.

Another important level of intertextuality connected the evolving news story
to *Runaway Bride* (1999), a film that worked to pathologize the bride with
"cold feet"—in that film, Julia Roberts' small-town girl, Maggie, is shown to
repeatedly abandon men at the altar because of her deep-seated identity crisis
(again the bride's trajectory is evasive rather than purposive).[78] In this respect
the film and the Jennifer Wilbanks case meshed perfectly and led on to what
would become the penultimate phase of the story where Wilbanks was recast
as troubled person, with an ongoing pattern of criminal/irrational behavior of

Figure 2.5 Follow-up tabloid coverage of "Runaway Bride" Jennifer Wilbanks featured a spectacle of community redress and contrition. (*New York Post*, August 10, 2005)

which her flight from a wedding she was uncertain about was just one more example. While there were strident calls for Wilbanks to make restitution for the money spent in searching for her, once she took up the place of a regretful, troubled woman who was (one imagines uneasily) reconciled with her fiancé, the Runaway Bride mediathon was just about over. In its final phase the story transmuted into a public mental and emotional health narrative with articles appearing about how the ever-growing scale and cost of an American middle-class wedding might well cause brides to do a runner before the big day—some stories even featured a set of "warning signs" about how to spot a potential runaway bride among family and friends. In the end in a hypermatrimonial, postfeminist culture, crisis most often converts to diagnosis even as our memory of recent mediathons fades out.

I've been addressing the media celebrity of an emotionally troubled woman who exploded into the public consciousness and quickly became a punchline via saturation media coverage. When she ran away from her planned wedding, Jennifer Wilbanks ran afoul of a powerful set of ideological groundrules for women in contemporary culture. Her story became rooted in her failure to pay homage to the notion that a large and costly wedding is the inevitable high point of any woman's life, and her scandalous deviation from the class codes of affluent whiteness (what, after all, is more tawdry than a Greyhound bus trip to Albuquerque with an unflattering homemade haircut?) Compounding the situation was the fact that Wilbanks had left behind a city (one that preferred the designation "hometown") that was particularly anxious to assert the power and value of community membership. National coverage of Wilbanks' story may have been heightened by a sense of bemusement that the "new south" narrative of bedrock family values, communal solidarity, and conservative ideological constancy was so blatantly out of sync with the developments of the case. It was certainly heightened by the emergence of a 24-hour-per-day news cycle that both takes for granted and feeds an increased information metabolism.

It is my hope that this case study of a particular kind of breaking news celebrity will throw into sharper relief a particular question: how does postfeminism now inflect the story when women attain (welcome or unwelcome, sought or unsought) celebrity? When it comes to female celebrity in recent popular culture there are, of course, the cautionary tales of female ambition run amok (domestic empirebuilder Martha Stewart), the ambivalent accounts of hypersexual yet affectless "bimbo" socialites (Paris Hilton), the often breathless coverage of the new multimedia teen moguls (Lindsay Lohan, the Olsen sisters), and as I have suggested the recurrent accounts of absent (exclusively white) women who are icons of victimhood (Laci Peterson, Natalee Holloway). Postfeminism broadly functions as a cover story for the reality that women's status and security remain in many ways tenuous and family values paradigms sort femininity into categories of value and abjection. The suspicion that these paradigms are widely misapplied and overgeneralized finds expression, I suggest, in the recurrent paradigm of the "missing woman story" in American media culture. One way in which this story is made to seem less exploitative is for the drama to be presided over by an authoritative female commentator, which is the case with both Greta Van Sustern on Fox News and Nancy Grace on CNN, both of whom exhibit aggressive, hectoring styles. Intriguingly, Margo Jefferson writing in *The New York Times* assessed these women's prominence in primetime as marking "the return of the shrew." She writes that Grace in particular:

has brought one of our oldest female caricatures, the Shrew, back to the culture. The Shrew used to be a staple of mass entertainment. She was the pushy wife who drove her husband out of the home or behind his newspaper. She was the spinster who hectored neighbors and school-children. She was plain and sexually deprived. No more. These women specialize in perfect marriages, idealized lovers and good sex. They turn facts into attacks. When they argue, their voices ascend to the 'shrill' notes once ascribed only to feminists.[79]

The primetime cable delivery of the missing woman story thus depends on a peculiar collision of victimized and apparently empowered female personalities (in addition to Van Sustern and Grace one might also include to a lesser extent Rita Cosby of MSNBC who also regularly reports such stories). Such coverage sets a particularly/peculiarly postfeminist scene as these authoritative cable per-sonalities symbolically "lead" the search for the lost woman. Thus, while it's clear that postfeminist media culture is making regular use of female celebrities who present across a spectrum from calculating to unwitting, it's much less clear if these uses represent any innovation in female representability. What is appar-ent is that the postmodern mediathon is giving rise to a new kind of female figure who is closely tracked, ideologically fraught, and highly overdetermined in her meanings. In a postfeminist cultural moment, Jennifer Wilbanks' transfor-mation from a valued to an abject social subject and her shift from geographical monogamy to geographical promiscuity tells us much about the investment in fantasizing stability and continuity through paradigms of gender.

Conclusion

In sketching out a set of suggestive connections between Hollywood romances, female-centered television dramas, and the social terrain of late 1990s and early 2000s retreatism, what I have not fully specified is the exact nature of the con-nections in play. Further analysis would be needed, for instance, to pin down more precisely the interaction between television fictions and sociological reali-ties. Are these series verifying a set of ongoing social practices grounded in an ideological shift in the nature and expectations of women's lives? My analysis has suggested that at times (perhaps particularly in a series like *Judging Amy*) these series demonstrate the capacity to dimensionalize and complicate high-profile social debates about femininity, domesticity, and agency in the early twenty-first century. Moreover, it is clear that in a range of texts postfeminism cooperates with a new regionalism which works to search out corners of "livable" territory amidst deep uncertainty in regard to current American economic and social conditions.

My attempt here to stitch together textual analysis and social history is nec-essarily limited in its ability to generate definitive conclusions. Nor have I fully pursued the questions about social health that arise from noticing a formula in television fiction whereby women deliver themselves (back) into safe, nurturing communities. What I do hope to have sketched, however, is the extraordinarily attractive combination of fantasy elements that unify this formula and the pervasive confusion of actual communities with the communities of sentiment fostered by postfeminism. The retreatist drama brings mothers and daughters back together (even after death), restores hometown sociality and intimacy, and grants its protagonists the putative freedom to be fully individualistic. Any explanation of the success of these series stressing only the industry's lemming-like tendency to duplicate hits may be neglecting their power to generate timely fantasies about gender and social life in America.

The extension of the hometown fantasy through popular romantic comedies to primetime dramas and through more diffuse media forms, such as the cable mediathon, indicates an extraordinarily durable and extendable ideological concept and underscores the frequency with which reteatism is presented as a pathway to the recovery of self. Meanwhile the Runaway Bride case illustrates that violations of the script for hometown femininity will be severely judged. It seems that in a postfeminist, retreatist culture some forms of female disappearance can be countenanced while others cannot. As we begin to witness the economic, financial, and social consequences of a culture of retreatism marked by anti-tax initiatives, educational, urban, and infrastructural decline (tragically brought to public consciousness in the aftermath of Hurricane Katrina), failing utility systems on both the East and West Coasts, the trend toward home schooling, and the proposed Bush social security plan in which individual investments would take priority over any commitment to social welfare, it is vitally important to reflect on the links between popular fiction and the material conditions of everyday life. Whether named as "downshifting," an "opt-out revolution" or the mommy or daughter track, retreatism heavily negotiates current economic and social dilemmas that disproportionately impact on women, while its romanticizing alibi, the hometown fantasy, remains distinctly evasive of social and economic realities.

Chapter 3

Time crisis and the new postfeminist lifecycle

In this chapter I analyze modes of postfeminist temporality, arguing that one of the signature attributes of postfeminist culture is its ability to define various female life stages within the parameters of "time panic." Postfeminism has accelerated the consumerist maturity of girls, carving out new demographic categories such as that of the "tween"; it has forcefully renewed conservative social ideologies centering on the necessity of marriage for young women[1] and the glorification of pregnancy; and it has heightened the visibility of midlife women often cast as desperate to retain or recover their value as postfeminist subjects. Crisis and fulfillment in virtually all these life stages center upon the discovery of personal destiny, the securing of a romantic partner and motherhood, and the negotiation of the problem of paid work (seldom its rewards). Those women who cannot be recuperated into one of these life-stage paradigms generally lose representability within a popular culture landscape dominated by postfeminist definitions of femininity.

These shifts have hardly taken place in cultural isolation, rather as Richard Sennett has argued, everyday life is increasingly driven by the temporal rhythms of corporate efficiency which demand interruptibility, contingency, and a general "time anxiety." As Sennett shows, in contemporary capitalist institutions "casualization, delayering and nonlinear sequencing—shorten the organization's time frame; immediate and small tasks become the emphasis."[2] Required to regularly demonstrate their dynamic character, institutions and the people who thrive in them, are expected to adopt a peripatetic and contingent approach, embracing change and flexibility as core values even in the absence of any evidence that change is called for. In the broad conversion from stability to fleetness, time is reconceived as something which is seldom linear or sustained and is broadly categorized as a threat. As the logic of corporate efficiency is increasingly (mis)applied to a range of human endeavors and interactions, even those whose daily lives are only indirectly structured by institutional affiliations begin to convert to this sense of time as threat, sometimes directly adopting institutional techniques of productivity and time management, such as is evident in a trend recently reported by *The New York Times* for families to write their own "mission statements."[3] My point here is that those who think of time nearly exclusively in terms of contingency will very naturally come to view time as a threat, and the transformation of experiences and conditions of temporality in contemporary culture is broader than I can attempt to show. However, what I do seek to establish as a necessary precondition to the analyses that follow in this chapter is that while a sense of time as threat is not exclusive to the experiences of women nor the media fictions directed at them, postfeminism particularizes and feminizes this broad shift.

Yvonne Tasker and I have noted elsewhere that "postfeminism evidences a distinct preoccupation with the temporal—women's lives are regularly conceived of as timestarved, women themselves are overworked, rushed, harassed, subject to their 'biological clocks,' etc. to such a degree that female adulthood is defined as a state of chronic temporal crisis."[4] Although harried, fragmented subjectivity is deemed a hallmark of postmodern culture, a closer look at mass media images and texts reveals a distinct feminization of the time crisis. Women are depicted as particularly beset by temporal problems that may frequently be resolved through minimization of their ambition and reversion to a more essential femininity. That reversion is often expressed through corporeal concepts and procedures— the "biological clock," intense adherence to regimes of diet, exercise, and personal grooming and the decision to have plastic surgery or a Botox injection are all manifestations of/responses to a postfeminist cultural climate. (Indeed, the intensification of a personal aesthetic regime that now normatively entails the services of day spas, nail salons, cosmetic dentistry, and tanning salons is one of the signal characteristics of the postfeminist economy as I discuss in Chapter 5). The achievement of a youthful appearance through consumerist "empowerment" is positively encoded even as it is disingenuously celebrated in some quarters as a genetic birthright and/or the natural outcome of a well-lived life. New exhortations for one to demonstrate that one is "aging well" employ such rhetoric as cover for the class and wealth bifurcation that enables an affluent minority to tap into a growing marketplace of products and services to forestall and camouflage the effects of the aging process. Popular culture formulations of age-beset femininity also fortify male heterosexual desire as the cynosure for women's concepts of self and their consuming behavior.

The postfeminist fixation on privileged young women and girls is in keeping with these temporal and consumerist habits. From the celebrity of Princess Diana in the US (dubbed in one account "a princess for the postfeminist generation")[5] to a plethora of princess-related marketing directed to young girls to the celebrity of super-rich young women promoted as stars in a culture of fully destigmatized nepotism, there has been an efflorescence of popular culture material glorifying feminine exemplars of inherited wealth and (spending) power.[6] A cycle of films imagines the teen girl as the new aristocrat—the highest-profile films of this kind are in the *Princess Diaries* franchise (2001, 2004) in which San Francisco high school student Mia Thermopolis learns that she is next in line to inherit the throne in the fictional country of Genovia, but the cycle also includes films such as *What a Girl Wants* (2003) (in which a young American goes to

England to meet her aristocratic politician father), *The Prince & Me* (2004) (a Wisconsin college student falls in love with a Danish prince), *Ice Princess* (2005) (whose protagonist's transformation from bookish student to skating star was hyped with the slogan "From Scholastic to Fantastic!"), and two films about a daughter of the US president (*Chasing Liberty* and *First Daughter*, both 2004). Reality television series including MTV's *Rich Girls* (2003) and Fox's *The Simple Life* (2003–) celebrate/despise the pampered daughters of the wealthy while reinforcing their participants' iconic status and furthering the recently renewed cult of the socialite. Meanwhile, the toy industry and new experiential girl-oriented leisure centers have also contributed to what *USA Today* has deemed "the princessing of America, a well-timed confluence of demographics, little-girl desires, parental indulgence, savvy marketing and fascination with European royalty."[7] Not only Mattel's Princess Barbie doll, but a new chain of mall stores called Club Libby Lu which offers princess parties and princess-themed makeovers to girls and a bombardment of princess-themed Disney merchandise from re-released classic films such as *Snow White* (1937) and *Sleeping Beauty* (1959) to *Disney Princess* magazine all cumulatively reinforce the thematization of privileged girlhood.[8] Recent signs suggest that the princesshood phenomenon is being extended to adult women with the marketing of a line of bridal gowns linked to female Disney characters and the notable success of films like *Enchanted* which concludes with its protagonist Princess Giselle opening a Manhattan boutique to sell clothing of her own design. Not only is the princesshood phenomenon another way of reinforcing the centrality and value of youth to femininity, it also customizes aristocratic fantasies for an America in which (particularly when combined with wealth) the precise combination of youthfulness, beauty, and style approaches the function royalty possesses elsewhere as valued social capital.

In the contemporary chick flick, temporal paradoxes abound. A film like *When Harry Met Sally* (1989), trailblazing in its use of the vocabulary and concepts of the self-help movement and deeply influential upon the genre, also took for granted female fear of the future and of the aging process as the death of romantic possibility. Upon learning that her ex-boyfriend is getting married, a distraught Sally has the following exchange with Harry:

Sally: "I drove him away. And I'm gonna be 40!"
Harry: "When?"
Sally: "Someday."
Harry: "In eight years."
Sally: "But it's there. It's just sitting there, like some big dead end."

In a more recent film (and one with stronger elements of fantasy) like *13 Going on 30* time is both more flexible and more subject to female volition. Here, an adolescent girl's intense yearning to experience the security of adulthood becomes a cautionary tale as Jenna is suddenly propelled (through the aid of "magic dust") into an adulthood of competitive careerism and emotional loss. The film's conclusion sees disordered time corrected to normative time and the heroine savoring the life she is meant to be living with a male partner who has loved her since childhood.[9] In order to achieve this end, however, the film must avail itself of a fastforward technique that stands at odds with its message of temporal conservatism.

While women's lives are represented as profoundly governed by the passage of time, postfeminism also extends the promise of new freedoms to transcend or cheat time. However, these putative temporal freedoms are countermatched by an intense calendarization of women's lives with a reinvigoration of demographic-defining rituals including sweet-16 parties, bridal showers, weddings, and baby showers which are positioned as markers of female identity legitimation in addition to life milestones. Women's lives are thus simultaneously ever more governed by notions of temporal propriety and conformity but also assessed in relation to women's perceived abilities to defy time pressures and impacts, and the ensuing paradox is one that a variety of forms of female-oriented popular culture seek to manage.

Such rituals, not coincidentally, all celebrate the achievement of sexual maturity, marriage, or motherhood, and thus one of the consequences of the heightened ritualization of milestones in the normative female lifecycle is that the lives of women without these experiences are temporally unmapped. This chapter will examine the spectre of female singlehood as it is staged in relation to a sense of time urgency. It will also consider the representation of motherhood as personal empowerment and achieved destiny. Finally, it will look at narrative resolutions to the contemporary problem of disordered temporality in films obsessed with a return to the past (notably in many postfeminist films, the 1950s) and with fantasies of time travel. In contemporary romances from *Blast from the Past* (1999) to *The Lake House* (2006) postfeminist romance is achieved through the resolution of temporal dislocation.

Ritualizing the female lifecycle

The conservative character of postfeminism's resolutions to the time crisis is closely connected to the other recidivist paradigms explored in this book. Recent arguments made by commentators such as Caitlin Flanagan about the value of reviving traditionalist models of marriage and motherhood speak to the popularity of re-casting traditionalism as innovation.[10] The frequency of this gambit, I argue, is derived from a sense of paralysis about the prospects for innovation and reform in American life that is in turn closely connected to the insularity and fear that currently predominate in so many features of national experience. When we can't confidently see a way forward we very naturally look back. And as Judith Warner has argued, when we are constantly told that we luxuriate in choices it becomes difficult to conceptualize systemic change or even to pinpoint the narrow channels through which "choice" is steered. In a provocative argument about learned helplessness as a feature of contemporary American culture, Warner contends that the perfectionistic motherhood that has emerged as a new social norm is associated with "a generation of women confronted by a world in which finding real solutions to improve family life seems impossible."[11] She goes on to identify this "Mommy Mystique" as "a social malady—a perverse form of individualism, based on a self-defeating allegiance to a punitive notion of choice; a way of privatizing problems that are social in scope and rendering them, in the absence of real solutions, amenable to one's private powers of control."[12] Other commentators, including Susan Willis, have made similar arguments about powerlessness as a defining feature of American citizenship, particularly in the era after 9/11.[13] There is no doubt that postfeminism gains ground through its acknowledgment of what one team of sociologists has identified as a bifurcation between "'the new impoverishment'—of time as well as income—of many American families" and "the growing affluence" of others.[14] However, as we have seen, its solutions tend to reinforce that inequality rather than challenge it.

Given the blinkered nature of contemporary American life with its sense of unmanageable terrorist, environmental, and other threats and a conservative political climate which advocates consumerism as a panacea for anxiety and an expression of good citizenship, it is perhaps not surprising that large numbers of Americans have come to invest deeply in ostentatious ritualizations of family life and female sexuality. In the expansion of bridal and baby culture, and in the return of celebrations of female sexual maturity like the sweet-16 party, we can track a certain myopic sensibility, a celebration of the present moment. Further, in an environment of rampant time anxiety, ritualization of the exemplary events of the female lifecycle serves to pin time down. Such rituals also essentialize femininity as a biological experience, reinforce the connections between femininity and domesticity, rationalize event-related consumer spending on a grand scale, and connect to the nakedly hierarchical culture that postfeminism helps to produce.

An article in the *Philadelphia Inquirer* documented some of the recent trends in affluent sweet-16 celebrations, describing one party in which the celebrant was mistaken for a bride and noting that "bigger, flashier and costing parents more than ever, the 21st-century Sweet Sixteen has become as elaborate as a wedding."[15] MTV's *My Super Sweet 16* (2005–), a reality series profiling the lavish celebrations of mostly female offspring of the super-rich, has raised the cultural profile of the Sweet 16 while also providing a forum for status envy and class resentment in an ever more economically-polarized culture. The series adheres to a simple formula in which the rich teen makes a series of elaborate demands related to the party, the parents capitulate, the celebrant glories in her social power, making precise guest list choices and humiliating the uninvited for their exclusion from a highlight social event, the party goes wrong in some way leading to a tantrum, but then it all comes together and the evening's apex is reached in the presentation to the teen of a luxury car.[16] As Moya Luckett has pointed out, the narcissistic spectacle at the heart of *My Super Sweet 16* is heavily sexualized but in an ambivalent, dualistic fashion. She notes that "most girls construct their party to stage simultaneously as both adult sexual figures (examples include Cleopatra, belly dancers, rap stars, Victoria's Secret models, and Paris Hilton) and as childish icons, typically princesses."[17]

While (as the anecdote above suggests) the intense ritualization of proms, sweet-16 parties and the like is in part to do with their status as "wedding warm-ups," new norms for showier, costlier bridal showers, rehearsal dinners, etc., are another sign of the extension and elaboration of bridal culture in American life. The intensified American bridal industry (a $32 billion a year "wedding-industrial complex" at the end of the 1990s, according to Chrys Ingraham,[18] but more recent statistics suggest this figure should be dramatically upwardly revised to about $161 billion)[19] and the heightened prominence of weddings within popular culture targeted to women, evident in television's lavish coverage of weddings on both niche cable (in such forms as The Learning Channel's *A Wedding Story*) and the networks (the greater frequency of weddings as television special events, particularly as season enders in primetime series and in programming such as *Today Throws a Wedding* on NBC's *The Today Show*), as well as in the emergence of the "wedding film" as a significant strand of the chick flick genre, have massively increased their cultural purchase over the last decade. While in 1999 Ingraham could legitimately observe, "clearly, weddings have become the most watched yet 'unnoticed' phenomenon in popular culture,"[20] in the past five years scholarship in such fields as sociology, cultural, and media studies on bridal culture in the US and the UK has grown exponentially.[21]

Research by Beth Montemurro reveals how a commensurate expansion in ancillary rituals like bridal showers and bachelorette parties has taken place in proportion to weddings themselves in the era of the "superbride." With multiple bridal showers becoming the norm and bachelorette parties now frequently taking shape as "mini-vacations" with the celebrants heading off to Cancun or Las Vegas, there is a new kind of seasonality to the bridal experience. As Montemurro explains, such events fit into "a larger trend in making the wedding into an extravagant and memorable celebration, extending from the time of the engagement through the honeymoon."[22] No wonder a number of brides report serious emotional anticlimax as they embark on their married lives after the ceremony. According to Jennifer Mendelsohn writing in *The Washington Post*, "The post-wedding letdown is the dirty secret of the bridal industry."[23]

For any such brides, however, motherhood is presented as the next normative plateau of temporal intensity and cultural celebration. In addition to such diffuse phenomena as the publicity campaigns for mother-focused sales strategies that include Target's "Lullaby Club" and the emergence of stork-designated convenient parking for mothers and pregnant women at supermarkets, there are a variety of other direct demographic symptoms of an intensified culture of "family values." At least one state antipoverty program endorsed by the Bush administration conceptualizes marriage as a social and economic diagnostic for impoverished women, and in a so-called "faith-based" initiative, the federal government has extended generous support to abstinence-oriented high school sexual education programs.[24] In order to qualify for federal funding, such programs are obliged to teach that sexual activity outside marriage is likely to be physically and psychologically harmful—their curricula often incorporate rituals that directly operate as "wedding warm-ups" such as "abstinence ceremonies" in which "purity rings" are worn.[25] With marriage now presented in prescriptive terms for the young and the poor, it is evident that the matrimonial mystique works to occlude a variety of social/economic/ideological problem spots.

The intensification of this mystique has been followed by a flurry of media coverage hyping the expansion of family size in a privileged demographic. In 1998 a *Redbook* article, "When Two Is Not Enough," chronicled a late 1990s "suburban boomlet" comprised of an uptick in the number of white, middle-class women electing to have more than three children.[26] More recently in its broadcast on July 3, 2006, *The Today Show* included a segment entitled "Are Three Kids the New Two?" reporting on a National Center for Health Statistics study that found a 10% rise in third children from 1995 to 2004. The broadcast editorialized from this that "having more children has become the new status symbol" and that "parents are starting to discover instead of careers and making money the abundance of big families." *The Today Show* segment had taken its cue from a May 28 *Boston Globe* article, "Three Is the New Two," which explored the family culture in the affluent Boston suburb of Wellesley, noting that in some families "Four is the new three." What is striking in these reports of familial plenitude is the repeated formulation in which a larger number is seen to have the same value held by a smaller number in the past. This formulation (which when it comes to women's ages, works on inverted but comparable terms as we shall shortly see) is presented as a form of contemporary one-upmanship, a strategy for conceptualizing time and age as flexible but also definitive.

Beating, cheating, and transcending time: disordered temporalities in recent cinema and culture

Postfeminism suggests that symbolic forms of time mastery (particularly management of the aging process) will provide the key to the reclamation of self. From self-help books on time-management to cosmetic products and technologies that celebrate "age defiance" as personal empowerment to hyped-up rhetorical/ideological formulations such as the "biological clock," women in a postfeminist culture are constantly exhorted to internalize and act on a sense of temporal urgency. To skim the titles of a broad swathe of books on couplehood and family life is quickly to register the centrality of time as threat in such publications as *It's about Time: Couples and Careers* by Phyllis Moen, *Working in a 24/7 Economy: Challenges for American Families* by Harriet B. Pressler, and *Competing Devotions: Career and Family Among Women Executives* by Mary Blair-Loy. Increasingly, the popular press generates alarmist coverage reinforcing "health panics" about women's susceptibility to time problems. Are midlife women behaving too youthfully? Are girls too mature? These worries are frequently crudely scientized in reports that the average age for the onset of menses has lowered or in accounts of a wave of "adult anorexia" that strikes women at a time when they fear they may be losing sexual desirability in the eyes of their husbands.[27]

The sense that women in particular cannot use time properly manifested itself in sensationalistic accounts in 2006 of a nation of sleep-deprived women worn out by their work and/or exhausted by the burdens of childrearing in a culture of perfectionistic motherhood. In a year when *The New York Times* reported on its front page that about 42 million sleeping pill prescriptions were filled over the preceding 12 months, the sleep crisis and its associated pharmacological dependency revived 1950s-era images of pill-popping motherhood through their installment of archetypes like the weary mother and the Ambien driver.[28] (By mid-2006 a popularly gendered mythology about Ambien-takers imagined male corporate workers falling asleep as they drove home from the office and female users waking in the middle of the night to binge on food, a particularly worrying side effect in a postfeminist culture of intense body maintenance.) The relevance of these kinds of concerns to everyday life was seemingly ratified when in the first season of the ABC television drama/postfeminist touchstone text *Desperate Housewives* an exhausted Lynette became briefly addicted to her son's Ritalin in an effort to keep herself going. Representations of this kind produce another variant on the theme of feminized temporal crisis.

Popular film registers the contemporary female time crisis in a variety of ways—one recurrent mode of response has been a nostalgic revisiting of 1950s culture as a scene of time abundance. While the need to restage the postwar period has been with us for decades (in the 1970s and 1980s the linchpin figure for reconnecting with that era tended to be the male pseudo-rebel incarnated by Arthur Fonzarelli in the TV hit *Happy Days* or Danny Zuko in *Grease* [1978]), Roberta Garrett has observed a more recent feminization of fiftiesness.[29] The clutch of chick flicks set in the 1950s includes *Far from Heaven* (2002), *Mona Lisa Smile* (2003), and *Pleasantville* (1999), which concludes with a time-traveling teen girl from the 1990s electing to stay in the 1950s rather than return to her contemporary life.[30] *Blast from the Past*, a film that dedicates itself to (re)finding a man from the 1950s for a contemporary "good girl," might be seen as a transitional text here. The film's bedrock belief in the need to recover original, essential archetypes of gender is suggested by the naming of its central couple Adam and Eve. Adam (Brendan Fraser), the child of Cold War parents who raised him in an elaborate underground shelter after becoming convinced a nuclear attack had taken place, is forced to come up to 1990s Los Angeles to obtain more supplies for the family and to find a wife. His encounters with Eve (Alicia Silverstone), a superficially trendy and cynical but fundamentally virtuous young woman, involve Adam's transmission to her of lessons in traditional courtesy and kindness and at the end of the film Adam and Eve (drawing on funds from cashed-in Old Economy stocks held by his father) build a secluded

Figure 3.1 Popular press reports of a feminized "time crisis" circulated with increasing frequency in the early 2000s. (*Newsweek*, April 24, 2006)

new home and bring his parents aboveground where the family will live together acting on Adam's conviction that normal family life involves care for all family members.

In addition to the nostalgia for social health and time abundance exhibited by some 1950s-themed chick flicks, another cinematic response to the contemporary time crisis can be seen in the recent rather robust cycle of time-traveling romances.[31] While the time travel plot has a long history in Hollywood films pitched to female audiences (from *Portrait of Jennie* [1948] to *Somewhere in Time* [1980] and *Peggy Sue Got Married* [1986]) there has seldom been a period in which this plot formula was so ubiquitous. The perceived commercial viability of this format is suggested by the involvement of several of the most high-profile chick flick stars (Meg Ryan, Jennifer Garner, and Sandra Bullock) in films of this kind such as *Kate & Leopold*, *13 Going on 30*, and *The Lake House*. Even as other forms of postfeminist culture seek to fix time, this form extends the promise of correcting disordered temporalities or of transcending or cheating time as I will argue.

It is important to note that in cinematic time-travel romances the heroine is frequently stuck in the present while the male lead is a temporal transit figure. This is the case in a range of films from science fiction romance *Starman* (1984), to *Somewhere in Time*, as well as recent films which feature a man from the past either literally (*Kate & Leopold*) or symbolically (*Blast from the Past*), a man from the future (*Happy Accidents*), or a man who moves between different temporal possibilities (*The Lake House*). Such time-shifting masculinities are not only infused with a sense of possibility and purpose, they are also particularly well suited to appeal to the time-beset female spectator.

The time-travel films stand in suggestive proximity to a set of "memory romances" including films like *The Notebook* (2004) and *50 First Dates* (2004) which crucially stage a heroine's disordered relationship to time. In the former, a largely World-War-II-era flashback narrative set within a contemporary frame story, the elderly heroine's Alzheimer's disease leads her husband to tell and retell her the story of their romance. That the heroine's memory problems (and associated emotional turmoil) are alleviated by the intervention of a male narrator who speaks memories for her/on her behalf may be seen to reflect a characteristically postfeminist mingling of male care and sensitivity with patriarchal authority. In *50 First Dates* Lucy (Drew Barrymore) has suffered a brain injury which eradicates her memory from one day to the next. While her father and brother work to manage Lucy's injury and shelter her from emotional distress by studiously pretending that time is passing normally (for instance, they re-celebrate her birthday with her every day) when Henry (Adam Sandler) meets and falls in love with Lucy he faces the challenge of trying to build a relationship with a woman who never remembers him. Henry's triumph in the film's flash-forward conclusion is to have engineered a situation in which every morning on waking Lucy finds a videotape that summarizes her relationship with (and now marriage to) Henry and imparts to her the news that they have a daughter. Lucy is also sheltered from confusing experiences by being isolated—Henry is realizing his dream of sailing around the world and consequently Lucy spends the vast majority of her time on a boat in the exclusive company of her husband and child. Strikingly, both of these 2004 hit films equate intimacy with male management of the knowledge and perception of a female character for whom time and memory have become incoherent.[32] In each case all the heroine knows is what her male partner tells her. In this way *The Notebook* and *50 First Dates* reveal the tendency of contemporary cinema to embed fantasies of patriarchal control within seemingly egalitarian romances deemed to be attractive to women.

Figure 3.2 In *Kate & Leopold*, the harried contemporary heroine finds respite in a time-traveling romance to the nineteenth century. (Meg Ryan and Hugh Jackman in *Kate & Leopold*, 2001)

They are in this sense to be specifically differentiated (on the basis of their centralization of the "romance of female forgetting") from other early twenty-first-century "memory films" such as *Eternal Sunshine of the Spotless Mind* (2004) and *Memento* (2000).

In *Kate & Leopold* the hard-edged New York advertising executive played by Meg Ryan meets an aristocrat who has traveled from the nineteenth century through a time portal into the present. Another in the long line of chick flick representations of disappointed professional women, Kate leads a harried life that is suggested by our first glimpse of her hounding her ex-boyfriend for the return of her Blackberry.[33] Despite her executive status Kate is trapped in an ethos of stultifying artificiality, spending her time manufacturing desire for synthetic products such as margarine through market testing and subject to the unctuous overtures of a boss who refers to himself unabashedly as a "people pleaser." Stuck in a superficial, alienated environment, Kate is by her own admission exhausted and disenchanted and this disenchantment culminates near the end of the film in her increasingly numb response to the news of her long-sought promotion. As in *Blast from the Past* the time-traveling hero arrives to school the heroine in a higher level of conduct steeped in the values of decency, kindness, and care the film represents as lost in the contemporary world and Kate is reduced to weepy appreciation of Leopold's thoughtful and considerate gestures during what he perceives as their courtship. Ultimately however, Kate's defiant justification of her work ("I'm tired and I need a rest and if I need to peddle a little pond scum to get one, then so be it") and attempt to use Leopold as a pitchman for the margarine product lead him to return to the nineteenth century. The concluding scene stages the only means of respite the film can envision for its heroine—a time-traveling return to 1876 where she rejoins Leopold. By giving up her life to become a nineteenth-century duchess, Kate is relieved of work in an atmosphere of sexual harassment, shallow promotional rhetoric, and crass salesmanship.[34]

In one of the most recent incarnations of the time-traveling romance, *The Lake House* (2006), *Speed* (1994) stars Sandra Bullock and Keanu Reaves are re-teamed to play Chicago-based professionals (a doctor and architect respectively) who find they can communicate through letters even though they are apparently living two years apart. While critics who deemed the more recent film "*Speed* in reverse" were probably sacrificing accuracy for glibness, the film does indeed abandon a conventional sense of a deadline in favor of a more complex struggle for time mastery on the part of its protagonists. Debates over whether the film was logically coherent tended to be showcased in its review coverage and on the Internet, but taken in a broader context such debates very likely miss the point. A movie such as *The Lake House* does not have to be logically coherent so much as it has to harmonize with the widespread perception that in everyday life time is somehow lacking, deficient, problematic, and blameworthy. Very much in keeping with the broader postfeminist rhetoric of female temporal crisis, *The Lake House* links the struggle for intimacy to a "time problem." It also engages quintessential chick flick themes such as the loneliness and isolation of female professional careers, the desire for home (in this case a glass house on a lake that both Kate Forster and Alex Wyler live in at different points), and the emotional need to restore/repair family roles. The revelation that the lake house was built by Alex's father, a prominent architect, suggests a core longing for the stable rootedness of a family home and shores up the film's validation of a patrilineal commitment to meaningful work (Alex, his brother and their father all practice the family trade of architecture).[35] In contrast, Kate's medical career is irrelevant apart from her unsuccessful attempt to save Alex's life (in one temporal dimension), and in the film's single scene of her doing her work she is represented as confused and rather hapless in her first day at a new hospital. Kate's urban melancholia (she confesses at one point "I sometimes feel as if I'm invisible, as if no one can see me at all") will be eradicated through romance and the promise that this ideal couple will live a life of emotional transparency in an all-glass house.

A year following the release of *The Lake House* Sandra Bullock appeared in *Premonition*, another fidelity drama linking female identity crisis to a fraught sense of multi-temporality. Here, housewife and mother Linda Hanson is trapped in a confusing temporal loop in which her husband, on the verge of initiating an affair with a work colleague, may or may not have been killed in a car accident. Each time Linda wakes up (and the film is remarkable for its heavy emphasis on its protagonist's perpetual sleepiness) she finds herself at a different point in time, with her husband sometimes already dead and sometimes still alive. The film makes clear that Linda's disordered sense of time stems from her failure (and it is hers alone) to emotionally maintain her marriage. Strikingly, the film's conclusion resolves Linda's sense of disordered time via a redemptive pregnancy; in a warmly-lit concluding tableau Linda wakes for the last time now heavily pregnant and surrounded by her children. Such a conclusion proffers procreation as one means of resolving time crisis, a gambit that appears very regularly in postfeminist popular culture as we shall see later in the chapter.

Deadline films: reforming and emancipating women under pressure

I want to briefly mention some examples of another narrative strategy that arises in the contemporary chick flick for conceptualizing time pressure and panic: the threat of impending death. This formula has several different variations. In one version of the "deadline film," the heroine is given to understand (wrongly as it turns out) that she has only a short time left to live. In contrast to a very different sort of "deadline film" such as the German-made independent hit *Run Lola Run* (1998) whose active heroine tests her own limits in an effort to save her boyfriend's life, these films usually entail a shoring up of the female protagonist's relationship to heterosexual romance and/or consumerism. That this can be a somewhat ideologically flexible narrative formula is borne out by an analysis of the contrasts between two particular films: *Life or Something Like It* (2002), which uses this deadline punitively against a transgressively ambitious female lead and *Last Holiday* (2006), which employs the device as an emancipation for its heroine. Both are seen as undertaking corrections to their life course as a result of their belief in their own impending deaths.

Life or Something Like It demonstrates the urgency of scaling back career aspirations in favor of a "real life" that is prohibited to high-level professional women. Lanie Kerrigan (Angelina Jolie), a Seattle TV reporter, opens the film fiercely ambitious to take her career to the national level. The film then employs an openly hostile plot device to compel her to rethink the meaning of her life; a homeless psychic, Prophet Jack (Tony Shalhoub), convinces her that her death is imminent. Lanie realizes that ambition has crowded out intimacy in her life and so chooses to stay in Seattle, temper her professional goals, and marry Pete (Edward Burns), a cameraman with a young son.

Released approximately one year after Hurricane Katrina and publicized with the tagline "Enjoy yourself . . . Time is running out!," *Last Holiday* stands in uncanny relationship to the (heavily African-American) population dispersion from New Orleans after Katrina's devastating impact. Its heroine Georgia Byrd (Queen Latifah) is a New Orleans shopclerk who has always lived cautiously and fully within her means, shirking romance with a fellow clerk out of reticence and engaging in symbolically maternal activities like cooking for neighborhood children. When mistakenly informed that she has a serious disease and only a very short time to live, Georgia liquidates her bank account and leaves her city for the first time, traveling to the Czech Republic where she undergoes a makeover, indulges her appetite to her heart's content, and finds herself mingling with a set of wealthy hotel guests that include the owner of the store where she used to work and a New Orleans politician. While imparting lessons to these characters about the psychic and communal costs of corporate greed and political duplicity, Georgia also bonds with a French chef. When the diagnostic error that led to Georgia's mistaken belief about her fatal illness is corrected, she finds love with her fellow shopclerk, returns to New Orleans and opens a restaurant, thus staging a tableau of hometown rejuvenation sadly at odds with the actual status of New Orleans in 2006.

Another sort of chick flick "deadline film" is the (in this case legitimately) dying woman drama, which further subdivides into two variants: one type is the coming of age story of a young woman in which an older maternal figure must die seemingly to make space for the heroine to come into her own and/or take up a proper place in a family structure. Films that hew to this formula include *One True Thing* (1998), *Stepmom* (1998), and *The Family Stone* (2005) while the other variant features a romance between a dying woman and a man who is initially unaware of her health status but who is tutored by the female protagonist in the values of intimacy and vulnerability (as is the case in *Sweet November* [2001] and *Autumn in New York* [2000]). Both variants are thus narratives of reform; in the former case an ambitious young careerist learns to put the value of family ahead of her own interests and desires, while in the latter a man is emotionally rehabilitated through the nobility of his dying partner. Both showcase the moral benevolence of femininity and celebrate a female capacity for selflessness through "time is running out" plot formulas.

Time is running out: abject singlehood in postfeminist fiction

In postfeminist culture the single woman stands as the most conspicuously time-beset example of contemporary femininity, her singlehood encoded as a particularly temporal failure and a drifting off course from the normative stages of the female lifecycle. Although Bridget Jones was the most high-profile and perhaps the pioneering figure of the new pathetic single woman, the spectre of singlehood abounds in print, film, and broadcast media. The ubiquity of this figure (invariably coded as desperate) has been observed by Roberta Garrett who notes

> the flipside of the pushy, competent careerist is not the pushy, perfectionistic homemaker, but that beloved figure of recent women's popular fiction: the hapless singleton. It is no coincidence that the phenomenal popularity of Bridget Jones and her many kooky, dizzy or commitment-shy sisters coincides with the vindictive treatment meted out to high-flying "career women" and smug housewives in female-orientated fictional forms.[36]

Under the terms of what social psychologist Bella DePaulo deems the "mythology of marital superiority," it is taken to be self-evident that single and non-parenting women's lives are empty, deficient, or not yet fully underway.[37] As DePaulo points out, "depictions of singles, interpretations of their motives and emotions, and conversations with them are driven by the assumption that for single people, the quest to become unsingle dominates their lives."[38] Such dynamics are acutely gendered in a postfeminist culture that directs an increasingly diagnostic gaze toward single women. On television the assumption that the single female is desperate to find a husband has served as the creative catalyst for numerous series particularly in reality genres. In matchmaking and courtship series from *The Bachelor* to *Meet My Folks* desperate (and often mercenary) single women make strenuous efforts to find a male partner. Two recent series are particularly worth noting here for their attempts to refresh the image of the desperate female single. In *#1 Single* on the E network, Lisa Loeb, the mid-1990s one-hit wonder pop star and iconic Generation Xer, moves to New York in the pilot to better her chances of finding a husband. Loeb's announcement to her audience that she is single because she has recently seen the second of two six-year relationships come to an end is critically processed when early on both her mother and celebrity interviewer Ryan Seacrest suggest she made poor use of her time by staying in long-term relationships that didn't lead to marriage. As she embarks on her quest, Loeb's (marginal) celebrity is trumped by her single status as she searches for her ideal partner. Along the way she attempts or addresses a variety of recent models of singlehood, interacting with or being advised by other B-list celebrities such as Ileana Douglas, Isaac Mizrahi, and

Adam Goldberg. The series takes on board topical lifestyling trends including Feng Shui, airplane dating, elaborate waxing techniques, etc., as the singer pursues her quest for love at age 37. The series pilot opens with an economical exchange between Loeb and Seacrest in which she outlines her quest (and not coincidentally the series' premise):

Loeb: I grew up in suburbia. And I sort of ran away from that in a way. I went to college. I moved to New York City. And now I'm here in Los Angeles and I really want to be a Mom. And I want to be married. And I want all that stuff that I sort of ran away from.
Seacrest: But why can't we just have fulfillment and peace of mind in the moment in a great relationship without thinking about next year and the next year?
Loeb: Ovaries.

In another episode at her mother's urging Loeb has lunch at the home of Rabbi Shmuley Boteach,[39] and one of the rabbi's seven children asks her age, starring in astonishment upon being told that Loeb is the same age as their mother. Loeb says to the Rabbi's wife "I'm so behind—you have all your children. Can I have one?" With its hip style and arch tone, *#1 Single* well illustrates the postfeminist tendency to use irony as a stylistic alibi for what is fundamentally deeply conservative material.

The standardization of formulae for depicting single femininity as a plight is further suggested by the primetime debut on ABC in June, 2006 of *How to Get the Guy*. The series profiled four single women who under the direction of two "love coaches" (a journalist and a television personality) pursue dating opportunities in San Francisco. Like *#1 Single* the focus is on an "empowered" response to the problem of singlehood. On ABC.com the series was described as follows: "The women take hold of their own romantic destinies and declare to the world that they are ready, willing, and able to do anything and everything they have to in order to find true love." The conjunction in such language between assertive self-interest and discovery of "destiny" is at once axiomatically postfeminist and thoroughly contradictory. Yet at the same time, such formulations speak to the most serious fear at the heart of such representations of desperate, questing, single women, one which takes vivid shape in the fear Bridget Jones gives voice to in the opening sequence of *Bridget Jones' Diary* (2001): that she is in danger of becoming socially worthless, a body whose abjection is so complete that upon her death it will go unnoticed and her corpse will be eaten by dogs. This hysterical sense of accelerated time that leads a woman in her 30s to fixate on her death expresses both the imminent social death for which the single woman is at risk and a sense of the centrality of her abject selfhood.

The fetishization and eroticization of pregnancy

In contrast to the time-beset single woman, the pregnant woman is often endowed with cultural permission to slow down and savor time. In a mainstream
popular culture that frequently equates motherhood with full womanhood,
pregnancy becomes "exemplary time" when women look, feel, and are their
best. Accordingly the pregnant female body has lost its taboo status and is being
subject to new forms of fetishization and eroticization. As Ruth La Ferla has
observed, "all at once, images of sexy, semiclad pregnant celebrities and new
mothers seem to be everywhere."[40] The Discovery Health Channel broadcasts
Runway Moms, a reality series profiling models who are either pregnant or have
recently given birth. Meanwhile, major designers now offer lines of pregnancy
coutures, and retail outlets such as A Pea in the Pod (in the US) and Mothercare
(in the UK) take an opposite tack from previous generations' sartorial efforts to
juvenilize or conceal the pregnant body and instead sell clothing to flaunt it.
The re-classification of the pregnant body as natural, normal, and healthy has
transitioned in recent years to a new physical and ideological exhibitionism that
is facilitated by fashion trends such as the belly-baring t-shirt. (These two layers
of exhibitionism were succinctly brought together in a well-circulated image
from pop star Britney Spears' first pregnancy in which the star was photographed
wearing a t-shirt that read "I've Got the Golden Ticket" with a downward arrow
pointing to her stomach.) From Catherine Zeta-Jones to Rachel Weisz many of
the most avidly-watched and highly-valued bodies on the red carpet at Hollywood events are pregnant ones. The trickle-down commercialization effect of
such high-status cultural events may be glimpsed in the recent trend toward
prenatal photography which has opened up a new line of work for professional
photographers, capturing images from the demure to the erotic of women dis-
playing their pregnant bodies.[41] A 2006 ad making the case for the longevity of
its product by presenting successive historical archetypes of American womanhood starkly illustrates the pregnant (white) woman's current position as the exemplar of idealized femininity. Here, the serenity and implied self-knowledge of
the most recent historical figure stands in comparison to the other figures who
merely seem to be posing/role-playing. This is in keeping more broadly with
the notion that motherhood confers authentic self-knowledge amidst a dizzying
array of potential identity categories.

Notably, the language we use to describe pregnancy is changing, with the delicate and oblique phraseology of the past (when a pregnant woman was described
as "expecting" or even "being in the family way") giving way to an emphatic
underscoring of the pregnant body (as in the now ubiquitous and transatlantic
"baby bump").[42] Within the newly exhibitionistic terms of pregnancy, the challenge is how best to showcase the pregnant belly rather than hiding it as was
once expected. Accordingly the aggressive eroticization of maternity fashion is
linked in the tabloids to female stars celebrated for their "glow" and deemed to

Figure 3.3 In an advertisement for Clorox Bleach, successive historical archetypes of American femininity lead to fetishized pregnancy as the
womanly ideal in our time. (© 2006, The Clorox Company)

be in a kind of competition for the most beautiful pregnancy. While the founder
of the Celebrity Baby Blog website claims the site is perused by more than 1.5
million people a month and has inspired a rash of knockoffs, Rebecca Traister
has dubbed the hyping of celebrity pregnancy "pregnancy porn," and intriguingly speculated on the reasons for its success. Amidst the breathless coverage
and intense hype that accompanies the celebrity pregnancy, it is worth observing that the broad fetishization of the pregnant woman and her centrality as a
lifestyle icon operate also as a means of quelling still-unresolved debates over
reproductive politics in America.[43]

Even as pregnancy has been hyped as a state of transcendent femininity, there
are signs that it is increasingly culturally acceptable to directly or tacitly limit
pregnant women's role in the workplace. Complaints of pregnancy discrimination filed with the Equal Employment Opportunity Commission (EEOC) rose
by 39% from 1992 to 2003 while observers like Ellen Bravo, the director of
a working women's association in Milwaukee, have asserted that "Pregnancy
discrimination is still alive and well and escalating."[44] Meanwhile, the kinds of
programs widely recognized to support working mothers such as flex time, tele-
commuting, and job sharing are being scaled back.[45] The incompatibility of
motherhood with paid work is also communicated in the press by conservative

columnists such as John Tierney who in 2002 espoused the position that Take Our Daughters to Work Day stigmatized at-home mothers.[46]

Celebrity Momism, bravura mothering, and motherhood as salvation

The postfeminist celebration of mothering reaches heights that would have been unimaginable a generation ago. In a range of films and television programs, in journalism, and in advertising motherhood redeems, it transforms, it enriches, it elevates. In recent years both the representational and social realms have fostered the display of hypermaternity among economically elite white women. As Ruth La Ferla has written, "To judge by the latest flurry of celebrity journalism and fashion advertising, for many women in the public eye becoming a mom is not just a momentous life passage but an opportunity to shine."[47] While the hyperprocreative family film has been revived/recycled (*Cheaper by the Dozen* [2003, 2005], *Yours, Mine & Ours* [2005]) and television magazine programs such as *Dateline NBC* regularly air adulatory features on families with multiple single-birth offspring, a conspicuous upper-middle-class "baby boom" is underway in some of the more affluent socioeconomic pockets of the country.[48] In chick flicks that stage motherhood as empowerment such as *Mrs. Winterbourne* (1996, where a homeless young woman earns a class promotion through motherhood and finds not only a wealthy husband but also a kind and caring mother-in-law) the decision to give birth is lauded as courageous and life-changing in every sense.

In a related development, film and television dramedies have repeatedly employed a crudely conventional plotline in which improvised and unexpected motherhood is foisted upon the unlikely or the unwilling for their betterment. In two particular examples the ambition of a professional woman is abruptly checked by her sudden inheritance of children. In the 2004–2005 Aaron Spelling series *Summerland* (Warner Bros.), for instance, single fashion designer Ava Gregory is living a busy life in Southern California when she learns that her sister and brother-in-law have been killed. The series originates with this event and then transitions to an emphasis on the challenges and rewards of motherhood as Ava finds herself the sudden guardian of three adolescents recently arrived from Kansas. (In this way the series regionalizes its sense of the value of traditionalism in a fashion that is reminiscent of a television series like *Providence*.) In a virtually verbatim plotline (though set on the East Coast rather than the West) the feature film *Raising Helen* (2004) showcases a rapidly rising junior executive in the fashion industry whose sister and brother-in-law are killed and who also bequeath to her three orphaned children. At the close of the film Helen (Kate Hudson) gives up her Manhattan career and marries a minister, dedicating herself to life in Queens and a lifestyle more suitable for childraising. In the film's flashforward close, we see that she has also had her own biological child and that the film's objective (bluntly conveyed in its title) has been achieved—Helen has finally achieved a meaningful state of female maturity because of her acceptance of her maternal destiny.

More recently, in *No Reservations* (2007), Catherine Zeta-Jones' brittle, emotionally isolated gourmet chef unexpectedly inherits her niece Zoe after the girl's mother is killed in a car crash. The little girl serves as a catalyst for Kate's transformation into a warmer, more caring person, earning Kate eligibility for romance with fellow chef Nick and the achievement of an idealized home life and a "family business" in which Kate is no longer an authoritative aesthete dedicated to serving precise and challenging high-end fare but a "team player" preparing breakfasts in a café with Nick and Zoe.

In many of the accounts of redemptive, transformative motherhood that circulate in the popular culture landscape, women repeatedly discover themselves when they experience an immediate and powerful sense of enchantment with their newborn. In Caitlin Flanagan's *To Hell with All That: Loving and Loathing Our Inner Housewife*, for instance, Flanagan writes that she always considered herself a failure until she gave birth to twin sons at which point she was transformed: "I had, at long last, done something right" she observes in postpartum wonder.[49] (Flanagan even repeatedly uses the language of religious epiphany and deliverance in describing her children's birth.) In an account such as that of Katherine Ozment writing in *The New York Times*, motherhood resolves depression and suicidal ideation. In a style section essay, the author recounts her lifelong struggle with depression and the immediate clarification of her illness upon the birth of her son, noting that the first days with her child "were as much the beginning of life for me as they were for the baby he was then."[50] Susan Cheever discusses the revelation of holding her newborn in similar terms: "The moment I held her in my arms, I became a different person. You could say that I joined the human race."[51]

Within the new maternalist paradigm, well-educated, high-achieving women are free to revert to a "signs and wonders" discourse in which they maintain magical communication/communion with their (sometimes as yet unborn) offspring and strongly perceive a sense of the higher calling/destiny of motherhood. Such is emphatically the case in Rebecca Walker's contribution to the literature of maternalist redemption, *Baby Love: Choosing Motherhood after a Lifetime of Ambivalence* (2007). An extraordinary account of self-glorification through pregnancy, *Baby Love* even goes so far as to figuratively extend the author's pregnancy to encompass 15 years of her life ("I didn't know that those 15 years constituted my real first trimester, and all that time my baby was coming toward me, and I was moving toward my baby").[52] What is particularly striking in Walker's account is her construction of a specifically generationally-marked contrast between what she represents as her utterly healthy and natural desire to be a mother and the negative legacies of her own mother who seeks (unconsciously or otherwise) to smother her daughter. This contrast is striking because Walker's mother is the Pulitzer Prize-winning feminist novelist Alice Walker, a woman whom her daughter seems to classify within a set of unnatural, angry "witch feminists" when she writes that "These mothers did not seem to know, with all their potions and philosophies, their desires to rehabilitate ancient scripts of gender and identity, that there is a natural order, and that natural order involves passing the scepter to offspring with unconditional love and pride."[53] In Rebecca Walker's account of her pregnancy, her mother functions as the poisonous feminist anti-maternal, the obstacle figure to her daughter's maternal ambition. At one point she even goes so far as to relate a recurring dream in which she perceives a little boy waiting for her in a cave (Walker knows she is a carrying a boy) but she is prevented from going to him by "an angry woman stabbing at my heart."[54] For Rebecca Walker, in another of postfeminism's perverse paradigms of "choice," one must be mother or daughter, but not both.

Such configurations of motherhood as salvation are also, of course, to be found in the testimonials of countless celebrity mothers. When Britney Spears decided to make known a change in her religious status, she used her website to announce, "I no longer study Kabbalah. My baby is my religion."[55] Angelina Jolie has attested that adoption of her son Maddox "made her a woman,"[56] while Céline Dion has sung of her feelings of triumphant self-discovery upon the birth of her son René-Charles. The commercial crossover possibilities of motherhood are apparent in Dion's hit "A New Day Has Come" which underscored the creative concept name for the star's Las Vegas show while linking her re-emergence after a professional hiatus to the rejuvenating effects of motherhood. The song's lyrics include the lines:

Where it was dark now there is light
Where there was pain, now there's joy
Where there was weakness, I found my strength
All in the eyes of a boy.

In advertising directed to women, the ostensible privacy of motherhood is often symbolically, commercially universalized. In 2003 DaimlerChrysler paid Dion about $14 million to sponsor a broadcast of the star's *A New Day* concert on CBS, and to have her appear in print and broadcast ads and make public appearances.[57] The ads tended to explain/source Dion's music as expressive of a broad maternal sensibility; for instance, as part of the campaign Dion cuddled her son while riding in a Chrysler minivan to the strains of "Have You Ever Been in Love?" Dion's bid for status as universal mother was further substantiated by a series of photos by Anne Geddes that paired the star with a variety of ethnically/racially marked babies whose otherness was meant to contrast with Dion's whiteness (in some of the photos the babies wore colored caps so that their "hair" would match the star's outfit and in one case this required an infant to appear to have green hair). This spiritualized presentation of the infant as style accessory and Dion as "global maternal" carried a specific commercial valence given that Dion had recorded a CD of lullabies called *Miracle* which had been cross-promoted on an episode of *The Oprah Winfrey Show* (titled "Miracle Babies") in which the two stars cooed over infants born prematurely. In a similar vein, new narratives of female celebrity benevolence often draw upon public knowledge of a star's maternity, suggesting that their capacity to feel for others in need is an extension of a full humanity facilitated by mothering as was the case in Dion's emotional pleas for support for the victims of Hurricane Katrina and in Jolie's ongoing efforts to draw attention to third-world poverty. Yet the lionization of motherhood in celebrity representations always teeters on the brink of open exploitation in which children are crudely presented as forms of capital. At the Emmy Awards in August, 2006, celebrity swag bags included t-shirts by the clothing company I Dream of Johnny that read "My Bling Is My Baby," and for infants and children "I'm the Bling."

The social currency of motherhood in postfeminist culture is hinted at in the extension and application of the term "Mom" well beyond the family context in which it originated as a shortened and informalized version of "Mama." Ben Yagoda has argued that "'Mom' is indisputably the word of the moment in the culture at large," citing the more than 320 million Google hits on the word as opposed to 192 million for "Dad" and the more than 3,000 books with "Mom" in the title listed by Amazon.[58] Yagoda draws attention to a subtle but significant change in the social usage of "Mom," with the term now self-applied by a large number of women (as in "I'm John's Mom," or "Speaking as a mom") and increasingly used in reference to particular women by people outside their families ("How's your Mom?").

"Mom," with its casual and intimate connotations, gives off the impression that maternal status now factors outside the family to a greater and greater extent. Demographic categories like "soccer mom," political ones like "security moms," and terms like "working mom" (whose warm sound would seem to alleviate the rampant ideological uncertainty about how this state is to be achieved) seem to reflect an understanding that the sentimentalization of motherhood is universal. As Yagoda aptly observes, "Mom" is the ideal term for a postfeminist era for "it finesses the feminist challenge to American motherhood . . . It cannot be a verb. It's just an identity, something we all seem to be looking for these days."[59]

Roberta Garrett has noted that "The 1990s could be characterized in the history of reproductive technology as a decade in which the institution of motherhood was publicly declared in crisis. Since the birth of the first test-tube baby in 1978, pregnancy's categorization as a 'natural' act has been contested medically and scientifically."[60] The terror that new technologies might shift the burdens of parenting and blatantly contradict the "self-evident" fact that mothers should be the natural priority (and near exclusive) caregivers of children helps to explain the emergence of the new bravura mothering in which postfeminist motherhood is equated with ultimate clarity and the will to achieve or endure. Flanagan concludes her book by relating her battle with breast cancer, providing an account in which her own doubts, fears, and uncertainties are continually emphasized by stating confidently: "Here's what I know: When I woke up from the final surgery, I didn't want to see the article I've written or the editors I've worked for. I wanted to see my sons and my husband. And I wanted to go home."[61] Such certitude is very much in the mode of Oprah Winfrey's sloganistic "What I Know for Sure," the title of her closing column in each issue of *O: The Oprah Magazine* and a mantra the star is careful to synergistically repeat from time to time on her television program. Such formulations appear to cut through postmodern ambiguity and ambivalence, giving credence to female intuition as a higher-order epistemology.

Temporal disorder and maternal righteousness are dramatically brought together in a film like *The Forgotten* (2005) in which heroic supermother Telly's (Julianne Moore) capacity to connect with her son and sustain his memory after his disappearance and apparent death empowers her to defeat a vague supernatural conspiracy that is testing whether parental love can be eradicated. Though nearly every logical sign shows Telly that her son is dead, the film's commitment to the power of private maternal certitude is such that she will move heaven and earth to recover him, leading to a joyous reunion at the film's close. With mothers now called upon to cultivate every iota of talent in their children, to protect them from the predators that are imagined to be all around, to guard their health (particularly in terms of new food allergies, asthma, and other ailments on the rise), and even (in an increasing number of cases) to bear the full burden of their education through home-schooling, cinematic narratives of bravura mothering may well register as realistic no matter how fantastical the genre in which they appear. Under the new bravura terms of motherhood, mothers are not only cast as expert decoders of all human behaviors, they are also frequently depicted as higher-level readers of illness and disability. In recent years press reports on the epidemic of autism in America have frequently included a crusading supermother who not only attends to her child's needs but also interprets her autistic child's value to society as a whole. The strains of such an interpretation are sometimes in evidence as in a 2005 *USA Today* profile of a family in which five of six children suffer from autism. The piece chronicled in detail the challenges of everyday life in such a family and the father's sense of stress and anger but concluded with the children's mother attesting that "They're here to teach me something I'm sure."[62] While such accounts of interventionist and advocate mothering embed a disturbing romanticization of disability, they nevertheless are grounded in a recognition that without advocacy educational and social systems may well overlook and disenfranchise the disabled. In the new social constructions of autistic and other disabled children who are spiritual beacons to their mothers, families, indeed their communities at large, mothers are important social intermediaries. Stories of this kind emerge from a cultural milieu in which femininity is re-sanctified by its association to children as "angels," figures of purity and innocence in a corrupt world.

The new terms on which motherhood is ennobled are not just ideological, they are of course financial as well. After all, the display of hypermaternity among economically elite white women is both a form of conspicuous consumption and a rationale for it. The supersizing of American cars and houses has taken place in exactly the era in which as Susan J. Douglas and Meredith W. Michaels observe "the new momism has become the central, justifying ideology of what has come to be called 'postfeminism.'"[63] In this period not only has the ante been substantially upped on what are considered consumer "necessities" for babies and children, a large luxury market for children, babies, and mothers has sprung into being that scarcely existed before.[64] As one commentator has observed (though somewhat ungrammatically), "many upwardly mobile parents have grown to accept that their child needs $1,000 cribs, $800 strollers and $30 booties for infants who cannot walk."[65] It is important, then, to bear in mind all the ways that "family values" operates as a consumerist script.

There's still time: the new midlife woman and the mature romance

Over the last decade a new matron culture has emerged driven by the expectation that mothers keep themselves fit and attractive in what another era would have deemed "middle age." Perhaps unsurprisingly, the eroticization of pregnancy is increasingly extended into the eroticization of motherhood, a trend that was chronicled in a 2005 *USA Today* article entitled "Mommie Hottest," which profiled a set of women who maintain impeccable grooming and fashion, who work out and who in general perceive themselves and are perceived by others as highly sexually desirable. Hijacking feminist rhetoric for postfeminist ends, the article maintained

> Mom has come a long way, baby. Of course, she's far beyond the ironed and buttoned-up June Cleaver archetype. But increasingly she's also moving past the soccer-mom look of the 1980s and 90s. She pays attention to trends . . . She indulges in a nip here, a tuck there. She stays fit, even buff.[66]

By the early 2000s popular culture was regularly invoking the figure of the "yummy mummy," or (less politely) the "MILF" (mother I'd like to fuck) in television and in popular music. Two pop hits of the period are notable in this regard, Fountains of Wayne's "Stacy's Mom," which as its name would imply speaks of the lust of a teenage boy for his friend's mother,[67] and Bowling for Soup's "1985" about a nostalgic suburban mother fixated on her memories of the 1980s. Youth films from *American Pie* (1999) to *8 Mile* (2002) have also showcased the desirable mother as a staple of the coming-of-age story.[68]

In recent years an aggressively postfeminist representational culture has intensified the sexual visibility of midlife women. Grandmothers can now be attributed with "gray glamour," romantic comedy heroines are played by female stars in their late 30s and early 40s, and, as noted above, a variety of slang terms have emerged in popular speech to designate sexually desirable mothers, feeding a

Figure 3.4 "Housewife chic" celebrates the new cultural permission for women to be erotic at midlife. (*Entertainment Weekly*)

popular culture that encompasses everything from pop hits to Hollywood films. As plastic surgery and other cosmetic technologies adjust the sliding scale of age-based conceptions of femininity, the correspondence between the new sexualities and the depreciating capital of female maturity deserves fuller examination.

Stephen Katz and Barbara Marshall have ably shown how contemporary lifestyle culture is shifting the meanings of aging with "market and lifestyle industries creat[ing] an idealized culture of 'ageless' consumers and active populations."[69] Entangled rhetorics of individual empowerment and consumer agency increasingly camouflage the diminishing of state care for the aging and vulnerable in a fantasy of age transcendence that rests, in fact, on an intensified stigmatization of those who show the effects of an aging process. As Katz and Marshall argue, vocabularies of risk and loss increasingly supplant any notion of the benefits of maturity. I am interested here in how postfeminism cooperates with "the new aging" and its emphasis on marketing, consumerism, and personal responsibility for fending off the aging process.

Fantasy constructions of the sexually seasoned midlife woman in popular culture increasingly stand alongside putatively feminist celebrations of newly-expanded conceptualizations of sexual attractiveness. A recent article listed a "top ten" of head-turning 40-something female celebrities including stars from Madonna to Geena Davis to Diane Lane to Sandra Bullock and cited the editor of *More* magazine (a lifestyle publication directed to women over 40) informing readers that "These stars are just a daily reminder that this is how 40 looks and this is what 50 looks like. It is certainly not the way your mother looked."[70] Such celebrations have to be approached with caution, not only for the way they obfuscate the class and consumer power that facilitates "age transcendence" on selective economic terms but also for the way they so often recast the pleasures/interests of adolescent boys as culturally universal, the defining barometer of mainstream taste and judgment. (One sign of this is the midlife woman's recent appearance in a rash of male sex comedies as I show below.) In her research, Suzanne Leonard finds, for instance, a number of contemporary films that "rely on the teenage gaze to posit the 30-something woman as an object of sexual desire, a move that privileges juvenile sexual proclivities and ways of understanding over articulations of female desire or agency."[71] Indeed, the expansion of teenage litmus tests for "hotness" into middle age is one manifestation of the way that "sexual freedom can be a smoke-screen for how far we *haven't* come."[72] That the films work in tandem with broader cultural shifts is suggested by the fact that a teen sexual vocabulary now appears to be the exclusive sexual vocabulary, applying to everyone, regardless of age, as I will elaborate near the close of this chapter through a brief discussion of one film's assessment on the Internet Movie Database.

It is in this sort of context that we can begin to explain the phenomenal success of the ABC series *Desperate Housewives* in recent television seasons. The series extends (and possibly culminates) a discourse of "housewife chic" that has been intermittently at work in both the US and UK media for some years.[73] This idealized category of femininity celebrates the affluent (usually white) stay-at-home mother for her retreatism which is to say her opting out of paid work and largely out of the public sphere in favor of a reconnection with essential femininity that is deemed to only be possible in domestic settings. While I have carried out a much broader analysis of retreatism as a cultural phenomenon in Chapter 2, it is worth noting here that *Desperate Housewives* revived the careers of three established aging TV actresses and made a star out of a Latina actress now in her early 30s (in line with the current heavy emphasis on Latina sexuality in US popular culture). The celebration of the sexuality of the 30/40-something woman that has been so central to the series' promotion is consistent with the new availability postfeminism extends to women of various ages to be youthful and girly at midlife. The personae of a variety of female celebrities such as Kylie Minogue, Goldie Hawn, and Sarah Jessica Parker also reflect this new cultural permission as (frequently) do the various women who are transformed and de-aged through makeover transformations on reality television.

One of the most striking features of the chick flick in recent years has been its extension at both ends of the generational spectrum so that it now encompasses everything from 50-something romances (*Something's Gotta Give*) to tween/teen ones. Like their younger 30- and 40-something counterparts, women in the 50- and 60-something age cohort are increasingly expected to maintain their sexual interest and sexual desirability further into life than in previous eras. Describing this shift, Dinitia Smith has written that "The generation of women liberated by feminism and the Pill in the 1960s aren't slipping quietly into post-menopausal celibacy; and books and movies are reflecting the change."[74] In an analysis of the recent "girling" of the older woman, Sadie Wearing has examined the rejuvenation narratives of reality television makeover series and of films like *Something's Gotta Give*, arguing that such texts "offer a fantasy of escaping (or evading) time, but one that places clearly defined limits on that escape." Ultimately, for Wearing, popular culture paradoxically presents the rejuvenation of older women as "simultaneously necessary and impossible."[75] In a study of what she calls the "middle-aged chick flick" Margaret Tally has similarly argued that in films like *Something's Gotta Give*, *The Banger Sisters* (2003), and *Laurel Canyon* (2003) "older women's sexuality, particularly that of the middle-aged mother, is given a kind of liberatory nod and affirmation,"[76] but is largely rechanneled into normative "family values" paradigms in the films' conclusions.

In a cycle of recent "mature romances" romance comes as a last-minute revelation to save the female protagonist from the fate of singlehood. The comeback stardom of Diane Lane in recent years has been particularly linked to the mature romance. In *Unfaithful* (2002) Lane's portrayal of restless midlife sexuality that undoes the family drew widely favorable critical notice, while subsequent performances in *Under the Tuscan Sun* (2003) and *Must Love Dogs* (2005) highlighted the actress' characterizations of sadly disillusioned women coping with the aftermath of divorce.

In *Under the Tuscan Sun*, a "tourist romance" of the kind that Hollywood has produced with some regularity in the 1990s and 2000s,[77] the protagonist's acquisition of a Tuscan villa and expatriation to Italy is the catalyst for her to re-imagine her life and transition from depression to vitality. In a key dialogue line centralized in the film's trailer, Lane's Frances testifies that "Unthinkably good things can happen—even late in the game. It's such a surprise." In *Must Love Dogs* Lane's Sarah Nolan is defined by her large Irish-American family and their desperate need for her to find love again. (The provocation that single femininity constitutes within a "family values" mindset is suggested in the film's first scene, an "intervention" staged by Sarah's family to try to get her to date though she professes not to be looking for a partner.) In a set of portrayals of restless housewives and emotionally questing divorcees, Lane's persona operates to take the measure of prospects and possibilities of midlife postfeminist femininity. Through plot lines featuring adultery and divorce, her films frequently underscore the problems that arise from failing to conform to the normative postfeminist lifecycle; but, on the other hand, they also frequently make guarantees about romance predicated on midlife viability.

The midlife woman is treated more ambivalently in films such as *American Pie*, a sex comedy in which one of a group of adolescent boys (whose sexuality is deemed aberrant by his friends) "graduates" to maturity through a sexual relationship with his friend Stifler's mother (Jennifer Coolidge, whose character's name is "Stifler's Mom"). The perceived use-value of the midlife woman as sex object in teen films (even those with a postfeminist gloss) is further suggested by Amy Poehler's portrayal of youthful Mrs. George in *Mean Girls* (2004) and Jenny McCarthy's embodiment of a similar role in *John Tucker Must Die* (2006).[78] Surely one of the most painful depictions of midlife femininity in recent popular film is that of Kathleen Cleary (Jane Seymour)[79] in the 2005 hit *Wedding Crashers*. The wife of the Treasury Secretary, Seymour's character bares her breasts to John, a male guest in her house, and compels him to fondle them while calling her "Kitty Cat." As the incident is paralleled with another in which John's friend Jeremy is the subject of aggressive advances by Kathleen's gay son Todd, the film means to display both mother and son as repugnant and perverted (if humorous) in a narrative that presents these characters as outliers to the film's world of superficially adventuresome yet ultimately conventional heterosexual sex. That this is habitual behavior for Kathleen Cleary is suggested when Todd casually asks John "Did Mom make you feel her tits?" and tells him to keep the incident quiet as the Treasury Secretary has used his power against previous recipients of his wife's advances.

Taken as a whole, recent representational trends regarding the sexed-up or romantically-challenged midlife woman suggest a culture in which, as Leonard contends, "notions of power and eroticism now surround older women with increased frequency, despite generally limited and facile notions of what empowerment really is."[80] In this regard, I would briefly mention two reality series which can be tellingly compared and contrasted in terms of their postfeminist age premises. The former, *Ivana Young Man*, achieved only the most marginal success while the other, *Age of Love*, became a cultural talking point in 2007. *Ivana Young Man* was commissioned and produced by Fox in 2005 which opted not to broadcast the series, selling it instead to the female-oriented Oxygen cable channel which aired it in 2006. The premise of the series was for socialite/businesswoman Ivana Trump to pair single 40-something women with younger men. Noteworthy for its apparent illustration of the ideological limits in the Fox reality television remit, *Ivana Young Man* interests me more for the squeamish reaction it elicited from the network and subsequent relegation to a low-ratings cable outlet. The series would seem to suggest that female-orchestrated scenarios of questing midlife female sexuality prove more problematic than those in which female agency is entirely absent or simply played for cheap laughs (as in *Wedding Crashers*).

By contrast, the success of NBC's *Age of Love* must be attributed at least in part to its employment of the well-established codes of the female-centered reality competition series and its centralization of male authority in the matchmaking process. The series' staging of a competition between a set of 20-something and 40-something women for the romantic attentions of 30-year-old retired tennis pro Mark Philippoussis was promoted using the tagline "Does Age Matter?" and seemed to hit a cultural nerve in terms of new scripts for midlife femininity as well as the kinds of female romantic desperation and competitiveness so often reflexively incorporated in postfeminist popular culture material. With the stress placed on Philippoussis' discernment and male decision-making redoubled through the placement of series host Mark Consuelos, *Age of Love* could safely broach themes of female maturity without incurring the hazards of female authority.

Postfeminist melancholia and the cross-generational romance: postfeminist uses of the "older woman"

The various manifestations and permutations of postfeminist hegemony in regard to time and aging proscribe female identity in punishing and heavily regimented ways. In closing this chapter, I want to examine how the figure of the "postfeminist melancholic" responds to this state of affairs. As I have argued, postfeminist culture keynotes a set of themes deemed central to contemporary women's experiences and concerns, and one of the most striking recurrent elements is the celebration of a new age flexibility in which traditional distinctions between youthfulness and adulthood are seen to be dissolving (even while the disapprobation accorded to the "aged" female body has intensified). Postfeminist media culture aggressively tropes femininities, with a predilection for typologizing them into (a frequently extended) girlhood or maternity. Age friction is certainly a regular feature of postfeminist representational culture, with countless contemporary chick flicks depicting the older female professional as a bad woman, an anti-role model for the protagonist, and a figure of calculation, deceit, and insecurity. However, in some lower-profile films a representational permutation arises that mediates between the polar extremes of postfeminist culture and adds depth and ambiguity to some of its age tropes. My concern here is with the midlife woman who features in a cross-generational romance plot, thus doubly defying postfeminist precepts that insist on demographic propriety and the dichotomization of women's experience into pre-motherhood and motherhood. A set of films showcasing that plot have appeared in the midst of a rather pronounced cultural preoccupation with the eroticized "mature" woman or mother.

The films under discussion here are very much to be differentiated from those examined by Kathleen Karlyn in her astute analysis of the prevalence of the incest theme connecting midlife males and young girls in recent popular cinema. Karlyn notes that:

> Incest provides a narrative structure—derived from Freud's work on the subject—that ideologically inverts the social realities of white male privilege. This structure redirects sympathy toward beleaguered midlife heroes by portraying them as victims of unhinged and vengeful wives, seductive, and manipulative daughters, or both. Not surprisingly, this narrative structure has been bolstered by an anti-feminist backlash against the working mother/wife. Paradoxically, however, films with this structure also make use of the increased acceptance in mainstream culture of young girls who, under the banner of Girl Power and third-wave feminism, are claiming the sexual entitlement boys and men have always enjoyed.[81]

Postfeminism has fully restored the (only very slightly dented) respectability of the young woman/older man couple through such legitimizing discursive terms as "trophy wife" and "starter marriage" and indeed has turned of late to celebrating the virility of the senior citizen patriarch.[82] Other paradigms of retromasculinity currently circulating include the harem-style male patron (Hugh Hefner) and the swinging male bachelor (even if lightly critiqued as in the *Austin Powers* franchise [1997, 1999, 2002] and recent remake of *Alfie* [2004]).[83] The sexual prerogatives of masculinity are apparently being extended to women in the cross-generational romance, though further analysis of the specific representational features of that romance is in order as I will show. Certainly there are other aspects of the popular culture landscape that reveal the intransigence of paradigms of disgust and moral condemnation in regard to midlife female sexuality "run amok." For instance, the romance of the older female teacher/male student has become an overreported template for moral panic in US broadcast media; the standardbearer here is the now decade-old case of Mary Kay LeTourneau, the Seattle elementary school teacher who fell in love and had two children with her young student, a case that has maintained an unlikely longevity in print and broadcast journalism. Meanwhile public scandals over older-women–younger-men relationships like the case of Debra LaFave, a Florida schoolteacher charged with having sex with a 14-year-old student, continue to be featured with some regularity.[84] Set in this context, it may well be that some of the fictional cross-generational romances are converting cautionary postfeminist narratives into exemplary ones.

Postfeminist representational culture is acutely age conscious; a variety of chick flick fictions from *Bridget Jones' Diary* to *13 Going on 30* and *Sex and the City* (which even in its cancellation exerts strong cultural influence) have shown themselves to be exceedingly precise about the ages of their 20- and 30-something protagonists. Meanwhile, the cult of youth is being technologically facilitated on a variety of fronts with myriad forms of reality television dedicating themselves to rejuvenating transformations and the fantasy that aging can be managed away through plastic surgery, exercise, and diet. In this context, the representation of the postfeminist female melancholic takes on a particular significance—in a cluster of recent popular film representations, the story of aging uncertainly but inexorably out of youth is marked by a deep and sustained melancholy. The films to be discussed here attempt to devise solutions for women's predicaments when conventional institutions of intimacy leave them dissatisfied.

The cross-generational romance is emerging as a regular formula in recent popular film, with emphasis on the particular status of the "older woman" in the romance. In addition to the films under discussion here, other contemporary examples include *Prime* (2005) and *I Could Never Be Your Woman* (2007), a May–December romance featuring Michelle Pfeiffer and Paul Rudd and directed by Amy Heckerling. However, my focus is on a cluster of films from the early years of the new millennium that seem to push against the trend toward unproblematic celebration of youthfulness. Like *The New Yorker* critic David Denby, I couldn't help noticing the distinctive similarities across several films dealing with this subject matter that were released in 2004.[85] These films centralize an adult woman whose erotic connection to a much younger man or boy arises from a stalled relation to the past. In *Birth* a widow who has just become engaged is pursued by a young boy who tells her he is the reincarnation of her husband, in *P.S.* a college admissions officer becomes romantically involved with an applicant who bears the name and identical physical appearance of her dead former high school boyfriend, and in *The Door in the Floor* a grieving mother has a sexual relationship with a much younger man who reminds her of the sons she has lost. In these films the experience of erotic intimacy by a female protagonist is defined purely as an access route to the past. With their connotations of necrophilia, pedophilia, and incest the films disturb the conventions of the romance in striking ways. Most crucially, the films' suspicion that the new rhetorics of age may disenfranchise women rather than empower them is articulated through the plot device of the intergenerational romance.

I should add that these films are not wholly without representational precedent; in fact the postfeminist melancholic has been around for a while although she has not always been centralized in the films in which she appears. Several such characters appear in late 1990s films where their emotional status is noted but is then subject to correction. In a set of highly generationally self-aware films including *Grosse Pointe Blank* (1997) and *Romy and Michelle's High School Reunion* (1997) the open nostalgia of the high school reunion narrative prefigured the nostalgia plots of the more recent romances. There are also moments of postfeminist melancholy in numerous chick flicks and I want to carefully stress the difference between such moments in conservative recuperative romantic comedies and the films I will deal with here. Locating the postfeminist melancholic requires a distinction between this figure and the numerous wistful, whimsical heroines of print, cinema, and television romance. While wistfulness is a politically and socially disengaged mode that serves postfeminist ideological aims by substituting mild emotions in favor of sharp ones and working to put across the recognition that the heroine is not "angry" or "shrill," it is fundamentally different in character from melancholy. I want to begin to theorize the difference between these two modes, observing that of late the postfeminist melancholic has a habit of appearing in reincarnation romances. Across a small spectrum, three films (*Birth*, *P.S.*, and *The Door in the Floor*) particularize the time travel romance by showcasing the ambiguous return of a deceased boy or man whose loss the heroine has never quite gotten over[86] and all feature an accomplished 30-, 40-, or 50-something female star (Nicole Kidman, Laura Linney, and Kim Basinger) paired with a far younger unknown or lesser known actor.[87]

These films participate in a general shift in postfeminist culture toward constructing femininity as romantically/sexually desperate. I want to examine how such desperation is generationally marked and where the postfeminist melancholic stands in relation to these dynamics.

P.S. and the youth romance fantasy

Reviews of *P.S.* often compared it unfavorably with director Dylan Kidd's previous film *Rodger Dodger* (2002) which also bridged a generation gap but one between male characters. Likewise, *Birth* was accounted a moderate disappointment for director Jonathan Glazer after his first film *Sexy Beast* (2000). As both of these directors' first films were about the entitlements of midlife masculinity and their second films about melancholic femininity, it is hard to avoid the clear implications about "quality material" and gender that arise.

P.S. focuses on Louise, an admissions officer for Columbia University's graduate program in art, and a woman in her late 30s whose social life consists mainly of platonic "dates" with her ex-husband Peter and visits home to her mother's house. At work one day she receives a package from an applicant named F. Scott Feinstadt, the exact same name of her high school boyfriend who had been killed in a car accident. Riveted by the coincidence, Louise contrives for him to come in for an interview although this is not normally part of the application process. The young man who appears not only shares a name with her earlier boyfriend but also looks, acts, and speaks like him. Scott and Louise have sex at Louise's apartment and although she does not initially tell anyone about it, this action seems suddenly to unlock revelations from those around her. Peter confesses to Louise that he is now dating a much younger woman but that during their marriage he suffered from an addiction to sex and was repeatedly unfaithful with both women and men. To recover from his addiction he sought out the counsel of Louise's brother Sammy who not only kept Peter's secret but also tells Louise later in the film that any consequences arising from her ignorance of the state of her marriage were her own fault. Just as Louise's intimacy with Scott seems to bring on this string of revelations from Peter, her high school best friend Missy intuits that something has changed in Louise's life and flies in from Los Angeles where she installs herself in a luxury hotel and tries unsuccessfully to seduce Scott away from Louise.

In the midst of this, Louise makes a visit back home to her mother's house where the inequities of her life appear in concentrated form. Although while he was a drug addict Sammy stole from his mother and abused her trust, she now maintains a state of readiness in case he visits, baking a pie should he choose to stop in at the house. Louise asks why her mother doesn't do the same for her and her mother suggests that Louise doesn't eat pie because she must watch her figure. In a conversation in the garden where Louise tells her mother about Peter's revelations, her mother dreamily discusses her love of gardening as a seeming metaphor for acquiescence and acceptance. "Do you know why I love it out here?" she asks her daughter. "All I'm responsible for is this little piece of dirt. No more saving the world, no more fighting injustice, just me and my babies [indicating her flowers]." With this section of the film contrasting maternal retreatism and male power plays, Louise has a conversation with Sammy in which he harshly dispenses advice and tells her to "Find the pattern and put yourself in a position of profit when the pattern repeats itself."

Louise goes to Scott and tells him about the uncanny resemblance he bears to her high school boyfriend. He rejects her desire to conceptualize him in this way, says that everyone has their heart broken at that stage of life and tells her that his real first name is Francis and he's usually known as Fran. Missy leaves to return to Los Angeles, telling her friend as she goes that "Some people just refuse to let anything good happen to them." The film suggests that with this Louise restores order and balance to her life and we see her working out at the gym, calling her brother to tell him that she's proud of him, and seeking out Peter to say "You and I are never going to work." Louise and Fran meet at Columbia where she gives him an acceptance letter and an ambiguous exchange of "OKs" between the two at the end suggests either a continuing friendship or the tentative further exploration of romance.

The film version of *P.S.* maternalizes Louise in ways that contradict the novel upon which it is based. Louise's cherished painting by her high school boyfriend has become not just a random abstract but a mother/child embrace that constitutes "proof" that Scott Fienstadt envisioned a maternal future for her, and in the film (unlike the novel) Scott makes an immediate post-coital phone call from Louise's apartment to his mother while Louise squirms. Most remarkable is a key conversation between Louise and Missy which presumes that one is either in perpetual longing for one's girlhood or one is a mother. Missy speaks of trying to access "the real me, the one I'd forgotten about, not the one that drives the kids to school in a fucking SUV"—and bitterly tells Louise "You are just not a mother." In the film, Louise is attributed with a miscarriage that is not in Helen Schulman's novel. In the voiceover commentary the film's director suggests that Louise has long been mourning this miscarriage. The link the film needs to supply between postfeminist melancholia and frustrated maternity is an important indication of its conservatism.[88] Despite Louise's resonant speculation

"Maybe that's what's wrong with the world. Everybody's just moving on," the film ultimately insists that Louise had better move on or subject herself to the inequities and brutalities of a postfeminist culture.

The limitations of *P.S.*' response to postfeminism are suggestively linked to its updating of the conservative critique of the melancholic Generation X member. The film's suggestion that Louise is out of step in her lifecycle links her to the arrested state of development so often attributed to Generation X, whose members may give voice to resonant critiques of existing institutional, economic, and ideological systems but in the end are made to accede to them in the name of "facing reality," "moving on," etc. *P.S.* is thus linked to a trend toward accelerated nostalgia in/around this generational cohort.

Birth and the reincarnation romance

Birth is the most credulous of the three reincarnation narratives I am analyzing here. In the film's first scene the death of an adult man named Sean is paralleled with the birth of a baby that we shortly meet as a ten-year-old boy. When that boy presents himself to Anna, the man's widow, and announces solemnly that he is her reincarnated husband, the film bluntly proposes that a revived romance (though on the most unlikely terms) with her first husband may be more meaningful for Anna than the marriage she is about to embark upon with her new fiancé, Joseph. Such a view is reinforced by the smothering overcloseness and control of Anna's family who close ranks against the boy they perceive as a threat to their intimacy and stability. Despite the closeness of the family circle (Anna and Joseph live in her mother Eleanor's opulent apartment, the site of repeated family gatherings) the film links family life to anger and intransigence. Eleanor, a stoic matriarch, seems most concerned that her family appropriately reflects her own affluence and grandeur, while Anna's heavily pregnant sister Laura is so offended by the boy's claims and the prospect that he may draw Anna into something unseemly that she at one point aggressively uses her own body to block her sister from going to see Sean.[89] In ways that are similar to *P.S.* and, as we shall shortly see, in *The Door in the Floor* this most extreme version of the cross-generational romance constitutes a radical disruption of family values and an interrogation of the postfeminist trope of "moving on" in the direction of marriage and procreation. Anna herself is candid in discussing her own state of mind and inability, even after ten years, to forget her husband. She tells friends, "It's taken me this long and I can't get him out of my system. I can't, I can't. It's not gotten any easier for me."

Anna's increasing belief in Sean's reincarnation claims is highlighted at a classical music performance given at Eleanor's home. When Sean repeatedly kicks the back of his chair in a little-boy challenge, Joseph explodes in anger, finally barricading the boy and himself in an adjacent room and beginning to spank him. This dramatic rupture in domestic propriety deeply shocks the family and their guests and causes Joseph to pack his things and move out, yet Anna nevertheless exchanges a kiss with Sean out on the street moments later. The film takes a turn, however, when Clara, a friend of Anna's, reveals to Sean that she had been having an adulterous affair with Anna's husband and contends that if the boy were truly reincarnated he would have known this. Sean is crushed that the ideal romance he believed he was restoring to Anna was actually highly tarnished and he sits in a tree in the park all night, contemplating his options. When Anna proposes that they run away together and in 11 years' time get (re)married, he abruptly tells her that he is not her husband after all and that he had been lying. At this point, Anna follows her mother's advice, seeking out Joseph and telling him that all she wants is a happy, peaceful life. The film's return to emotional austerity and Anna's fulfillment of her family's wishes culminates at the conclusion with Anna and Joseph's wedding.

When compared to the relentless celebration of the wedding in contemporary female genres and the broader hypermatrimonial turn in popular culture, *Birth*'s closing sequence depicting Anna's bereft state on her wedding day registers as both stark and powerful.[90] The sequence highlights the presentational and performative work of weddings as social theatrical events, placing a strong stress on photography and image-making. Married in compliance with her mother's request to hold the event at the beach house that was the scene of her parents' wedding, Anna at first appears content and tranquil. She is seen in long shot surrounded by her bridesmaids while her mother, sister, and other female relatives look on in satisfaction. Yet as the photographer continues his work and the film's own camera takes up a closer position, we see Anna's struggle to maintain her composure and at last she flees the scene, running onto the beach and into the waves in her wedding gown. Throughout this section we hear the ten-year-old Sean in voiceover reading a letter he has sent to Anna. Although ostensibly a repudiation of his actions and assurance to her that he is back at school and behaving appropriately as a child, the letter is nevertheless sprinkled with rather knowing references including one that hints at his disruption to Anna's family's behavioral norms ("Tell everyone I'm sorry I made a problem for them") and closes with the offhand but resonant "Well, I guess I'll see you in another lifetime." The effect of the voiceover is heightened by intercutting between Anna posing for the photographer at her wedding and Sean having his school photo taken—as the flashbulb pops, he produces a generic schoolboy smile that contrasts markedly with the solemn, precocious demeanor he exhibits through the film. The clear suggestion of this linkage is that both Anna and Sean have elected to perform their appropriate social roles in defiance of their actual emotional desires. Sean's recollection earlier in the film that he first met Anna at the beach further dimensionalizes the significance of Anna's breakdown there. Moreover, this sequence culminates a set of birth references through the film, seeming to suggest that Anna wishes she too might be reborn.

Birth's horror film aesthetics—its sustained camera shots and depth of field call to mind the films of Stanley Kubrick and Roman Polanski[91]—heighten its sense of the uncanny while the film's austere tone and Sean's ghostly demeanor feed the suggestion that Sean appears only as a manifestation of Anna's own unconscious wishes. The need to retrieve a pure, uncontaminated version of masculinity that runs rampant in postfeminist fiction is pushed to its limits in the formula of the cross-generational romance. In *Birth* the pushing past those limits seemingly caused the film to be rejected by both audiences and critics (reviews largely lambasted the film), with the radical age variance between the adult Anna and the ten-year-old Sean leaving it open to the rhetoric of disgust that accompanies moral panic around the "misdirected" sexuality of adult women.

The *Door in the Floor* and the cathartic cross-generational romance

The Door in the Floor focuses upon a couple still grieving years after the deaths of their two sons in a gruesome car accident. Despite the birth of another child conceived in an effort to solidify their marriage, Ted and Marion Cole are deeply (though not acrimoniously) estranged and about to start a trial separation. This film differs from the two previous examples in that it does not generate a (quasi)supernatural explanation for the symbolic return of a lost, loved male figure. In fact, the arrival of Eddie is quite prosaic, with the strong suggestion (one which is openly spelled out near the film's conclusion) that Ted has hired him as his assistant very deliberately as a surrogate for one of his lost sons. The film has a habit of undercutting Ted's intentions and sense of patriarchal centrality, however, and there are suggestions early on that associate Ted's masculinity with the ridiculous and the pathetic. Roused out of bed when his daughter hears a noise in the middle of the night, he carries her back to her room in the nude and the little girl observes "Your penis looks funny." "My penis is funny," Ted replies.

Eddie's attraction to Marion is cemented from the first moment he meets her as she collects him at the ferry; expecting Ted, it is clear that when she speaks to him he believes/hopes he is being propositioned by an attractive older woman. He takes a photograph from a hallway "shrine" to the dead boys and tapes paper over the images of her sons, isolating Marion as the only visible figure and symbolically de-maternalizing her. When she discovers him masturbating to pieces of her lingerie and becomes aware of his attraction, she speculates about whether her sons ever had sex before they died and then initiates Eddie into lovemaking.

Ted, having deduced what is going on with his wife and his assistant, is ambivalent; the self-destructive and angry behavior he manifests through his own adulterous relationship with a neighbor, Mrs. Vaughn, intensifies and is explained by Marion who relates to Eddie the stock pattern of her husband's relations with other women. An author and artist, Ted begins by sketching conventional portraits of a mother and a daughter, then sketches each alone, with the mother nude in representational phases that move from innocence to degradation. Ted's obsessive need to render maternity as sexually sordid is contextualized when he explodes in anger in the car as Eddie tries to turn off a rap song about female sexual degradation. "I love that song," he yells at Eddie, and then proceeds into the house, channelsurfing on television to images of violence and sexuality, including notably an ad for *Girls Gone Wild*, the video franchise in which "regular women" are induced to flash their breasts and other body parts at the camera.[92] At this point, postfeminism enters the film directly as it illustrates that Ted's management of the losses in his own life through the disparagement of women is culturally authorized and supported by a popular culture that increasingly features women showcasing their own desire for debasement. This section of the film is deeply sad, however, and intercuts Ted's behavior with Eddie and Marion making love for the last time, her eyes fixed on a portrait of her dead sons and tears streaming down her face. While Marion recognizes that she has to interrupt the patterns of dysfunction and emotional frigidity that characterize her marriage and makes a choice to leave, Ted is locked into a cycle of repetitive behavior. Chased out of her house and down the beach by a furious Mrs. Vaughn when she realizes how he has abused her, Ted finds refuge in a small bookstore where he is fawned over as a literary celebrity and encounters a mother and a daughter whom he lines up for his next series of portraits. The film concludes with Marion gone and Ted and Eddie briefly left alone. Ted tells the boy the story of the car accident in which his sons were killed and when he does so, it calls to mind an earlier section of the film in which we have also seen him in the role of storyteller. At a public reading of one of his children's stories (one which Eddie calls his favorite) Ted recites "The Door in the Floor," a fiction about the repression of terror and horror in the world in the form of a mother/son narrative. As Eddie leaves we last see Ted on his squash court alone, opening a hatch door in the floor and descending, it would appear, into the horror his short story has chronicled. In this way, the film flips its original image of Ted as a stoic father and Marion as a woman traumatized by grief; Ted is caught up in a cycle of repetition in which his image of himself as an artist and a father is predicated on the degradation of adult women. Though he tries to present himself to Eddie as a procurer and thus diminish the relationship Eddie had with his wife, the film insists that not only was that relationship legitimate and cathartic for Marion but also in no way was it managed by Ted.

Further evidence of the centrality of the semiotics of the aging female body to postfeminist culture can often be culled from review and fan discourses. For instance, it is telling to discover that when one looks up *The Door in the Floor* in the Internet Movie Database, the most extended strand of discussion about the film centers not on the film's major characters or plot but rather on the aging body of actress Mimi Rogers who as Mrs. Vaughn is glimpsed in one of Ted's sketching scenes in full frontal nudity. This posting strand included a full 47 posted comments on this subject as well as nine messages deleted by the system administrator (presumably for sexual content deemed offensive). The evaluations of Rogers' body, the shape and sag of her breasts, etc., come in for detailed analysis here with postings that range from assessments that the actress ought to have cosmetic surgery (in fact the leadoff post reads "Mimi Rogers—the surgeon is waiting") to numerous defenses of the beauty of women's natural bodies and several testimonies ranging in degrees of explicitness to the desire to have sex with Rogers. Many of the postings deploy postfeminist sexual terminology in which the woman's subjectivity is erased, sex is figured as an act of dominating violence, and a woman's body is openly dehumanized (several posters expressed their sexual interest in Rogers with colloquial phrasing like "I'd beat it up," and "I would so hit that!"). Another striking feature of the postings is the absolute certainty with which audience members discriminate between bodies that have had plastic surgery and those that have not. Notably, one poster specifically calls Rogers "a total MILF [Mother I'd like to fuck] in this movie."

The films examined here represent merely one strand within a larger cultural weave of women's genres preoccupied with reincarnation and time travel. (And though she functions somewhat differently there, the postfeminist melancholic is also a feature of more conventional chick flick time travel narratives including *Kate & Leopold* and *13 Going on 30*.) In highlighting *Birth*, *P.S.*, and *The Door in the Floor* in my discussion I have not taken up other proximate examples which would include films such as *The Good Girl* and *Irresistible* both of which also feature older woman/younger man romances, though ones in which the age difference in the couple is not as pronounced.

My sense is that these three films raise the stakes above the miraculous/ magical interventions of recent time-traveling romances like *Kate & Leopold* and *13 Going on 30*, interrogating to varying degrees some of the precepts of postfeminist culture in ways those films do not. *P.S.* is least able to break from the conventions of maternalism, *Birth* occupies a melancholic middle ground and *The Door in the Floor* is most direct in its use of a non-romanticized cross-generational relationship to free the protagonist from a stalled and impossible family life. In two of the films a transitional cross-generational romance works to move the protagonist to a new stage of her life, while in *Birth* Anna's tragic accommodation to gender and class norms belies her own desire for a greater, more intimate existence.

Interestingly, all three films highlight male anxiety, aging, and co-dependency through a character proximate to the romance (Peter in *P.S.*, Joseph in *Birth*, and Ted in *The Door in the Floor*) whose emotional limitations and weakness have exerted a controlling, limiting impact on the protagonist. The midlife woman/younger man romance unlocks this state of affairs in an increasingly decisive way from *Birth* to *P.S.* to *The Door in the Floor*.

At their best these films begin the project of adapting mainstream conventions to alternative ideological ends. In so doing they also feature a marked and explicit eroticism not regularly found in vehicles for mainstream female stars. In these films women are legitimately melancholic about their respective predicaments as single, widowed, and unhappily married women in a postfeminist culture. Their erotic encounters with phantasmatic boys figure their own unlocking of stalled states and ways of accepting and facing what they know about their own conditions. In this way the films begin to find a means for bypassing the pervasive postfeminist typologization of contemporary culture.

Conclusion

In a cultural environment in which temporal anxiety predominates, postfeminism fits that anxiety to experiences of femininity in precise ways. By emphasizing rituals that anchor and mark time, by fictionally highlighting the experience of temporal dislocation, and by promising that commodity culture can erase the impact of time, popular culture operates as a zealous timekeeper for women. Ritualizations attendant to sexual maturity, marriage, and motherhood have risen in prominence in tandem with these dynamics as women are cued to understand that "exemplary time" is biological, emotional, and consumerist. A new exhibitionism of pregnancy and motherhood may work to compensate a generation of women raised with feminist expectations for the actual setbacks in women's public stature and laborforce status.

Postfeminist temporality consistently raises issues of memory, ritual, generational affiliation, and aging. It promulgates matrimonial panic, proposes motherhood as the all-purpose site of adult female subjectivity and celebrates a maternal certitude that operates in counterpoint to contemporary anxieties/uncertainties. Even as it hyper-idealizes marriage, pregnancy, and motherhood, postfeminist popular culture links all three to various archetypes of time-beset femininity. In this way women are subject to a contradictory discursive complex of exhortation and reproach in regard to how they spend, manage, or "defy" time. Clearly, those women who are most likely to solve "time problems" are white, rich, young, and/or married, procreative (and as we shall see in Chapter 5) virtuoso consumers of beauty products and technologies. Postfeminism, it seems, can celebrate some women for their time victories while (implicitly or directly) castigating others for their failures. In the final section of this chapter I have examined a set of films (none box office successes) that in certain ways look to challenge postfeminist rules of temporal/age propriety, but these may be decidedly seen as exceptions that prove the rule when it comes to the strict ideological control postfeminism seeks to maintain over the female lifecycle. I have sought to make a case here for all the reasons why "time" is such a fraught concept in female-oriented popular culture, but to that case I would like to add one further speculation: postfeminist texts so often obsess about the temporal because they half suspect postfeminism's own historical misplacedness, that is they recognize at some level the premature and deceptive nature of any conceptual system that declares feminism obsolete.

Chapter 4

Postfeminist working girls
New archetypes of the female labor market

This chapter centralizes the postfeminist relationship between women and work, first noting the large number of recent Hollywood romances in which a female protagonist is situated in a low-paying, low-status (though often nurturing and symbolically domestic) mode of employment, then considering professional women who discard their jobs and/or repudiate their "female" professions (as in films such as *How to Lose a Guy in Ten Days* and *Someone Like You*) and finally analyzing a set of adjustment narratives in which working women must downsize the importance of work in their lives. In addition I will analyze the inverted but related dynamics that give rise to a postfeminist preoccupation with certain kinds of women's work. Thus, later sections of the chapter examine the new respectability (even, at times, idealization) of the female sex worker, the representational prominence of nannies, and the emergence of flight attendant chic in a variety of forms of popular culture.

The selectivity essential to the organization of this chapter should not, I hope, exclude recognition of the wide variety of ways in which a range of postfeminist media texts frequently negotiate the "problem" of the working woman by minimizing the realities of women's workforce participation. Although the retreatist epiphany is a major strategy for addressing this problem as I will show, it is not available in every instance and a variety of other negotiating practices emerge within popular culture. One is to trivialize the female income earner or to de-emphasize her earning status by subsuming it within a broader framework so that it tends to be eclipsed by other factors. For example the quintessentially postfeminist MTV reality hit *Newlyweds* (2003–2005), profiling the lives of pop star Jessica Simpson and her then husband Nick Lachey, negotiated the reality of Simpson's breadwinner status by constantly emphasizing her ignorance, youth, hyperfemininity, and domestic incapacity. Near the end of the series as Simpson's fame grew disproportionate to Lachey's, *Newlyweds* struggled to maintain this formula as Simpson was increasingly called away for promotional appearances and film shoots and Lachey frequently appeared to be trying to win back his wife's attention with gifts and dinners. The lopsided power dynamic between the couple and Simpson's increasingly rare appearances at home deprived the series of its trademark gambit (opportunities for its female star to be tutored and protected by her older husband) and *Newlyweds* effectively culminated with the couple's divorce.

Essential to my arguments here is recognition of the high degree of ambivalence with which postfeminist culture treats women in the workforce; some of this ambivalence dissipates when such work is seen to be expressive of women's essential femininity. The contemporary chick flick has regularly offset the threat of the urban "career woman" by establishing her use of workplace resources as a means in the pursuit of romance. For instance, journalist heroines played by Meg Ryan and Robin Wright Penn in *Sleepless in Seattle* (1993) and *Message in a Bottle* (1999) respectively use the tools of their profession to make contact with a man who is the subject of their romantic interest. In this way the films are linked to a broader context in which, as Suzanne Leonard contends, "Feminist-inflected discussions of the importance of finding suitable, lucrative, and relevant labor have thus receded in a postfeminist culture far more concerned with reminding women of all the personal and romantic goals their laboring might put in jeopardy."[1] But a number of films of the last ten years go further in celebrating female protagonists whose work places them in a clearly subordinate role and for whom any display of ambition would be out of character. The ubiquity of the sweet, decent, traditionalist whose non-threatening work status is one of her hallmark features can be glimpsed in a short list of such roles in recent films:

- *Along Came Polly*, Polly, a waitress described on the Internet Movie Database as "a sweet itinerant"
- *Monster-in-Law*, Charlotte ("Charlie"), a dog walker and temp
- *Spanglish*, Flor, a housekeeper
- *Shopgirl*, Mirabelle, a sales clerk
- *Elizabethtown*, Claire, a flight attendant
- *As Good As It Gets*, Carol, a waitress
- *In Her Shoes*, Rose, a lawyer who resigns and becomes a dog walker
- *Sideways*, Maya, a waitress and wine pourer
- *While You Were Sleeping*, Lucy, a subway tollbooth attendant
- *Return to Me*, Grace, a waitress
- *Must Love Dogs*, Sarah, a pre-school teacher
- *The Wedding Singer*, Julia, a waitress
- *50 First Dates*, Lucy, an art teacher
- *Bruce Almighty*, Grace, an art teacher.

In the vast majority of cases these characters are romantically paired with an affluent male professional (though he may be in crisis about the value and status of his career). The female protagonists' names are often implicit markers of their traditionalism since they tend to be called by Anglo-Saxon names that imply racial and class capital (Grace, Lucy, Julia, and Rose among those on the list above). The chick flick does not feature protagonists named Michelle, Dawn, or Linda, though in keeping with its arthouse status a film like *Sideways* can exoticize the trend a bit with a name like Maya. These subordinate women are often placed to speak the truth to a man in crisis, and they are represented as in possession of a serenity and composure that is essentially feminine. Their lack of a professionally threatening career, their symbolically or literally nurturing work, and the promise implied by their old-fashioned names combine to powerfully idealize these women on postfeminist terms.

In Chapter 2 I argued that the "retreatist" plot showcases the rewards of an adult woman's return to a hometown space and decision to downshift her career. In corresponding fashion, a number of chick flicks feature the protagonist's revelation that professional work is unrewarding or even impossible. Indeed, the contemporary chick flick stages the discovery over and over again that the professional life is a "bad bargain" and in so doing the films simultaneously give expression to widely perceived sensibilities about the duress of the contemporary workplace *and* pander to hoary antifeminist notions that women's involvement in paid labor disturbs the natural order of things. They therefore frequently include a plot device where a kindly male boss roots for the heroine as she moves toward a change of heart in which romantic commitment will displace work. He may look on with concern at his driven employee, urge her to go home when she is working late, even compel her to take a vacation (as in *Hitch*), or simply respond with utter sympathy and understanding when she quits (*Picture Perfect*, *13 Going on 30*). By contrast, the role of the middle-aged "bad" female professional whose interests are antithetical to the heroine's has become distressingly regular in the contemporary Hollywood romance, and it is often played by well-known and accomplished actresses. Ellen Barkin plays this role in *Someone Like You*, Stockard Channing serves this function in *Life or Something Like It* while Candice Bergen does so in *Sweet Home Alabama*.

Such stock characters serve to anchor a set of standardized representations which act to elongate the distance between public and private spheres for women through a "logical" formulation in which female retreatism is salvation for women whose public roles are provisional, contingent, and fundamentally unimportant. Two recurrent plot devices enact this theme:

- The discovery that the professional sphere of work is meaningless, shallow, venal, and in many cases "wrongly" feminized and aberrant (*Someone Like You, 13 Going on 30, Life or Something Like It, Raising Helen*).
- The abandonment of a job that was fundamentally menial and service-class rank to be glorified through romance and family (*While You Were Sleeping, Monster-in-Law*).

In addition, as I shall show in this chapter, "adjusted ambition" narratives work to discredit the meaning and value of work in the heroine's life or at least to insist that it be made secondary to romance.

In a postfeminist culture healthy and urgent debates about the nature, function, and reward structure of the contemporary culture of work are in part foreclosed by a minimization/ghettoization of these subjects into the sphere of "women's issues" while feminism is cast as "straw man" (so to speak) for social changes that are much more directly attributable to other factors such as the power of profit-minded behemoth multinational corporations to chip away at social health and intimacy. Prevailing identity paradigms identify women as uncertain about what we want, troubled by the dissatisfactions of the public sphere, and looking homeward to try to rebuild. In this way, postfeminism sees itself lifting a supposed "feminist" taboo on human longings for dependency, succor, and nurturance.

In Chapter 2, I examined the recurrent role of retreatism in postfeminist culture, noting postfeminism's tendency to acknowledge the ideological impasses of contemporary culture and then detour around them deploying platitudes about essential female desires/needs. For instance, films like *Life or Something Like It*, *You've Got Mail* and *How to Lose a Guy in Ten Days* incorporate a critique of unbridled capitalist aggression but shift that critique onto women who must rediscover their essential roles as other-focused, nurturing, etc. In all three of those films, a resolution is achieved when the female character downsizes her ambition, leaves her job, and/or finds a more private mode of working. Typically, in the postfeminist protagonist's ongoing search for a stable sense of home, work is posed as a realm of competition, uncertainty, fear, and corruption, in short, the antithesis of domestic safety. Of course, not all contemporary romantic comedies adhere to the retreatist paradigm. In this chapter I will be looking more closely at the kinds of work chick flick protagonists do, the films' assessments of it, and the kinds of adjustments that are required when a major female character cannot be entirely severed from the working world through retreatism.

Analysis of contemporary postfeminist culture suggests the need to radically reimagine the contemporary culture of work. The retreatist formulation depends heavily on an elongation between the private and public spheres for women and a cynical belief that the public sphere is competitively anti-social and corrupt. As Johanna Brenner writes:

> the image and idiom of the family privilege ties of solidarity based on personal life and denigrate those based on other kinds of relationships. If we envision, for example a radically democratized organization of production which allows individuals to "be themselves" at work, which breaks down the division between work and play, which makes work self-affirming instead of soul-destroying, and which allows individuals to build a sense of community and collegiality on the basis of the common purposes and shared decisions of their efforts, can we not then envision work as a place where we are "at home?" . . . Extension of the values now located exclusively in family life—solidarity, respect, and a commitment to others' development—across a society requires the elimination of "the family" in its meanings as a special place for those values.[2]

Women and the postfeminist workplace

Throughout this book I have sought to show that there are real uncertainties and ambivalences embedded in postfeminist fiction yet these are also most
often subject to easy and artificial modes of textual resolution. It is crucial to
emphasize that the contemporary postfeminist chick flicks I analyze here situate
themselves in relation to stalled if not reversed patterns of women's social health
and resonant middle-class anxieties. On January 12, 2005 Nicholas D. Kristof
reported that in 2002 (for the first time since 1958) America's infant mortality
rate increased. For Kristof such information is "part of a pattern of recent statistics dribbling out of the federal government suggesting that for those on the
bottom in America, life in our new Gilded Age is getting crueler."[3] Grist for a
millennial middle-class "fear of falling" was provided by a rise in the poverty rate
in the early years of the twenty-first century as well as the increasingly precarious status of healthcare, insurance, and pension plans for many Americans.[4] In
a series of articles for *The New York Times* analyzing the contemporary classed
landscape of American life, contributors found that despite widespread belief
that class differences are no longer decisive, class position was becoming more
influential upon health, lifespan, admissibility to a four-year college, choice of
where to live, and of marriage partner.[5]

The position of women in the workplace has been disproportionately affected
by a renewed social conservatism which sometimes translates into discriminatory
policies with anecdotal reports of female dress codes, required makeup, and a
generalized sense of appearance-based discrimination proliferating. A 2005 *USA
Today* article concretized these trends somewhat, reporting a New York University study in which an increase in a woman's body mass correlated with a decrease
in her family income and job prestige, with men experiencing no such negative
effect.[6] In a related development Stephanie Armour has reported that pregnancy
discrimination complaints filed with the federal Equal Employment Opportunity
Commission (EEOC) jumped 39% from 1992 to 2003.[7] In striking ways, a set of
job market data is emerging to substantiate trends that had previously resonated
primarily as "lifestyle" shifts and as the subject of pop sociological accounts. In
The New York Times Eduardo Porter reported on the faltering pace of women
entering the job market, noting that "since the mid-1990s, the growth in the
percentage of adult women working outside the home has stalled, slipping somewhat in the last five years and leaving it at a rate well below that of men."[8] Much
of the research cited in the article suggested that the tendency of women to
balance time on the job with relationship-building, childraising, and domestic
chores had led to an impasse in which they simply have no more hours to give.
Consequently, as Porter reports, "the gender revolution at work may be over."[9]

As has been suggested at various times in this book, postfeminism always
maintains a highly selective engagement with the features of the socioeconomic
landscape. At the same time, postfeminism may be seen to give cover to a set of
deeply divisive and oppressive social and economic conditions, and to demon-

strate compatibility with the new majoritarian politics. Such politics are a defining feature in what Jonathan Simon has characterized as "a new political order, one that stresses personal responsibility (rather than collective risk spreading) and minimal protections against economic harm with a highly moralistic criminal law enforced harshly with a promise of almost total protection against crime (combined with continued emphasis on how dangerous it still is)."[10]

In general, postfeminism partners well with other conservative formulations such as a corporate culture that reinforces divergent social privileges. With its heavily classist character, postfeminism flourishes under the conditions of private wealth and public austerity that currently prevail in the US. Toward this end, it maintains a relentless representational focus on the interests, concerns, and prerogatives of elites.

Women's positions are distinctly impacted by the growing income inequality of what Robert H. Frank and Phillip J. Cook have identified as "the winner-take-all society."[11] In an era of heightened middle-class anxiety and "reshaping of income distribution toward the top,"[12] the culture of work is particularly unsettled in its meanings. Indeed, Mark Ames has gone so far as to assert that "Most Americans today take it for granted that the workplace is unbearable, stressful, fearful, and, organized to transfer much of the wealth up to a tiny, privileged class of executives and shareholders at the expense of the many."[13] One of the features of contemporary work culture that is most actively repressed by postfeminist representations is a new pervasive white-collar job insecurity. As Barbara Ehrenreich has noted "Starting with the economic downturn of 2001, there has been a rise in unemployment among highly credentialized and experienced people."[14] In the late 1990s and early 2000s, rhetorics of corporate prosperity came to be more and more at odds with a broad middle-class anxiety, an anxiety closely linked to the draconian cost-cutting measures that prevailed in the corporate workplace. As Jill Andresky Fraser has provocatively deemed it, "the white-collar sweatshop" emerged as a function of "corporate America's campaign to replace postwar employment practices with ever more demanding, stressful, and unrewarding workplace conditions."[15] These conditions often entail a belief in the utter and complete dedication of the worker to the enterprise at hand in the staging of a scenario for corporate success that Fraser characterizes in the following terms:

> If they (our visionary corporate leaders) and we (their fortunate employees) all work as hard as we can, to the utmost of our capabilities, *every single moment of every single day*, we all may thrive—at least for a while—in a new economy that is difficult and demanding, but potentially rewarding.[16]

Against this psychological backdrop of cynicism, desperation, and mandatory dedication, the corporate scandals of the early 2000s, the astronomical (and increasingly well-publicized) rise of salaries, bonuses, and perks in the top income brackets, and the US government's seeming complicity in a "cash and carry" economy all factor to produce a culture in which the meanings of work are negatively impacted. Scholarship in sociology and social policy suggests that psychological adjustment to what Richard Sennett deems the "culture of the new capitalism" has broadly stressed passive acceptance. Sennett maintains that over the past decade his interview subjects "have tended to accept structural change with resignation, as though the loss of security at work and in schools run like businesses are inevitable: you can do little about such basic shifts, even if they hurt you."[17]

Moreover, as Micki McGee has cogently argued in her study of self-help industries and the conceptual power of the makeover as a mode of response to economic insecurity, many Americans now find themselves peculiarly "belabored," a term she uses to describe the appearance and attitudinal work undertaken by millions to maintain their eligibility for the job market. A substantial number of Hollywood romantic comedies now take for granted audience understanding of the belabored condition, and a significant percentage dedicate themselves to moving the heroine out of a position of professional solipsism and into what they define as a more fully relational sphere. In *Just Like Heaven* (2005), for example, the well-worn concept of romantic destiny is blended with a critique of the female professional's overdedication to the workplace. As the film opens, medical resident Elizabeth Masterson (Reese Witherspoon) has been on duty for 26 hours but is still willing to take on fresh cases until her supervisor insists she goes home. Surrounded by colleagues in the ladies' room discussing their personal lives, Elizabeth looks soberly at herself in the mirror when informed "you're so lucky that all you have to worry about is work." After learning of her promotion to attending physician (she wins the post over a thoroughly mercenary male colleague) Elizabeth begins the drive to her sister's house and a planned dinner in which she will be introduced to an eligible man. In an ambiguous sequence in which the multitasking Elizabeth is seemingly at fault due to her own use of a cell phone and adjusting of the radio, her car collides with a large truck in what appears to be a catastrophic accident.

In the succeeding scene David (Mark Ruffalo), a widower searching for a place to live, discovers a random flyer on the street advertising Elizabeth's apartment for sublet. Having rejected a succession of other apartments, he's attracted by the location and the furnishings, and shortly moves in, only to discover that the apartment is, in effect, "haunted" by Elizabeth who does not believe she is dead and cannot account for her existence beyond the times when she appears to David. Drawing upon aspects of star Reese Witherspoon's "controlling and achieving" star persona (which sustains a certain tension with emphasis on her dedication to her family) the film derives comedy from the idea that perfectionist Elizabeth can be "summoned" by David whenever he threatens to perform a domestic infraction (such as failing to use a coaster) in the tastefully appointed apartment. The couple's testy relationship begins to deepen as Elizabeth rouses David from the depression he has suffered since the death of his wife (though a landscape designer he appears to spend his days sitting around the apartment), and he assists her in her quest to learn her fate after the car accident. In a moment that clinches their compatibility, both simultaneously object when a visiting psychic criticizes the apartment, each emphatically insisting that the apartment is beautiful. (Among other things *Just Like Heaven* is a film about the power of high-end urban real estate.) As a sign of the viability of romance and as a function of the emotional rehabilitation required of female professionals in the chick flick, Elizabeth increasingly articulates uncertainty and dependency, telling David "When I'm not with you, it's like I don't exist," and "I'm trying to figure it out, I just can't do it by myself."

Following a series of clues to who Elizabeth was and hearing repeated testimonials from other women about her workaholism and emotional isolation,[18] the couple finally learn that Elizabeth has lain comatose since the accident in the very hospital in which she had worked. An attempt by David and Elizabeth to re-fuse her spirit and body is unsuccessful and Elizabeth's professional rival (who now holds the promotion previously awarded to her) is zealously making plans for her to be removed from life support. In an exchange crucial to the film's gendered politics of achievement, Elizabeth deduces from a monitor that "my brain activity is decreasing every day," and David tells her "Well, maybe that's not such a bad thing, you're kind of a smarty pants." As the two join forces to try to prevent her death, David pays a visit to Elizabeth's sister Abby in an (unsuccessful) effort to persuade her to withdraw consent for the removal of the respirator. Where up until this point, the film has emphasized that Elizabeth is visible only to David and further that her body is uniquely responsive to his touch (when he holds the hand of her comatose body lying in the hospital bed she can feel it), this scene suggests that Elizabeth's young niece also perceives her presence. Chased out of the house by a knife-wielding Abby who thinks David is a lunatic when he claims that Elizabeth is standing beside him, the couple try to strategize further options but Elizabeth is distinctly less assertive here and wistfully tells David "I think I would have liked to have been a Mom." The couple draw closer when back at the apartment David reveals that he had taken a photo of Elizabeth from her hospital room and the photo he chose reflects an idealized image of her "freed" from ambition and professional achievement. The photo was taken on the evening that Elizabeth learned that she'd failed her MCATs and at Abby's insistence went out and got drunk. Staring at it, Elizabeth reflects that "the one time I completely failed at something, I had more fun than I ever did in my life."

Lacking any further options David concocts a plan to steal Elizabeth's body from the hospital before she is removed from life support and here *Just Like Heaven* settles into a standard misadventure sequence which culminates with a display of love's energizing force. Apprehended by staff and security at the hospital, David can't prevent the removal of Elizabeth from the respirator, but his frantic efforts to revive her produce a "miracle" and she begins breathing on her own. When she reveals that she has no memory of him, David rehabilitates the bare rooftop of her apartment, transforming it into a sumptuous garden. Sometime later Elizabeth returns from work and discovering the transformed rooftop her memory is restored and she and David embrace to close the film. The resolution here clearly suggests that Elizabeth's devotion to work will be counterbalanced by romantic intimacy but it also illustrates that David has gone back to work (his display of love for Elizabeth entails the re-embrace of his landscape design vocation).[19] In this way the film's conclusion joins together a sense of romantic symmetry with a symmetry of gendered work roles. Elizabeth's career can be tolerated as long she does not exaggerate its importance and proper role in her life and as long as she is romantically partnered with another achieving professional. Elizabeth's authority as a doctor must not be allowed to interfere with the "natural" roles as wife and mother the film looks ahead to for her. The film's minimization of Elizabeth's competence is signaled in part by the fact that the only display of medical prowess in the film occurs when David aids a dying man in a restaurant, making an incision into the man's ribcage under Elizabeth's invisible guidance that allows him to breathe.

Another film that does not entirely separate its heroine from achievement but minimizes her accomplishments by making them incidental to emotional transformation and the attainment of intimacy is *Wimbledon* (2005). In this romance between tennis-playing professionals Lizzie Bradbury (Kirsten Dunst) and Peter Colt (Paul Bettany) it is suggested that the killer instinct necessary to rise to the top of the tour is for men, a positive revelation of character, and for women, a worrisome step in the direction of unwomanliness. While Lizzie is a star from whom much is expected at the highest-profile Grand Slam tournament, Peter is an aging player whose highest-ranked days are well behind him and whose announcement of his imminent retirement from the sport is greeted with indifference in the press room. The romance between the two players is celebrated by the film via Lizzie's unexpected loss and Peter's unlikely winning of the Wimbledon championship. As a result of these events (which are deemed favorable by the film), Lizzie establishes a healthy separation from her controlling "tennis father" who has projected his ambition onto her, while Peter's emergence as a national hero through the tournament leads to a reconciliation between his estranged parents. *Wimbledon* suggests that female professional achievement is expressive of an unbalanced life and family relations that have slipped out of order while male achievement constitutes "proof" of a clear sense of identity and the (re)establishment of appropriate social/familial roles. The reconciliation between Peter's parents is "inspired" by their son's display of tenacity on the court but also, it seems, by a show of manliness on the part of Peter's father who has been spending his time living in a treehouse on the family property. While watching Peter win a match, he gives a Tarzan yell while beating his chest, thus attracting the attention of his wife who falls completely under his spell when he reveals that he has caught, and is presently grilling, the rabbit that had been bedeviling her in her garden.

Peter's success is paralleled by an increasing level of anxiety about Lizzie's devotion to her sport. When she tells Peter, "I love winning too. More than anything. More than anyone," it is implied that her professional dedication may present too great an obstacle for any permanent romance. When the couple are reconciled shortly before Peter's championship match, the film works its way toward the kind of conclusion it is comfortable with—tennis star Lizzie turned spectator watching her boyfriend win the tournament. This sequence is also in part symbolic of the sexual sanitization *Wimbledon* needs to effect with regard to Lizzie, who prior to meeting Peter, had casual sex with a number of male players on the tour. Peter's victory is achieved at the expense of one of Lizzie's form-ers lovers, a man who had insulted her at a party. (Even as the film links Lizzie's champion status to promiscuity, it also links it to a loss of femininity; at the same party she greets a manager by asking "How are they hangin'?" and he responds "Fine and yours?")

With Peter's championship victory restoring his sense of self, revitalizing his parents' marriage and symbolically expunging Lizzie's promiscuous past, the film can move to a tableau scene of familial continuity. In a flashforward conclusion, Lizzie and Peter play with their children on the same tennis court where Peter had once been tutored in the sport by his father. In voiceover, Peter tells us that Lizzie has gone on to win several Grand Slam titles, but her real achievement, it is suggested, is her motherhood and role in ensuring familial continuity. While in playing with her daughter, Lizzie still exhibits a touch of the killer instinct to win, her hypercompetitiveness is seen to have been tamed and balanced by marriage.

Narratives of adjusted ambition

As I have discussed elsewhere, one of the most consistent attributes of post-feminist cinema is the drama of "miswanting" in which the heroine comes to realize that her professional aspirations are misplaced.[20] A film like *Picture Perfect* (1997) illustrates well the conventional concerns of the contemporary "working-woman" chick flick. In it New York advertising executive Kate Mosley (Jennifer Aniston) is initially turned down for promotion on the grounds that she lacks "maturity," which she is bluntly informed is constituted by a husband and family. To boost her social capital at work, Kate asks a man whom she has met at a wedding to masquerade as her fiancé. Nick, a blue-collar videographer who will shortly make headlines for rescuing a child during a fire, agrees to the plan and takes up a place in the narrative as an exemplar of stable, authentic masculinity in opposition to the chicanery and shallowness of all the men Kate knows through her job. At dinner with Kate's colleagues Nick makes a character defining speech about the joys of his work and the immense privilege of being on hand to witness and record important family events. Inspired by this image of familial retreatism, Kate nevertheless continues her vigorous climb up the cor-porate ladder[21] until a late stage epiphany leads her to abandon the office for a romantic reconciliation with Nick.[22] While *Picture Perfect* is careful to ensure that Kate won't have to leave her job (and in this way the film differs from more fully retreatist romances) it nevertheless remains deeply uncertain about how to put her back in the workplace, emphasizing instead an ideological transformation utterly in keeping with the drama of "miswanting."

Picture Perfect enables me to begin to pinpoint a set of films in which the heroines retain their role in the workforce but are psychologically distanced from ambition, and the central significance of work for them is diminished in what I would deem "narratives of adjusted ambition." To consider how such films function, it is instructive to examine several other recent examples. *Hitch*, one of a new breed of male-centered chick flicks that began to emerge in 2005 (along with films such as *Wedding Crashers* and *The 40-Year-Old Virgin*), showcases the confidence and charisma of Alex "Hitch" Hitchens (Will Smith) an entrepreneurial "date doctor" who schools male clients in how to charm beautiful women they are in love with.[23] To the extent that Hitch and the film assume that women need to "open their eyes" to a greater range of available men, concepts of female miswanting are already latent in the plot which will go on to pair Hitch's client Albert (Kevin James), an asthmatic, overweight junior accountant, with Allegra (Amber Valletta), a beautiful socialite and heiress.[24] Hitch himself falls for Sara Melas (Eva Mendes), a gossip columnist at the fictional *New York Standard*, and a woman defined by her world-weary presumptions about male infidelity and deceptiveness. As the film opens, Sara has returned early from a vacation mandated by her boss who tells her "you are becoming a sick workaholic lunatic" but modulates his concern when Sara reveals that she has obtained a new scoop on her holiday. Pleased as he is by the choice item of gossip, Sara's boss nevertheless counsels her "You know, kiddo, there is more to life than watching other people live it . . . I think it's great you're so good at your job, I'm just a little worried as to why." In this way the film introduces its gendered valuation of work: Sara's singlehood implies the illegitimacy of her career, but there is no such judgment extended toward Hitch. As *Hitch* develops, it is made clear that Sara's work has made her bitter and suspicious while Hitch's is an outlet for a fundamental optimism. As a tabloid journalist, Sara constantly exposes revelations of infidelity and duplicity while Hitch seeks to create legitimate romantic partnerships. While the possibility that male manipulation and deceit might exist is shunted off onto a minor character (a prospective male client seeking uncommitted sex whom Hitch chides for "hating women") the film centralizes female cynicism and myopia as the driving factors in the uncertainty and difficulty of contemporary romance. When Sara begins a reproach of Hitch, "You're a scam artist. You trick women into getting—" she is neatly cut off by his interjection "into getting out of their own way so great guys like Albert have a fighting chance."

Hitch illustrates a belief that for men work can be a healthy expression of self/individuality but for women it leads to confusion and bad faith. As it moves to a conclusion the film requires an apology from Sara who tells Hitch "I made some assumptions about you based on nothing it turns out," and for Hitch himself to take on the vulnerability and openness to love demonstrated by his male clients. Hitch's epiphany arrives when he is the subject of a distinctive critique by

Albert who tells him "You're selling this stuff, but you just don't believe in your own product." For Hitch to achieve authenticity then, he has to fully merge the personal and the professional (the obstacle is lingering romantic trauma from when he had his heart broken by a callous woman).[25] For Sara, on the other hand, it is imperative that she unlearn the lessons of her profession. *Hitch* typifies a new postfeminist emotional economy in which female-oriented fabrication has to be detected and corrected. In the end, Hitch's work is more emotionally legitimate than Sara's (which the film designates mere "gossip"), and the legitimacy of Hitch's entrepreneurial efforts is reinforced when we see that he is continuing to ply his trade even in the film's closing wedding sequence.

In Her Shoes (2006), the Curtis Hanson-directed adaptation of a bestselling novel by Jennifer Weiner, is another female-oriented fiction that hinges on the necessity for its characters to establish a healthy relationship to work. Its pursuit of this narrative goal entails engagement with the distinctly postfeminist themes of consumerist gratification, female competition, and generational tension. While Rose Feller (Toni Collette) begins the film as a harried, overweight but accomplished professional with a showplace apartment and Maggie Feller (Cameron Diaz) as an unemployed, promiscuous, secretly dyslexic woman who finances her chaotic life by tapping other people for money, the film suggests that in their different ways the sisters are equally troubled. In a film that deeply romanticizes female connectedness it will become clear that the early suicide of their mother has left both Rose and Maggie without a vital ingredient for knowing who they are, for overcoming the challenges of life, and for establishing healthy heterosexual intimacy.

Rose incarnates one of the most regular postfeminist archetypes of the female professional: the abject, deeply vulnerable woman exhibiting a dawning sense of regret about the dissatisfactions and sacrifices that accompany her success. To the tune of Garbage's pop hit "Stupid Girl," the film opens with images of Rose at work at her law firm.[26] A short while later, she says "My life is about working long hours, planning trips I never take and settling for love found on the pages of romance novels." When Rose catches Maggie in bed with Jim, the law firm colleague she herself has been dating, the sisters' vehement quarrel leads Maggie in search of new financial sponsors. In her father's house the chance discovery of a set of unopened cards from a grandmother she never knew leads Maggie to Florida where she takes up residence in the senior living center her grandmother resides in.

Meanwhile, Rose takes a leave of absence from her job and through seemingly random circumstances becomes a dog walker. The film suggests that freed from the reflexive workaholism of her law career, Rose finds beneficial work that provides her with the exercise she needs and gives her the time and space to begin to discover her true self. In a series of walks around Philadelphia, Rose looks freer and happier; in a repeated sequence she and the dogs energetically ascend the stairs in front of the Philadelphia Museum of Art famously climbed by Rocky in his training regimen. The film further suggests that in her professional life

Rose had closed herself off to legitimate romantic prospects; on leave of absence she runs into Simon Stein, another firm lawyer whom she had previously scornfully rejected. This time she agrees to a date with him and the ensuing romance certifies Rose's restoration to health; a gourmand who tells her on their first date "you'll wanna eat with me for the rest of your life," Simon embodies the sanctioned pleasures of food within couplehood. Instead of the ice cream and other junk foods the film associates with emotional eating early on, Rose transitions to happy meals with Simon where they consume multicultural delicacies like sushi and Jamaican jerk chicken. One evening Simon asks her about her decision to leave her career and Rose tells him that she now realizes her job was only a means of escapism, characterizing her fears in the form of a question she then goes on to answer: "What would happen to me without those people to please and those tasks to get done? Maybe those were the things holding me together and without them I'd fall apart."

In Florida Maggie hangs around the senior center pool before taking a job at a nursing home. A blind retired professor in the home asks her to read to him and through patient coaching enables her to transcend her dyslexia and become a competent reader. Like her sister, Maggie comes into her own through care work, not a high-wage status profession, and the achievements of both sisters are communicated through what is deemed a healthy, essentially feminine consumerism. While Rose has been compulsively buying expensive high-heeled shoes, she only begins wearing items in her collection once she falls in love with Simon. The film, in effect, approvingly communicates that she is now woman enough to wear such beautiful shoes. Maggie, cured of her selfishness through exposure to her grandmother and her set of friends, now also "accidentally" finds healthy work. After successfully shopping for an elderly woman who wants a nice outfit for her son's wedding (and in so doing resisting the temptation to abuse the woman's credit card as she would once have done), Maggie finds herself much in demand among the other elderly women of the community and becomes a personal shopper. (In this way the film doubles Maggie's experience of the care work that will help her to find herself; significantly her nursing home job and her personal shopping job bring solace and pleasure to the elderly.) The emotional legitimacy of Maggie's work is confirmed when after a reconciliation with Rose, Maggie proudly and confidently asserts her skills by telling her sister that her bridal gift will be the selection and purchase of the wedding dress, stating "I'm good at this, trust me." Maggie's transition from sexpot outfits to a more demure style and her association with the tasteful clothing she buys for the affluent elderly women of her grandmother's set help to establish the suggested symbolic transition she is making out of the sordid, hypersexual culture that has been trivializing her, and her elevation into the kind of woman who would make a fine wife for a doctor. (Maggie's nursing home patient has a doctor son whom she briefly but suggestively meets, for in the contemporary romance such chance meetings of two eligible single people are never insignificant.) It is a sign of the film's ideological limitations that it proposes the reason why a middle-class

20-something woman would have difficulty finding rewarding work is due to untreated dyslexia, rather than due to any other systemic issues. It is similarly telling that *In Her Shoes* comes to closure via an emphatic sentimentalization of women's connections to each other, their fundamentally traditionalist orientations, and their deep-seated consumerist desires.

The sex worker next door

In addition to the move away from work as a defining feature of the establishment of identity in the contemporary chick flick, I want to analyze several other representational developments regarding the kind of female work roles popular culture does sanction. One such development is tied to the recent reclassification of pornography as hip, ironic, and mainstream, in terms vividly conveyed by a 2003 *USA Today* article that noted "a wave of mainstream projects on TV and film and in books, peeling back the plain brown wrapper from the world of pornography."[27] One of the most striking features of the postfeminist epoch has been the simultaneous rise of a self-proclaimed family values culture and a culture in which the sex industry is flourishing in new ways and many of the traditional stigmas of participation in that industry (as performer, and especially as consumer) are being eradicated. Perhaps the most conspicuous development in this regard has been the national "proliferation of 'gentleman's clubs,' a euphemism for the high-dollar, upscale strip clubs that cater to businessmen, couples and even women."[28] The new proscription against critique of such industries is sometimes accompanied by (straight) women playing the role of consumer in such spaces as a testament to their postfeminist moxie.[29] The association of pornography with an exclusive definition of potent and attractive female sexuality has powerfully taken hold in recent years such that as Ariel Levy points out,

> Because we have determined that all empowered women must be overtly and publicly sexual, and because the only sign of sexuality we seem to be able to recognize is a direct allusion to red-light entertainment, we have laced the sleazy energy and aesthetic of a topless club or a *Penthouse* shoot throughout our entire culture . . . We skipped over the part where we just accept and respect that *some* women like to seem exhibitionistic and lickerish, and decided instead that *everyone* who is sexually liberated ought to be imitating strippers and porn stars.[30]

Under such terms male sexuality is dominantly displayed while female sexuality is ever more a quotation of itself. Since the job of a lap dancer or stripper is to feign sexual arousal, when the female sex worker is cast as the universal model for female sexuality, women's sexuality is played out in an imitative mode and women's actual sexual pleasure is at a further and further remove.

A number of critics have taken note of the destigmatization and migration of pornography to the mainstream in recent years. For instance, in *Pornified:*

How Pornography Is Transforming Our Lives, Our Relationships, and Our Families, Pamela Paul has explored how "pornography's ubiquity and acceptance are affecting American society."[31] Even as pornography has surged into a \$10–20 billion slice of the American economy,[32] its social status has changed, with interest in and attraction to pornography largely becoming universalized in American culture. As Paul notes, "something that used to be considered seedy and hidden is now considered a healthy exercise in fantasy."[33] For present purposes (I return to the subject of pornography's mainstreaming in a different context in the next chapter) I want to establish that in tandem with this, representation of women sex workers has emerged in such disparate cinematic categories as the adult drama (*Closer*) and the teen romance (*The Girl Next Door*). Recent years have seen the publication of bestselling advice literature by stars of the pornography industry (Jenna Jamison's 2004 *How to Make Love Like a Porn Star*) while another sign of the absorption of pornography into mainstream culture has been the revival of the Playboy brand by various means including an E television series *The Girls Next Door* (2005–). That series ironically inverts concepts of hometown femininity being re-idealized elsewhere, as the "girls" in the series are the members of Hugh Hefner's harem. As Moya Luckett has demonstrated, the series "plays with significant ideological contradictions as it tries to address the prevailing popularity of the Playboy bunny image with a new generation of women while trying to remove any taint of sexual exploitation from its girls."[34]

The correlation between power and femininity that has arisen in pornography is in one respect, I argue, a function of the postfeminist susceptibility to confusion between empowerment and role restriction. Yet in another sense there is an economic logic at work here too in terms of the new authority that working-class women are granted to "own" their sexual labor in the marketplace. As Imelda Whelehan reminds us, the "only sphere in which women's pay consistently outstrips men's is in the realms of heterosexual pornography."[35]

What is certainly clear is that the female sex worker is becoming one of popular culture's most regular archetypes of paid labor, perhaps particularly in those genres and forms that play to a younger demographic. In a *New York Times* account profiling the new sexual behaviors of teens, Benoit Denizet-Lewis opens his article relaying how, at the boy's suggestion, he met a male teen informant at a Hooters restaurant (where scantily-clad waitresses are trained to flirt with customers). When Denizet-Lewis called Hooters to ensure that teens were allowed to patronize the restaurant, he reports, "the woman who picks up seems annoyed I would even ask. No, we're a family restaurant, she says"[36] In an article which goes on to sketch a culture of casual, utterly uncommitted teen sex in which girls often perform oral sex on boys without any sexual gratification of their own, this choice to open the article with a reference to the postfeminist sexual culture symbolized by Hooters is surely telling. Moreover, this anecdote (whether intentionally or not) hints at some of the ways that in a postfeminist culture the ideological and economic privileging of "family" often employs the term as a codeword for male entitlement.

In *The Girl Next Door* (2005), a self-conscious update of landmark teen film *Risky Business* (1983), Matthew Kidman, an ambitious but unpopular high-school boy, discovers that Danielle, the girl of his dreams, is living next door but that she is a porn star. Initially nonplussed, he adjusts quickly to the idea and when it becomes clear that Danielle loves him and wants to dedicate herself exclusively to making him happy, he falls in love with her. The film's broader project is to demonstrate that mainstream sexual culture is so suffused with pornographic codes and concepts that pornography itself can no longer be seen to constitute any degree of difference. (An opening sequence in the film has a photographer coaching his offscreen subject in a sexualized mode of display; when the camera pulls back we see that this is a high-school yearbook photo session.) Moreover, pornography has been thoroughly de-stigmatized and operates as a profit source fully compatible with any other capitalist venture. When in *Risky Business* Joel Goodson becomes a pimp to raise the funds to repair his father's Porsche, the film suggests that in his coming of age he has irrevocably lost his innocence and a degree of his humanity. The film's highly melancholy (even despairing) conclusion questions what it means to come of age in a society marked by exploitation and stacked competition. By contrast in *The Girl Next Door* the profits from a porn film shot by Matthew's friends and starring Danielle's friends become the means of replenishing the funds he has raised to bring a brilliant Cambodian student to America. The student, it is suggested, is so brilliant that his future scientific discoveries may be of great value to humanity. In this way, the film accommodates a double rescue fantasy: Matthew gains a sense of himself by ushering both the white woman and the minority male into the roles they "deserve."

The Girl Next Door updates some of the formulas of *Risky Business* for a postfeminist era by deceptively (and only initially) stressing a certain egalitarianism. Whereas Joel had fantasized about entering the house of a neighborhood girl and finding her in the shower, Matthew peers out the window at Danielle while she is getting dressed and she immediately comes over to his house, introduces herself to his parents and tricks him into taking a drive with her as a means of payback, leaving him standing naked in the road. However, from this point forward the film gives up any egalitarian project as Danielle demonstrates no attributes other than her pure love for and dedication to Matthew.

While *Wimbledon* finds it necessary to rehabilitate its female professional for romance, no such need is apparent with respect to the porn star in *The Girl Next Door*. The reason that this is the case is that Lizzie is an ambitious high-earner whose work has made her wealthy and famous, while Danielle operates as a profit source for a variety of men. *The Girl Next Door* acts as a barometer of the current norms of youth sex culture and depicts a world in which everyone (except Danielle) speaks the language of brutal self-interest, using a vocabulary of sex as power. Dialogue references to "Getting fucked" are frequent in the film and mean a variety of things but pornographic femininity is strangely idealized.

In the remaining sections of this chapter I look to investigate the cultural logic by which two particular archetypes of the woman worker have recently risen to prominence: the nanny and the flight attendant. Both operate in traditionally gendered milieux and yet their potential access to power and authority often figures as a concern in their representation. Anxiety about the former is managed through a caricaturing maternalization and in the latter through erotic trivialization/disparagement. Occasionally, these figures speak the rhetoric of a postfeminist "power" that stresses care for others and authority over procedural matters. Both are also almost inevitably represented as single women and so it will be important for me to analyze their representation within that context as well, with the nanny often cast as an accessory to a smoothly functioning family life and the flight attendant as a symbol of respite from the travails of business culture. At the same time, the representation of nannies and flight attendants reflects the characteristic overemphasis of the experiences, concerns, and dilemmas of the wealthy in a postfeminist representational regime. Their recent over-representation reflects something of the ways in which as the experience of middle- and working-class life becomes more fraught, popular culture representation restricts its view to the affluent elite.

Nanny nation: postfeminist work and the new female domestic

There is, of course, one form of female worker that has become particularly conspicuous of late, and that is the nanny. In "an America that has invented a new nanny culture,"[37] this figure has been centralized in TV series such as *Supernanny* (ABC) and *Nanny 911* (Fox), in films like *Nanny McPhee* (2006) and even on Broadway in an adaptation of *Mary Poppins* for the stage. As we will see, the phenomenal status of the nanny resembles flight attendant chic in its prominence and representational duration. The prevalence of nannies in current popular culture is consistent with postfeminism's tendency to focus our view upon the concerns and options of the affluent, and Caitlin Flanagan is indeed correct to pinpoint the nanny as a manifestation of "the current upper-middle-class practice of outsourcing even the most intimate tasks."[38] At the same time, the nanny is crucially linked to new fantasies of accessible luxury and symbolic aristocratization within the middle class. Thus, in the television series and film noted above, the nanny appears as a temporary transitional agent who leads a comfortable but not wealthy family toward a correction in their domestic behavior.

The nanny's work is reassuringly domestic and (often) suburban; at the same time it gives credence to postfeminist notions of female power (in approved realms such as childcare) and advances concepts of traditionalist parenting leavened with contemporary compassion. At the same time, the invariably, white, middle-class (and seemingly obligatorily British) nanny is an inverted double for the minority and third-world women who are in fact most likely to take work as nannies. This form of labor has been particularly susceptible to globalization as Barbara Ehrenreich and Arlie Russell Hochschild have shown, expanding a national labor economy into a worldwide one as impoverished women increasingly take up jobs as nannies, housecleaners, and modern-day servants in the affluent West, sometimes at the cost of a wrenching departure from their own children.[39] While the nanny helps to underscore the vital importance of a seemingly self-sustaining, highly productive and aspirational Western family model, she is thus also a nodal point to the broader global economic forces that help to hold that concept of family (precariously) in place. As Flanagan observes,

> In our time and place, the forces that bring nanny and employer together are, respectively, the collapse of the third world, which has flooded the United States with immigrants desperate for work; the rise of the two-career couple, which has doubled the income of many professional-class families and created the large-scale need for child care; and an intense preoccupation with the emotional lives of children, which puts a premium on top-quality care for them.[40]

The nanny figures repeatedly as a supporting character in narratives centering on the infatuation of the affluent with their offspring and concern for their wellbeing in an era of inflated rhetorics of safety and security. In such scenarios the vital imperatives of children's health, nurturance, and development may require a team of caregivers. In Flanagan's account of the concerns of the affluent at-home mother she goes so far as to pinpoint the emergence of the "executive child," the center of the well-off household. The executive child, intensely scheduled nearly from birth, requires a mother advocate to ensure that he/she will not miss an opportunity for development and growth. Describing a domestic milieu in which she has the sense that "the children . . . are engaged in the most important work of the household,"[41] Flanagan writes, "I have Miss Moneypenny's romantic attachment to my little bosses, as well as her sterling loyalty and eagerness to stand in the shadows, taking pleasure in the achievements—impossible without her steadying, invisible hand—of the loved ones. In short, I am a modern mother . . . "[42]

To a limited extent the nanny also figures in the new social norms regarding the erotic vibrancy of the midlife woman that I discussed in Chapter 3. The nanny's more menial work frees the affluent mother to do the work on herself that is required if she is to adhere to new standards of glamour and physical fitness. As Flanagan acknowledges, "the at-home mother has a lot on her mind; to a significant extent, she has herself on her mind. She must not allow herself to shrivel up with boredom. She must do things *for herself*. She must get to the gym, the spa, the yoga studio."[43]

A decade ago the notorious case of British nanny Louise Woodward seemed to give shape and credence to a kind of "nanny panic" in the US. Such panic, many media accounts suggested, was justifiable in an era in which more two-career parents elected to bring a stranger into their household and entrust the care of their children to her. Woodward, put on trial for causing the death of Matthew Eappen, the infant in her care, by shaking him to death, became a representative figure for a shift in the practices of elite domesticity. Specifically, the case (which culminated with Woodward's exoneration and return to England) centralized for many observers the public judgments that could be summoned against a "working mother" (in this case Deborah Eappen) who relinquished her maternal obligation, and conventional wisdom about the case held that the defense's ability to shift guilt for the child's death to Deborah Eappen played a substantial role in Woodward's acquittal.[44] The sense that a nanny-hiring mother bore a responsibility for the death equivalent to or greater than the nanny herself and that blame of Deborah Eappen could be mobilized toward a successful defense is all the more striking given the widespread public belief (despite the acquittal) that Woodward had, in fact, killed Matthew Eappen.

In the mid-1990s the association between nannies and a hazardous balancing act of career and domesticity was further reinforced in several aborted attempts by Bill Clinton to appoint an Attorney General. Clinton's first nominee, Zoe Baird, saw her case scuppered after her employment of undocumented household help (a Peruvian couple who worked as nanny and chauffeur) was brought to light. The likely second nominee, Kimba Wood, withdrew her name from nomination revealing that her baby-sitter had been in the country illegally when she was first hired in the 1980s. In commentary first published in the *Harvard Law Record* Rebecca Eisenberg notes that ultimately the post of Attorney General went to Janet Reno, a woman who (conveniently, in Eisenberg's eyes) was childless. She writes that the scrutiny of nanny selection as a condition of appointability is a "standard uniquely applied to women" and notes "Unfortunately, for many of us, particularly women, the Zoe Baird incident will linger in our memories. For the first time in US history, hiring the right nanny became a prerequisite for serving our country."[45]

The Woodward case and the Baird scandal followed by just a few years the high-profile cinematic cautionary tale, *The Hand That Rocks the Cradle* (1992), in which sinister nanny Peyton Flanders (Rebecca De Mornay) plots to destroy the household into which she is incorporated. The film was one of the most conspicuous of a reactionary set of late 1980s/early 1990s fictions dubbed "yuppie horror" by Barry Keith Grant (such films were devoted to thematizing the covetousness of the underclass and the righteous re-possession of material and familial assets by the wealthy).[46] Arguably, this cycle of films has been revived in the early 2000s with abduction narratives such as *Breakdown* (1997), home invasion thrillers such as *Panic Room* (2002), and films such as *One Hour Photo* (2002) in which Robin Williams' store clerk fantasizes his inclusion within a family whose idyllic life he believes is documented in the photos he develops.

In the 15 years since *The Hand That Rocks the Cradle* and the Woodward case helped to shape the crucible of public opinion about nannies in American life, the choice to include a nanny in one's household has been destigmatized and "nanny panic" has receded if not dissipated altogether. The nanny is clearly a highly intelligible cultural figure, her role consistent with a more generalized repression of the subordinate female labor that is so often required to sustain a high-powered career, a showplace home and family, or a balance of the two. In many ways it would appear that the nanny's usefulness as an accessory figure within a framework of luxury lifestyling has trumped earlier fears that she violated the sanctity of family. The fact that a case such as Louise Woodward's would probably no longer work in the same way is the kind of proof of social "progress" that is so often marshaled in postfeminist terms. Yet while the discourse over "working mothers" has shifted from direct condemnation to a focus on "choice," the new rhetoric is laden with anxious remonstration and isolates individual women and families from a social and economic context.

Meanwhile, the nanny industry has expanded even as the place of the nanny has moved to a prominent one in the public imagination. In addition to her representation on television and in film, the nanny has factored in recent celebrity scandals (such as the breakup of Jude Law and Sienna Miller after the actor admitted to an affair with his children's nanny) and a flurry of bestselling books including Suzanne Hansen's *You'll Never Nanny in This Town Again* and Barbara Kline's *White House Nannies: True Tales from the Other Department of Homeland Security*. Elizabeth Hale has identified a strain of chick-lit that encompasses bestsellers like *The Nanny Diaries* which draw from the codes of Victorian literature, sketching scenarios where a morally superior but economically inferior young woman describes her employment in a wealthy household, documenting in meticulous detail the cruel and indifferent parenting she observes there. Such nanny fictions are marked by what Hale refers to as "damp squib" endings in which the exploited, undervalued, and underpaid nanny goes quietly, her dignity intact (and moral superiority confirmed) when she is unjustly fired at the conclusion.[47] Even where the nanny does not drive the narrative, she may also factor as a significant figure in relation to the working woman protagonist as in such bestselling chick-lit as Allison Pearson's novel *I Don't Know How She Does It*. Public interest in this incarnation of the postfeminist working woman is suggested by the success of nanny fiction and nanny non-fiction alike; Hansen's book, for example, sold out in its first 2003 printing.

Such examples of "underling lit" as *The Nanny Diaries* and *The Devil Wears Prada* have been successful enough to spawn film adaptations (in 2007 and 2006 respectively). While *The Devil Wears Prada* at times complicates and even interrogates this category's class and generational premises, *The Nanny Diaries* conforms scrupulously to them, even intensifying the postfeminist conceptualizations upon which its source text is based.

Kline's account of her career running an elite nanny placement service in Washington DC innovates chick-lit paradigms of luxury lifestyling and the "female" dilemma of work/life balance while conservatively refraining from any critique of a work culture that makes it exceedingly difficulty for two-career couples (Kline's primary clients) to spend time with their children. Moreover, Kline's occasional caustic assessments of the mothers whose children her nannies care for suggest a gender-unbalanced assessment of parental responsibility. While fathers are occasionally inappropriate toward nannies or are worryingly distanced from their children, Kline communicates that maternal failures are the ones that really matter. When contacted by a pregnant journalist whose experiences after the birth of her child take center stage in the book, she writes "Our superstar will probably visit motherhood long enough to do an eyewitness report as if it's just another assignment. She'll be back on the air so soon after giving birth, we'll barely have missed her."[48]

The central profile of the book (which is interspersed with vignettes from Kline's lengthy career) examines a White House correspondent and law firm partner couple adjusting to life after the birth of their son and highly dependent upon their heroic nanny. Kline's book closes with the promise that the Huntington-Wilder household will find a way to continue to cope when the husband downshifts his career, and Kline anticipates the birth of another child, adding to her business.

Kline's account is meant to astonish with the lengths to which high-profile parents and their domestic staff go to manage the balancing act of work commitments, childcare, family time, and basic errands. In this account, family life is a vigorous manifestation of the commitment and dedication of a high-achieving elite able to purchase a category of service that (just barely) enables them to hang on to their sanity and large incomes.

A different view is on display in Hansen's memoir of working as a nanny to high-profile entertainment industry figures such as Michael Ovitz and Debra Winger. Hansen's book continues very much in the same vein as a previous bestseller, *The Nanny Diaries*, which notably helped to pioneer a category of female-authored underling lit. Operating in fictional, non-fictional, and sometimes hybrid modes, these books have powerfully imprinted cultural understandings of "women's work" over the last ten years.[49] Like the authors of *The Nanny Diaries*, Hansen decries the petty economies and loveless family lives of the super-rich. Her innovation is to situate her account in a Hollywood that aggressively promulgates "celebrity momism" with the promise of exposing hypocrisy "in the diaper trenches of Hollywood."[50] Hansen writes "I realized that I had met or knew the nannies for most of the celebrities I saw in television interviews. And the mothers' descriptions of their own homemaking and childrearing prowess were vastly different from what their nannies described. If any of the employees ever came forward with the truth about what the *stars* really did behind closed doors, they'd probably need to be placed in a Nanny Witness Protection Program."[51]

Alongside the proliferation of non-fiction nanny texts has been a stream of fictional ones. At one end of the representational spectrum, the nanny registers as mysterious, uncanny, a not-quite witch whose charged status arises from her break with conventionally gendered codes of authority (despite the fact that her stay will be a temporary one and her authority resides exclusively in the feminine domestic sphere). Family film *Nanny McPhee* (2006) for instance reinstates the supernatural component of the nanny narrative that had been in place in earlier film hits such as *Mary Poppins*. In the film, widower Mr. Brown (Colin Firth), the anxious father of seven ungovernable children, is turned down for any further service from his local nanny agency after his children traumatize the agency's most able worker. At his wits' end and financially dependent upon an imperious aunt who stipulates that he must marry within the month or face the loss of her patronage, Mr. Brown is suddenly visited by the magical Nanny of the film's title. As played by Emma Thompson (who also wrote the screenplay) Nanny McPhee is a wart-ridden witch figure with a magic staff that she taps on the floor to influence events. Nanny's role in bringing the household under control entails leading the oldest child Simon into an awareness of how to use his intelligence for the good of his family and effecting the transformation of a scullery maid, Evangeline, who is both beautified and educated under the tutelage of the aunt.

Of course, one sign of the film's cognizance of the postfeminist ethos is its inclusion of the ubiquitous postfeminist makeover. This nanny is also a bit of a fairy godmother and Nanny McPhee's key skill is her ability to perform a magical makeover that promotes the beautiful young servant into a marriageable state, thus "completing" the Brown family. Further, as in reality series *Nanny 911* and *Supernanny*, the nanny's Britishness here is partly a sign of the work that she does in class terms, symbolically elevating the household into a more elite position. Postfeminism's habit of re-activating previously problematized stereotypes of femininity is also relevant here; the sexless singlehood of the contemporary nanny serves to generate functional value for the new spinster.

The prominence of the nanny in an emphatically postfeminist culture is illustrated in her recurrent appearance in a wide range of popular culture forms. The conceptual potency of the nanny clearly exceeds her actual economic role. In the nanny resides the hope for resolution of what I have argued is one of postfeminism's defining dilemmas—the achievement of a work/life "balance." At the same time, however the nanny operates as a fraught figure who may expose the illusion of perfectionistic domestic performativity. Nanny fictions underwrite the idea that the care of children remains inevitably a female task, even if that care is outsourced. The conspicuous presence of nannies in scenarios of perfectionistic domesticity suggests an awareness of the "impossibility" of what has been cast as a problem of female ambition, under the auspices of "having it all." The significance and scope of this problem is suggested by the titles of the books by Hansen and Kline which intriguingly embed an assumption that the nanny communicates at a social or even political level.

Popular media, postfeminism, and the return of flight attendant chic

In this study of the ways recent media culture has been actively engaged in troping postfeminist femininities, I have frequently looked to those representational strategies that seem to retrieve a prefeminist mindset or relocate into a prefeminist moment. As has been suggested, one of the most singular characteristics of

Figure 4.1 A flurry of early 2000s films, television programs, and books centralized the thrilling figure of the nanny, a particular kind of working
woman who embodies the promise of domestic order through outsourcing. (*Nanny McPhee*, 2005)

postfeminist representational culture is its ability to objectify women as figures of
erotic fantasy while casting those very same women as subjects of their own self-
determination. A common strategy for naturalizing this contradiction is to raid a

prefeminist past, recovering and recycling earlier feminine archetypes. This section of the chapter will examine how the retrograde image of the hyperfeminine flight attendant was brought back into active cultural circulation in 2002–2004 in American and British cinema, popular music, print fiction, and related forms of corporate branding.[52] Although I won't be discussing them here, by 2003 the high profile of the female flight attendant seemed to be confirmed with the publication of a flurry of books that showcased nostalgia for an earlier era of aviation. The titles of these books often emphatically reinstated stereotypes of the flight attendant's glamour and sexual availability. They included two memoirs *Glamour and Turbulence: I Remember Pan Am 1966–91* by Aimee Bratt and *Coffee, Tea or Me: The Uninhibited Memoirs of Two Airline Stewardesses* by (puzzlingly) Donald Bain, Trudy Baker, and Rachel Jones as well as a broader history *Come Fly With Us: A Global History of the Aviation Hostess* by Johanna Omelia and Michael Waldcock.

The texts I will be examining include *View from the Top* (2003), a chick flick self-discovery narrative in which a working-class "white trash" woman remakes herself via flight attendant training and a subsequent career working for "Royalty Air." I will also consider how some of the period's most high-profile pop stars, including Britney Spears and Kylie Minogue, associated themselves with flight attendant chic in their music videos and concert performances. I conclude with a brief discussion of Hooters Air, the notable 2003 airline start-up venture which expanded the Hooters chain restaurant brand into aviation and resexualized the flight attendant as "Hooters Girl."

In part through a focalization and revalidation of some of the most retrograde stereotypes of femininity (the servile flight attendant, waitress, or secretary, the housewife, the "dumb blonde") postfeminist culture is finding ways to politically neutralize "women's work," celebrating the range of choices women now enjoy even if those choices may cluster disproportionately in the service and sex industries. Yet an understanding of such postfeminist recidivism should not obscure the reality of two recurrent and deeply contradictory discursive tropes about gender in the culture—one celebrates female empowerment and agency (in certain realms) while the other invokes neotraditionalist definitions of femininity. The flight attendant, I suggest (or at least her fantasy incarnation) is a useful figure in resolving the contradiction between these two.

Emotional labor, sexual iconography, and flight attendant chic

In the early decades of commercial air travel the flight attendant was an icon of non-threatening female independence. As Ayesha Court has written, "being a stewardess was right up there with being a model or actress . . . Before women's liberation, the chance for young ladies to live independently, travel and meet men was rare."[53] In her position as doubly answerable to a male pilot and a largely male passenger clientele, the flight attendant's "independent" role was

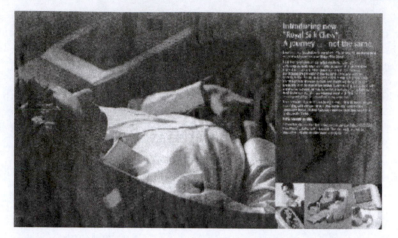

Figure 4.2 Airline advertisements frequently cast the flight attendant as an accessory figure in the drama of male corporate achievement (Royal Silk advertisement).

Figure 4.3 The reassurance of traditionalist femininity is a frequent element in "approved" forms of postfeminist labor (Singapore Airlines advertisement).

surely always heavily compromised. But it is clear that an early image of the flight attendant was available to anchor broader fictions of female agency, as was the case for example in the *Vicki Barr Flight Stewardess* series. This set of 16 mystery novels published between 1947 and 1965 featured the adventures of a blonde, blue-eyed crimesolver (sort of a Nancy Drew of the skies) whose position as a flight attendant enabled her to detect and thwart a variety of criminal plots.[54]

While in the 1960s the determining cliché of "coffee, tea or me?" underscored a new image of flight attendant sexual availability,[55] this image was modulated in later decades to encompass a rhetoric of sexual self-determination; popular culture increasingly imagined the flight attendant as a hip international swinger.[56] In the 1980s and 1990s with air travel vastly expanded and service diminished after deregulation, and with new cultural and sexual norms (arguably) inhibiting use of the broadest female sexual stereotypes, the flight attendant became decidedly less representable.[57]

Now in a postfeminist culture widely revalidating what had until recently seemed quite anachronistic images of femininity, the flight attendant has re-emerged perhaps in keeping with an ideological trend in which female care labor is mobilized to repair a variety of crises of uncertainty. Just as the masseuse assuages uncertainties over the body in an era of stress and overwork, and the parachuted-in nanny of reality television shores up the viability of current family values proscriptions, the nostalgic (re)discovery of an essential femininity in the flight attendant speaks to widely-felt uncertainties about class and security in contemporary America.[58] In this light, flight attendant chic reads as an oblique effort to stave off the realities of aviation terror and a brutally segmented air travel market. The social meanings and significance of air travel have been radically revised and bear significant stress as Crispin Thurlow and Adam Jaworski have observed:

> Ironically, the sharp increase in the number of people enjoying air travel, its democratization and mass-marketization, especially due to "cheap," "no-frills" air carriers, leave most traditional "flag-carrier" airlines, with their slim profit margins, confined aircraft space, restricted weight allowances, and so on, struggling to maintain their image as dispensers of luxury and glamour. Thus, having very little to work with, they must necessarily rely on ever more sophisticated, semioticized means in order to stay competitive and profitable.[59]

It is clear that the vast majority of air carriers market essentially two products at once: a mass experience at (relatively) reasonable cost in the coach cabin and a luxury experience (at high cost) in business and first class. In doing so as Thurlow and Jaworski maintain, "there is something unapologetically retrograde about the appeal to pre-modern and old class systems."[60] The delicate role of the flight attendant in this context would be hard to overlook and the conspicuous contradictions of air travel at the moment are evident in the way she is often positioned as a guarantor of old-fashioned, personalized service even in an era in which (for coach travelers anyway) those features of air travel that used to be considered necessary for human dignity now appear only occasionally as "perks." This would help to explain the trend toward retro-styling that has taken place on carriers including British Airways, which in April 2004 debuted new staff uniforms reminiscent of those displayed in *Catch Me If You Can* (2002) that were meant to "provide a nod to the glamorous pioneering days of aviation."[61] Indeed, traditional flight attendant iconography persists quite widely, particularly in advertisements for first and business class travel which heavily privilege the comforts of the corporate male traveler, particularly on long haul and international routes.[62] At a time when "business class" often operates as a gendered designation and a trend is emerging toward all-business class service on some flights, the higher-price ticketholder is likely to experience a level of service that is symbolized by flight attendant chic.[63] It is worth pointing out that within the promotional rhetoric of airline advertising, Asian flight attendants seem to be particularly available as icons of solicitous service, symbolically guaranteeing, it would appear, a white male "safe passage" into far-flung (but growth) economies.[64]

If on the one hand films like *View from the Top* and to a lesser extent *Catch Me If You Can* invoke the flight attendant as warm traditionalist, other recent configurations suppress awareness of this figure as emotional laborer and incline us to see her as a sex toy, prop, or living corporate logo (even as the hypersexualized flight attendant also works to suppress the realities of an aviation industry in crisis). The image of the flight attendant as providing subservient feminine labor is radically destabilized in a number of texts, particularly those of pop divas Britney Spears and Kylie Minogue. In *On a Night Like This*, a concert broadcast on MTV in the UK, Minogue performed a number in costume as a flight attendant, telling her audience, "Thank you for flying KMAir." Similarly, Spears' pop hit "Toxic" is supported by a music video in which the star appeared as a revenge-wreaking woman whose efforts to poison an ex-lover are facilitated by her role as a flight attendant. Meanwhile in 2004 British boy band Busted hit the charts with "Air Hostess," a ribald account of sexual interest in a flight attendant.[65] Situating the flight attendant as figure of erotic fantasy, "Air Hostess" suggests also that she is a consoling figure with lyrics that include:

> Air hostess
> I like the way you dress
> Though I hate to fly
> But I felt much better
> Occupied my mind
> Writing you a love letter.

Flight attendant chic is undoubtedly connected to the revalidation of a broad set of social practices associated with male homosocial and corporate culture, notably the proliferation of "gentlemen's clubs," the emergence of the destination bachelor party, and the broad ironization of pornography that works to neutralize feminist critique. From a business standpoint, the most high-profile and sustained recent placement of the flight attendant as a figure of erotic interest and corporate hospitality has occurred via the emergence of start-up airline Hooters

Air. The 2003 expansion into aviation of the well-known chain restaurant brand was marked by the presence onboard of "Hooters girls" (supplementing a regular crew of flight attendants) outfitted in the restaurant's signature orange short shorts and white tank tops. Some reservations were expressed at the time that Hooters Air was launched, though perhaps not of the kind one might expect; an Association of Flight Attendants spokeswoman voiced concerns that in an emergency passengers might look to the Hooters Girls for assistance, which they are not trained to provide.[66] Another report observed that "today's cabin crews face challenges above and beyond simply delivering a cocktail," pointing out that it was American Airlines flight attendants who in late 2001 helped to subdue shoe bomber Richard Reid.[67] The apparent absence of any broader commentary regarding the airborne Hooters Girls is telling of a postfeminist culture in which feminist critique is seen as passé, overserious, or simply trumped by considerations of profitability. Meanwhile, the start-up airline's steady expansion was regularly and breathlessly hyped by USA Today travel commentator Ben Mutzabaugh. On December 8, 2004 under an item titled "Will Hooters be next big airline?" the travel commentator wrote "the restaurant-themed carrier has been adding new cities at breakneck speed. The carrier said Wednesday that its flight attendants and Hooters girls will now service Pittsburgh." Mutzabaugh delights in such sexual puns, producing additional items titled "Is Hooters Hot for US Airways?" and "How does a bigger Hooters stack up?"

Flight attendant chic seemed to give rise simultaneously to two contrastive images; one is of the virtuous and straightforward "good girl" and the other of the sexually-knowing postfeminist "working girl." The impossibility of any more complex rendering within current popular culture may be illustrated in the characterization of Amelia Warren, Catherine Zeta-Jones' flight attendant in The Terminal. Throughout much of the film Amelia is an icon of idealized female virtue and innocence to Viktor Navorski (Tom Hanks), a "citizen of nowhere" who finds himself taking up long-term residence in an American airport. While The Terminal at first positions Amelia as a symbol of its desire to return to values of civility, compassion, and kindness and suggests that she is romantically victimized by her married lover, the film later abruptly reverses course in its moral assessment of her character (a reversal that is accompanied by the telltale revelation that she is deceptive about her age). First Viktor receives a grim warning from a friend who tells him "You better be careful—you know those flight attendants ain't like regular women. Flying back and forth between all those time zones kind of messes with their biological clocks or something. They're always ready for sex—why do you think they can't stop smiling?" Later the film tacitly validates this characterization as Amelia tells Viktor that he has misjudged her and we learn that she has male "friends" who can do favors for her. The suggestion of romance between Amelia and Viktor is quashed as we accept that she is morally unfit to be the partner of this deeply virtuous man who has chosen to live in an airport for months rather than neglect a promise made to his father.

Another text which sustains both images of the flight attendant (in the UK) is the Living TV series *Trolley Dollies*, a behind-the-scenes reality profile of British-based flight attendants. Named in a way that typifies postfeminist reactivation of sexist terminology previously discredited by feminism, this series' voiceover rhetoric (ironically) activates associations of glamour and travel to exotic destinations, setting these expectations against the realities of cramped space, bad food, and uncertain scheduling. *Trolley Dollies* works to retain the femininity of the profession though the cabin crews featured are manifestly not unisex; disproportionate attention is given to the female flight attendants and it is suggested that male staff are in transition to other, more appropriate lines of work. One episode, for instance, focuses on a 20-year-old flight attendant, Adam, who is learning to be a pilot (emphatically celebrating his "coming of age moment" when "he learns that he has what it takes") while another showcases a young junior member of staff who is fussed over and mothered by female co-workers who urge him to remember to eat and drink during shifts. Meanwhile, a female flight attendant is shown accepting a gift and phone numbers from a passenger in scenes that reinforce the sexual availability of women the series refers to as "mile-high honies."

Trolley Dollies draws our attention to the endurance, forbearance, and work ethic of the male and female flight attendants. Actively managing the sense of customer frustration in an industry plagued by delays and diminishing service, *Trolley Dollies* binds together the perspectives of airline workers and customers as co-constituencies (both are trying to "survive the savage skies") in an era of exigent travel. In this series we see the reality TV flip side of the chic presentation that predominates elsewhere. *Trolley Dollies* generates certain discursive contradictions in seeking to sustain both a discourse of workplace teamwork and sexualized, exoticized experience.

Broadcast interest in the figure of the flight attendant meanwhile also manifested itself in an April 2005 Channel 5 history entitled *Fly Me*, while in the US the Travel Channel debuted an 18 episode series called *Flight Attendant School* which followed the efforts of a group of candidates in Frontier Airlines' six-week training program. In autumn 2005, two high-profile film releases further highlighted the flight attendant as one of the most prevalent images of the contemporary female worker. In the Jodie Foster kidnapping drama *Flightplan* the precise movements and clipped speech of flight attendants are linked to a sense of foreboding as Foster and her young daughter board the flight on which the little girl will shortly seem to disappear. *Flightplan*'s unflattering depiction of flight attendants as grimly controlling antagonists thwarting the efforts of Foster's desperate mother to find her lost child on board the plane drew protest from national flight attendants organizations.[68] In contrast, the Cameron Crowe-directed *Elizabethtown* features Kirsten Dunst as Claire Colburn, an ebullient flight attendant who reaches out to a passenger, the deeply depressed Drew Baylor (Orlando Bloom), a formerly high-achieving executive whose failed sneaker design has led to his being fired shortly before he learns of the death of his father. In what the film depicts as a restorative journey homeward, Claire plays a major role in comforting Drew during his grief then finally elaborately choreographs and scores the road trip she tells him he needs to take to "find himself." In this highly sympathetic depiction the flight attendant acts as moral ballast to the traumatized hero in a world gone awry, re-orienting him and teaching him how to recover a meaningful sense of identity.

Flight attendant chic and post-9/11 configurations of the airport

With hindsight it appears that flight attendant chic may have operated as a transitional phase in the process of the airport shedding some of its traumatic associations post-9/11. Just as representations of the eroticized flight attendant began to diminish somewhat, popular culture seemed to pick up the airport as a scene for reality television and feature films. While comedies including *Meet the Parents* (2000) and *Anger Management* (2003) showcased the airport as a site of male rage, in 2002 *Catch Me If You Can* invoked a glamorous, thrilling era of flight in which the commercial airline pilot was endowed with an image of virility and cosmopolitanism. In 2004 while ABC heavily hyped a new primetime series *LAX* starring TV stalwarts Heather Locklear and Blair Underwood, BBC America decided the time was right to adapt/indigenize British reality series *Airport* for US audiences. *Airport*, it should be noted, concentrates our attention on a broad view of a range of activities that go on in airports, but is strikingly inattentive to the impact of terrorism on these spaces.[69] Instead it trains our gaze on the rather miserable experiences of front-line low-cost airline staff (in so doing studiously avoiding any consideration of the airline and airport management whose decisions lead directly to the scenarios of conflict between passengers and staff profiled in the series) and typically ends its sequences with the seeing-off of a flight. With these considerations in mind, flight attendant chic may be seen to have arisen in tandem with a culture "slowly absorbing the sense that in a post-9/11 world, airports are neither what they once were, nor fully evolved into a singular something else."[70]

Flight attendant chic accompanied a pronounced tendency in recent film, print, and television fictions to place the professional woman in such a way that she is subject to postfeminist correction, coming to grips with her professional aspirations as a form of "miswanting" and/or retreating from the world of paid work. This development has taken place alongside a robust representational trend in which professional and/or aspiring men in crisis are redeemed by a woman who is stalwart in her service role as occurs in films from *White Palace* (1990) to *Sideways* (2004). Notable also is the trend for recent romance films to unapologetically stage romance between unequals, where a high-status male is paired with a female service worker. Maureen Dowd contends that films such as *Spanglish* (2004) (male celebrity chef/Spanish-speaking maid) and *Love Actually* (2003) (British prime minister/tea lady, businessman/secretary, writer/Portugese-speaking maid) mimic social trends toward the coupling of powerful men with young women whose job it has been "to tend to them and care for them in some way: their secretaries, assistants, nannies, caterers, flight attendants, researchers and fact-checkers."[71] The recent idealization of the flight attendant can thus be understood in relation to a broader postfeminist trend in which women's participation in the labor force is represented as at best an opportunity to display skills of emotional care and nurturance that will "earn" them the reward of romance.

This chapter has offered only several selected case studies of the ways in which "women's work" is being recoded in a postfeminist era. The recent surge of flight attendant chic reflects two forms of nostalgia that expediently intersect: the desire for a prefeminist certitude about "women's place" in the workforce and the longing to revert to an earlier moment before air travel acquired traumatic connotations. A variety of media forms synergistically fed a brief but intense representational phase in which the flight attendant was troped as a multipurpose postfeminist icon: for a British boy band, she could be erotically trivialized, for female pop stars whose meanings are crucially dependent on claims to empowerment, the invocation of flight attendant iconography proved that they could ironically stage their own subservience to better consolidate images of erotic power. In an era of diminished service in which the air passenger is bluntly informed that the cabin crew "are here primarily for your safety," a start-up airline cannily seized upon postfeminist recidivism and post-9/11 security jitters to invent a new hypersexualized form of female in-flight service worker.

Contemporary popular culture manifests a new unapologetic interest in (both symbolic and literal) menial female labor, and the rise in such representation has been accompanied by a wave of suspicious portrayals of female professionals. In this chapter I have sought to show that a postfeminist mindset operates to broadly trivialize and minimize women's work while maintaining a perverse fascination with women workers who can be conceptualized as accessory figures to male public achievement and idealized female domesticity. The cause for concern in all this has to do in part with the substitutability of femininity for political and economic anxieties; it has to do as well, of course, with the fact that such narrow casting works to obscure all the variety of ways in which women are at work in the world.

Chapter 5

Hyperdomesticity, self-care, and the well-lived life in postfeminism

Imelda Whelehan has shrewdly noted that:

> At the beginning of the new millennium, feminists have been positioned as the cultural oppressors of "normal" women against which a younger generation of "new" feminists offers as antidote a marked individualistic kind of "radicalism." This radicalism pretends the power of self-definition is all about "being in control" and "making choices," regardless, it seems of who controls the "choices" available. Being "in control" became one of the catchwords of the 1990s in the parlance of women's magazines, but control always seemed to be about the right to consume and display oneself to best effect, not about empowerment in the worlds of work, politics, or even the home. It was an expression of withdrawal from a wider political arena.[1]

While earlier chapters of this book have explored postfeminism's conceptualizations of home, time, and work, this chapter has a somewhat more diffuse focus. My concern here is with what might be deemed postfeminist status anxiety and the expression of that anxiety through perfectionistic domestic pursuits, shopping as a lifestyle practice, and new concepts of corporeality (in the postfeminist era it seems the body is relentlessly owned, claimed, and managed but it is simultaneously as fragmented and ruled by social norms as it has ever been). The themes, values, and lifestyles associated with postfeminism often entail a consumerism that is not only guilt-free but associated with a renewed moral authority. Analyzing the ways that luxury consumption functions within a postfeminist culture, this chapter considers how a vaunted consumer emancipation is presented as a substitute for more meaningful forms of emancipation in early twenty-first-century culture.

I want to be clear about what I consider the specifically *postfeminist* features of luxury lifestyling and its associated promise of personal serenity. At a general level, the attractions of luxury hold a specific function in an era of diminishing social/ state care for the individual. As Samantha King points out, "By every administration since the election of Ronald Reagan in 1980, the American people have been told that the state can no longer be relied upon to mitigate the social effects of capitalism."[2] Avoiding at all costs any formulation that would deem capitalism problematic, it instead becomes salvation; crucially, growing income inequality, and the downward mobility that affects so many Americans is made to dissipate under the terms of postfeminist consumerist enchantment. The consumerist spectacles associated with postfeminism work to neutralize and camouflage looming crises of natural resources and the persistence of poverty while cooperating with the re-emergence of unapologetic class stratification in America. Such hyperconsumerism is postfeminist in the sense that among the other evasions of institutional, social, and political power it facilitates is specifically an evasion of the critiques of power and passivity associated with feminism. At a basic level, postfeminist culture manages the decline of social health by emphasizing the importance of personal (physical and emotional) health in an individualized, isolated context. This meshes rhetorically and ideologically with a financialized culture in which "personal responsibility" operates as a kind of voodoo incantation.

To a great extent this chapter will be concerned with the domestic aggrandizement of the last decade—by this I mean the vast expansion in popular culture material devoted to the celebration of cooking, cleaning, childcare, and other activities that take place largely in the home. The specifically postfeminist quality of this new lifestyle script can be glimpsed in the way that it presumes female managerial capacity and choice and remakes domesticity around these qualities. Domestic practice gains a "value added" status as highly capable, managerially-minded women are invited to devote themselves to home and family in a display of "restored priorities" after the social fracturing attributed to feminism. In contemporary culture women are charged as guardians of lifestyle which is itself all-defining in an era in which living the fully aestheticized life has become a significant priority in mass media representation. In exploring how the semantics of luxury function in a postfeminist context I want to take seriously the power of a well-kept home and well-kept body as the new indices of achieved adult femininity in America.

A growing slice of the American consumer marketplace is devoted to personal services related to health and the body. The effects of such services are in some respects less showy than the beauty treatments of earlier eras, and tend to manifest in a general appearance of health and wellbeing rather than more specific and overt corporeal signs. This corresponds to the way in which health in America increasingly appears as a class entitlement. In an article entitled "Life at the Top in America Isn't Just Better, It's Longer," Janny Scott has investigated the class divisions that operate with respect to healthcare and the important role lifestyle plays, leading to a state of affairs in which "many risk factors for chronic diseases are now more common among the less educated than the better educated."[3] In a profile of affluent, middle-, and low-income heart attack victims, Scott paints a stark portrait of the variations in immediate management of these patients' healthcare crises at very different hospitals and of the social and economic factors that influence follow-up care. Her analysis chronicles a class-bifurcated millennial American society in which health is increasingly a commodity like any other.

Eroticism, exercise and the making of the postfeminist body

One of the most distinctive features of the postfeminist era has been the spectacular emergence of the underfed, overexercised female body, and this ideal has drifted into middle age (and beyond). In sketching the preoccupations and interests attributed to the self-surveilling postfeminist subject, a key development with which I am concerned is the rising social expectation for American women to adhere to an intense regime of personal grooming (waxing, tanning, manicures, pedicures, facials, Botox treatments, etc.) and at younger and younger ages.[4] Notably, contemporary beautification discourses place strong stress on the achieved self. Typical of the marketing rhetoric that accompanies grooming products in the postfeminist era is a recent series of ads for Nair Pretty, aimed at 10- to 15-year-olds, which "suggest that the depilatory is a stubble-free path to empowerment."[5]

The fact that men are also sometimes subjects of the new treatment industries should not obscure the fact that femininity faces new stipulations about its consuming/display practices. The vast expansion of these industries in the 1990s and 2000s underscores the material/economic changes that subtend postfeminist ideological shifts. Jennifer Steinhauer has observed that, "From 1997 to 2002, revenues from hair, nail, and skin services jumped by 42 percent nationwide."[6] In an article documenting the rise of high-end urban day spas, Natasha Singer notes that from 2002 to 2005 the number of day spas in the United States almost doubled (from 4,389 to 8,734) and that spending on treatments rose in a two-year span from $10.7 billion to $11.2 billion.[7] These figures give only a partial glimpse of the scope and scale of new luxury practices dedicated to restoring, improving, and perfecting the female body.

Over roughly the last ten years, a growing frankness about sexuality and the body have accompanied an ever more specific sense of what ideal femininity should look like. Just as nail salons and day spas have conspicuously proliferated in the American commercial landscape, a variety of salons and spas have also expanded their waxing services, with the brow, lip, and bikini waxes of the past now being supplemented by elaborate regimes of pubic hair waxing. The fashion in recent years for Brazilian waxes (in which all female pubic hair is removed) as well as specialty shapes (from heart shaped to "landing strip" styled pubic hair) is predicated on a commitment of time, money, and physical discomfort for the sake of fashion that is axiomatically postfeminist. Pubic hair waxing is only one of a number of female beauty and exercise trends that originated in pornography (as I explore below); it not only stylizes the female genitalia so as to appear prepubescent, it also reflects a misogynist belief that female genitalia are excessively complex and need to be simplified and made visible for the comfort and pleasure of a male sexual partner.

Some researchers have begun to examine the cultural as well as economic dimensions of the labor involved in the expanded sphere of body-oriented service interactions. After all, in privileging the care of the (generally white and affluent) female body, day spas, nail salons, and other businesses depend upon the unglorified working bodies of other women, who are frequently (particularly in nail salons) immigrants. Miliann Kang has considered how the purchase of such services "not only expands the boundaries of the service economy to include formerly private regimens of personal hygiene" but how it generates encounters between highly unequal bodies.[8] The obligation of workers to produce an emotional environment of entitlement to leisure, comfort, and bodily care for clients intensifies the emotional performativity involved in such exchanges. As Kang writes:

> Body labor not only demands that the service worker present and comport her body in an appropriate fashion but also that she induces customers' positive feelings about their own bodies. This is a highly complicated enterprise in a culture that sets unattainable standards for female beauty and pathologizes intimate, nurturing physical contact between women, while it normalizes unequal relations in the exchange of body services.[9]

Of course, another essential element of postfeminist body culture is cosmetic surgery, which has been conspicuously mainstreamed over the past decade. Citing data from the American Society for Aesthetic Plastic Surgery, Abigail Brooks observes that "In the United States, 6.9 million cosmetic procedures were performed in 2002, a 203% increase from 1997."[10] A recent *USA Today* article reported that from 2000 to 2005 the number of women choosing to have their breasts enlarged with implants rose 37%. The same article cites shorter recovery times due to improved surgical techniques, aggressive direct-to-consumer advertising by implant manufacturers and a broader sense of the desirability of large breasts among "average women" in predicting a continued rise in such numbers. According to the article, "once the domain of strippers and starlets, breast augmentation appears to be catching on with increasing numbers of soccer moms."[11]

Such a description seems especially apt in light of the emergence of a particular plastic surgery package that was popular enough to be chronicled in 2007 in *The New York Times* in a commentary entitled "Is the 'Mom Job' Really Necessary?" For the author of the piece, the "Mom Job" offers evidence of the way that the marketing of plastic surgery "seeks to pathologize the postpartum body, characterizing pregnancy and childbirth as maladies with disfiguring aftereffects."[12] In ways that suggest the considerable limits of the postfeminist celebration of the maternal, the "Mom Job" (a breast lift and/or augmentation, "tummy tuck," and liposuction) functions to expunge all traces of the maternal body and restore a taut and youthful figure. If motherhood figures as a state of exalted subjectivity in many forms of contemporary popular culture (as I have argued in Chapter 3) its corporeal effects quickly give way to patriarchal norms dictating the shape and size of the female body.

Whereas in the public imagination not long ago cosmetic surgery meant primarily rhinoplasty and facelifts, it is now just as often associated (in concept and practice) with such procedures as breast and buttock enlargement. At its most extreme the spectrum of normalized cosmetic surgery also involves surgeries to tighten the vagina (though not among the practices detailed above as the "Mom Job," this is usually done after childbirth) and reshape the labia. Potential female clients are exhorted to consider such surgeries on the basis of arguments that hold natural female genital development to be unsightly ("many women want to enhance or improve appearance of 'butterfly' or asymmetrical labia") or an impediment to exercise or fashion (the labia "often interfere with biking, working out, and wearing tight-fitting clothes"), and/or to beautify themselves as a means of improving self-image ("Feeling good about how you look often builds self-confidence and self-esteem").[13] Such procedures thus come to represent not only a new commercial frontier for a rapidly expanding and highly lucrative sector of the medical field, but a reflection and reinforcement of the body norms associated with postfeminist perfectionism. As Sandy Kobrin has observed in an article based on interviews with plastic surgeons, it seems more than coincidental that labiaplasty and "vaginal rejuvenation" procedures have attained normative status in tandem with the mainstreaming of pornography. Indeed, in sharp contrast to the promotional rhetoric of the cosmetic surgery industry with its emphasis on female self-empowerment and presentation of the cosmetic surgery patient's behavior as inevitably self-initiated, according to the surgeons Kobrin interviews most clients elect for surgery after critical commentary by a male sexual partner.

Sometimes overlooked in cultural explanations of postfeminist body perfectionism is the function of a broad promotional rhetoric that (re)assures female clients that they are demonstrating agency and self-management when they avail themselves of such services rather than capitulating to regressive (sometimes misogynist) appearance norms. Yet the general return by the late 1990s to regimes of personal grooming unseen since the 1950s (with the attendant boom in the beauty salon and nail industries, etc.) did indeed elaborate the care regimen required of women in ways that demand ideological examination within the context of social and economic change.

Similar rhetorical formulations emphasizing self-esteem and health have been central in phenomenalizing two of the most high-profile female-oriented exercise trends of the early 2000s: strip cardio and poledancing. A 2004 *USA Today* article sketching the growing popularity of poledancing observed, "Once reserved for the privacy of a men's club, poledancing is turning up in unexpected places. Health clubs and dance studios offering the slow grind are attracting women who might have otherwise settled for a step class."[14] The presentation of such activities as means for the reclamation of an essentially female interiority is suggested in the conclusion to the article's profile of a women-only Los Angeles poledancing class which notes that "The class is as much about being female as about being fit."[15] Likewise, Jeffrey Costa, a Los Angeles dance instructor credited with inventing the "cardio strip" workout, characterized the trend toward strip exercise routines as reflective of a turn toward an innate femininity. He asserts that through strip cardio "I've had so many makeovers with moms and wives and [women playing] every other role besides being a woman that they get into the class, and it's a rebirth for them."[16] For Costa "'It's empowering, when they see how good they look all hot and sweaty in their sexy underwear. It makes them feel good about their bodies.'"[17]

In a celebrity culture that demonstrates intense attentiveness to the material rewards of wealth and a microscopic level of attention to celebrity consumerism, the concept of Hollywood as a lifestyle center has powerfully taken hold. Exercise routines emphasizing the emulation of the performance codes of pornography are further idealized through their association with a celebrity clientele. As one article enthused, "What do you get when you're in a roomful of sweaty people in boas and fishnet stockings peeling their clothes off? Get your mind out of the gutter. It's totally legitimate and the hottest new workout trend: strip aerobics. Teri Hatcher, Lucy Liu, Christina Applegate, Jennifer Love Hewitt and even *Bachelor* Bob Guiney are already devotees."[18] Indeed, strip-oriented exercise has proved a lucrative ancillary activity for (predominantly) female celebrities including Carmen Electra who in 2003 introduced an aerobic striptease DVD collection. Sheila Kelley, a film and television actress married to Richard Schiff, a star of *The West Wing*, further elaborated the links between "celebrity fitness," poledance routines, and the triumphant rediscovery of essential femininity through her 2003 bestselling book *The S-Factor: Strip Workouts for Every Woman*. In November, 2004, the website iparenting.com profiled Kelley as its "Mom of the Month," celebrating her for launching "one of the nation's most popular workout routines" while raising two small children and nurturing her family. The piece highlighted Kelley's extension of her interest to her children: "Kelley's love of fitness is continued in her family's home, and Kelley makes sure her kids learn to love their bodies and to care for themselves properly."[19] Specifically, as the actress explains, this entails luring her 9-year-old son away from the computer to baseball and karate and reinforcing the interests of her 3-year-old daughter who "adores swinging on the pole" and "may be following in mom's footsteps."

Not only is "exotic dance" reclassified as a postfeminist form of empowering exercise, it is increasingly associated with the experience of female sociality. In addition to health club classes promoted as an opportunity to reconnect to femininity in the company of other women, services to provide strip dance instruction at female-oriented social occasions have proliferated. For instance, the online party service partypop.com offers "The Exotic Party" as an option for bachelorette parties and bridal showers in nearly every large American city. Its website avows that

The Exotic Party is the newest phenomenon in girls' night out. It is a private exotic dance class party for you and your girlfriends. Whether it's teach [sic] the bride-to-be some new moves for her honeymoon, to celebrate a birthday or because girls just want to have fun—The Exotic Party is designed to be a fun-filled hour and a half class.[20]

The emphasis on the sexually performative female body in accounts such as these is thus grounded in familiar postfeminist rhetorical codes and tropes: self-care, personal empowerment, essentialized femininity, devotion to family, the celebrity as lifestyle guru and the entitlement to female sociality. The postfeminist commodification of corporeal perfectionism achieved through disciplined (though also erotic and playful) regimes of exercise as well as such practices as plastic surgery and vaginal grooming, gives evidence of the ways that "the body is forever being creatively reimagined in ways that ratify existing social premises about gender."[21]

In a postfeminist consumer culture the makeover is a key ritual of female coming into being and so it is not surprising that this once occasional element of American films as varied as *Now, Voyager* (1942), *Vertigo* (1958), *My Fair Lady* (1964), and *Grease* (1978) has turned ubiquitous in contemporary film and television. The impact of the makeover as personal empowerment trope was noted in a 2003 lifestyle article in *USA Today* which noted that "Makeovers are more visible than ever these days. Long a staple of daytime TV and women's magazines, they have become their own genre."[22] While other critics have more fully explored the cinematic makeover, I want to briefly register the usefulness of this trope for staging the kind of transformative consumerism so valued by postfeminism.[23] A large number of chick flicks employ it, among them teen films and franchises such as *Clueless* (1995), *She's All That* (1999), and *The Princess Diaries* (2001, 2004), as well as adult-themed films including *Pretty Woman* (1990), *Never Been Kissed* (1999), *Miss Congeniality* (2000) and *Miss Congeniality 2: Armed and Fabulous* (2005), and *My Big Fat Greek Wedding* (2002). This set of films tends to make strong but unsubstantiated claims for personal empowerment.

In *The Princess Diaries* Mia Thermopolis, a West Coast American high school student, learns that she is actually a princess who stands in line to inherit the throne of the fictional kingdom of Genovia. As an "average" high schooler Mia is invisible to the point that her teachers don't know her name and other students perceive her as simply vacant space (she tells her best friend "someone tried to sit on me again"). However, with a makeover engineered by her grandmother the Queen (Julie Andrews), Mia transforms from invisibility to hypervisibility as a beautiful young sovereign in the making. This Gary Marshall-directed film is clearly moving in well-covered territory for the director who kicked off his makeover filmmaking with *Pretty Woman*. Whereas the fairy princess transformation was symbolic in that film, it is more literal here and in keeping with the ideological mandates of the cluster of recent chick flicks that showcase transformative fantasies of European aristocratization (in addition to this film, *What a Girl Wants* [2003] and *The Prince & Me* [2004, 2006]). What is also noteworthy here is that in general newer chick flicks tend to lovingly detail the transformation process in sequences of close consumer fetishization. Unlike a classical melodrama such as *Now, Voyager* which documents Charlotte Vale's physical transformation but does not really elaborate it, *The Princess Diaries* features an extended scene in which Mia's unruly hair and eyebrows are tamed by a team of stylists as she is groomed and dressed to perfection and the film deems it important that we can glimpse the brand names of the products being used to beautify its star.

In the large number of television reality programs dedicated to the makeover as the scene par excellence of postfeminist identity making, there is a similar sense that the makeover entails not change, but a revelation of the self that has "been there all along." In the staging of the makeover as truthful revelation scene, such series as *Extreme Makeover*, *The Swan*, and *What Not to Wear* allay broader concerns about the stability and coherence of self and body. In an article analyzing such series, Brenda R. Weber links the imperative of personal transformation implicit in plastic surgery makeovers to the terror of the body out of control and defines it as a response to a millennial crisis of citizenship. In her astute and illuminating essay she argues that in the makeover processes of reality television "personal transformation is the first and most necessary step in self-improvement and thus, to a sort of sublime American entitlement."[24] For Weber "What we're seeing in both *Extreme Makeover* and the present media and makeover genre more broadly, then, is not programming dedicated to individuated enhancement, but a clustering of makeover shows working to underscore collectively the imperative of high-glamour appearance."[25]

Luxury lifestyling and the semiotics of elitism in the "New Economy"

In *The Wedding Planner* (2001) a lonely San Francisco professional elaborately stage-manages affluent weddings while nursing a broken heart from her own pre-marital abandonment some years earlier. However, things begin to turn around for Mary (Jennifer Lopez) when she is dramatically rescued from serious injury by Steve, a handsome pediatrician. The scrupulously accessorized Mary is crossing a street when a careless driver sideswipes a trash dumpster, setting it in motion toward her. At just that moment, Mary catches the heel of her pump in a manhole cover and even as she sees the dumpster careening toward her, she can't bring herself to abandon her designer shoe. As she tugs at it, bemoaning "my new Gucci shoe!" Steve dramatically comes to her rescue, knocking Mary out of harm's way and in the process his body suggestively coming to rest on hers. In this quintessentially postfeminist example of the "meet cute," Mary's unwillingness to sacrifice her Gucci shoe even to the point of seriously endangering herself is the catalyst for her meeting Steve. Through this example we get a glimpse of how adherence to the norms of luxury consumerism often brings a (direct or indirect) reward in intimacy in the chick flick.

As Yvonne Tasker and I have argued elsewhere, "postfeminism increasingly operates as a rationale for the brutalities of the emergent 'New Economies' of both the United States and the United Kingdom."[26] Crucial to the logic of such "New Economies" is the primacy of status commodities with a general consumerist emphasis on "luxury, expensiveness, exclusivity, rarity, uniqueness and distinction."[27] In many cases, as Virginia Postrel contends, "Furnishings once reserved for rich afficianados are now the stuff of middle-class life."[28] In the culture of aspirational elitism, as Crispin Thurlow and Adam Jaworski have observed, the "chasing of ever more inflated consumerist ideals" is matched with an emphasis on the strategic promotion of "a state of perpetual, covetous lack."[29] To a great extent, contemporary culture is organized around the semiotics of elitism with a heavy stress on luxury commodities and experiences as transformative, renewing, and life-affirming. Yet as Thurlow and Jaworski note, "Social norms and practices that order the world into status-based categories are not natural orderings; rather they are ideological and discursive, and established by a complex combination of material *and* social capital."[30]

A number of critics, most prominently Juliet Schor, have taken note of the escalation of luxury expectations among the American middle class over the last decade. In the midst of the late 1990s "boom," Schor wrote that "Trophy homes, diamonds of a carat or more, granite countertops, and sport utility vehicles are the primary consumer symbols."[31] Significantly this list tilts toward items that function as consumerist tokens of marriage and family life and at the same time symbolize the depreciation of natural resources and/or assaultive environmental practices. The importance of these signifiers of the new American Dream also suggests the centrality of what we might call a postfeminist situational ethics which accommodates abstract or occasional commitment to issues of resource sustainability as long as such commitments represent no real challenge to an affluent way of life and the idea of wealth as moral entitlement. In this way we can understand the lip service paid to recycling and "green" culture in the American upper middle class even as its lifestyle choices consistently function to subvert environmental health. It is in this same light that what King refers to as "the emergence of an ethicopolitics of self-fulfillment and community action through volunteerism and philanthropy" appears in which individualist/familialist lifestyles selectively engage with a broader communal sphere but only on self-aggrandizing terms.[32]

What I want to underscore here is that many of the commodity accoutrements of postfeminist lifestyling signify "a radically individualistic citizenship"[33] that belies the imbrication of those commodities within brutally exploitative and heavily standardized global economic and cultural regimes. As David Campbell has shown, "the unbundling of domestic territorialities" has occurred "in the context of new global networks."[34] Campbell sees SUVs as "the embodiment of a new articulation of citizenship that effaces its social and global connectivity."[35] As we will see, the serenity industries and magazines like Oprah Winfrey's *O* consistently promise to restore that sense of connectivity though on highly blinkered terms. Broadly speaking, postfeminist family values presents itself as the moral framework in which winner-take-all earning and spending patterns are seen as reasonable and justified. It is therefore particularly associated with a situational ethics in which wealth is a moral entitlement. This cultural context has yielded the emergent "sanctimommy" (a term designated by *The New York Times* as one of the buzz-words of 2006) archetype to designate the mother who practices maternity as a display of social entitlement, a phenomenon discussed in Chapter 3.

In the "New Economy" we see a redefinition of reference groups with a greater fixation on the habits of the wealthy. As Schor observes:

> today's comparisons are less likely to take place between or among households of similar means. Instead, the lifestyles of the upper middle class and the rich have become a more salient point of reference for people throughout the income distribution. Luxury, rather than mere comfort, is a widespread aspiration.[36]

Contemporary mass media and particularly those forms of media directed to women are frequently characterized by what Diana Kendall has referred to as "emulation framing," in which the close consideration of affluent lifestyles is accompanied by the emulation imperative. As Kendall puts it, "This type of framing offers people in other classes suggestions as to how they might emulate the lifestyle of the rich in small ways such as by buying a bar of 'luxury' soap or designing a room so that it will 'look like a million' and thus share in the lifestyle of the rich and famous."[37]

In the "aspirational gap" culture we are more and more aware of status commodities yet for the majority such things remain financially out of reach (or attainable only on hazardous credit terms). Thus, identification with a level of luxury consumption far out of proportion to one's actual financial circumstances is emerging as a hallmark of contemporary experience. Complicating matters is the fact that the growing gap in income inequality has been accompanied by a general diminishing of the traditional sartorial markers of personal status. As Jennifer Steinhauer observes, Americans appear "to be blending into a classless crowd, shedding the showiest kinds of high-status clothes in favor of a jeans-and-sweatsuit informality."[38] In many respects the new markers of luxury in American culture are significantly less ostentatious than in earlier eras. In the new postfeminist status anxiety that has emerged in tandem with these shifts, two particular factors are worth noting: one is the enhanced emphasis on the slim, fit body and the other a corresponding moderate de-emphasis on the visibly made-up face. This is not to say that the beautiful female face is no longer important, far from it. Rather, in conforming to contemporary beauty norms, women are under particular obligation to efface the signs of their own labor; they are expected to know how to use makeup in such a way that they do not appear to be made-up. This entails a greater emphasis on brow grooming and depilatory functions and a far greater emphasis on moisturizing and sunscreen products to retain the health of the skin and guard against signs of aging. In makeup itself, recent trends emphasize natural color palettes and the avoidance of the harsh blushing products and bright eyeshadows of the past (unless engaged in self-conscious retro styling), and cosmetics companies like Aveda, Origins, and Fresh have built their brands around the appeal of subtlety, green consumerism, and a powerful rhetoricizing of "nature." Bernadette Wegenstein goes so far as to contend that in contemporary culture "any body part can now gain the status once exclusively enjoyed by a face as a window to the soul. It is not necessarily behind faces that we expect the person to be revealed. Faces are becoming obsolete."[39] This overstates the point somewhat in my view but Wegenstein's commentary does usefully underscore the conceptual shift away from the face as the exclusive barometer of character. In postfeminism, the morality of the fit body is coming to the fore.

Discourses on the heroism of the relentlessly self-disciplined, fit female body tend to camouflage the centrality of that body in the reinforcement of traditional heterosexual desirability. As the achievement of health/fitness becomes a marker of middle-class white femininity and a sign of virtue, inequalities are magnified; recent American culture has increasingly emphasized the triumphantly healthy body within a semiotics of survivorship. In 2004–2005 the Lance Armstrong-promoted yellow Livestrong wristband, for instance, became a key fashion accessory promoting the "awareness" of cancer survival. For many, however, the rubber wristband seemed to operate as a token of personal virtue, an emblem connoting the compassion and care of the healthy and fit wearer for those less fortunate. In a similar way, the "ribboning" of American culture in the 1990s and 2000s (pink breast cancer awareness ribbons, yellow "support the troops" ribbons, etc.) often occludes complex political questions. As Samantha King has observed, the "awareness" that such ribbons are meant to betoken is often vaguely defined and heavily conformist in character. In *Pink Ribbons, Inc.*, King provides a compelling study of the making of breast cancer charity in the direction of corporate, neoliberal interests that centralize a heroic survivorship and the primacy of the "national maternal" rather than disease prevention or analysis of the environmental factors that may be at play in the soaring disease rates among American women. Her discussion of the growth of charity run/walk events on behalf of causes like breast cancer draws attention to the various ways in which the fit (postfeminist) body seeks scenarios of symbolic functionality and moral aggrandizement.

Postfeminist homemaking

Television has manifested a renewed fascination with the homemaker in recent seasons, both in fictional primetime series (*Desperate Housewives*) and in reality formats (*Wife Swap*, *Trading Spouses*, *Meet Your New Mommy*, and *The Real*

Housewives of Orange County). All these series are underwritten by a broad agreement that domesticity doesn't work without some version of the female homemaker in place. Such an assumption, I would argue, is bolstered by a myriad of factors at work in the postfeminist landscape.

Postfeminist culture places a premium on showplace domesticity, with the achievement of a comfortable domestic life also a marker of personal virtue. In this realm also, status correlates with the achievement of/entitlement to comfort, composure, and serenity, giving rise to the great seriousness now often accorded to domestic atmospherics. Accordingly, the 1990s and 2000s saw a strong consumerist emphasis on the expressive, designative power of small (though frequently costly) aesthetic touches in the home such as throw pillows, throw rugs, candles, and fresh flowers in various rooms. (Lest the home become too overtly feminized, this same period saw an enlargement in upper-end homes of spaces associated with masculinist comforts, with the wine cellar and home humidor coming into fashion.) The period also saw a rise in the number of companies positioned as niche purveyors of goods and services designed to help set the scene of perfect domesticity, such as florists that deliver fresh floral arrangements to a household each week. Entertaining was also subject to this upping of the consumerist ante, and the period saw the expansion of catering into events which in previous eras were both smaller scale and more reliant on homemade foods and decorations. As the signifiers of domestic tranquility also came to include products like room sprays and scented waters for ironing clothes in an increasingly micro-focused domestic economy, we see a broad fetishization of "old-fashioned" housekeeping, one sign of which has been the trend toward retro domestic appliances such as hand mixers and blenders styled to look like those of the 1930s and 1940s. Major retail outlets such as Crate & Barrel and Pottery Barn have been key purveyors of this sort of merchandise and to a degree their own store environments operate as conceptually themed spaces that put into practice the value of stylish cookware and retro appliances, with an island at the center of each store including not only cash registers but working grills and ovens so that shoppers smell (and very occasionally taste small samples of) grilled meat or cakes.

Just as the postfeminist body displays increasingly subtle signs of status, the postfeminist home now stages a quiet but no less calculated presentation of luxury. While William Roseberry has commented on the "widening spectrum of foods— including wines, beers, waters, breads, cheese, sauces, and the like—through which one can cultivate and display 'taste' and 'discrimination'"[40]—the luxury consciousness which he identifies has now extended to not only what we consume but even apparently the most mundane of household fittings. As plumbing supply company Kohler has consolidated its category strength and association with dreamhome luxury through its corporate slogan "Art Innovation Life" it has also diversified its holdings and sought ways to more emphatically connect its plumbing products to lifestyling concepts. The company maintains two resorts, one in Wisconsin and the other in St. Andrews, Scotland, both of which centralize spas that showcase high-end Kohler products. Indeed, the Wisconsin Kohler Waters Spa uses sensuous language to entice potential guests to identify closely with water as the essence of life (rather than as the raison d'etre of the company's bath and toilet products): "Our bodies are, in essence, water. And it is with water that Kohler believes we can restore and replenish them."[41] In a remarkable display of the corporatization of everyday life, the company also maintains the planned community of Kohler, Wisconsin, which it touts as an ideal site of social health and harmony.

In a postfeminist domestic environment even those functional objects/machines which would seem to most resist aestheticization are available to be customized and stylized. The air conditioning company Trane employs a distinctively post-feminist lifestyling pitch and notably its website features a stylish young mother supervising the homework for (or possibly homeschooling) her children beside a caption that reads: "Your family. Your comfort. What means the most to us is providing better, healthier air for those that mean the most to you." Implicit in the ad is not only a new female domestic managerialism but also the intense health/environmental consciousness so often disingenuously rhetorically paired with luxury domesticity.

In 2006 Trane regularly ran a series of television ads for its outdoor central air conditioning generators. Situated on a manicured lawn or tucked into a tidy flower bed, the ads revealed that Trane generators come in a range of styles and colors so as to harmonize with the overall domestic aesthetic of the affluent home. The highlighting of guaranteed access to pure water and air that runs through the ads by Kohler and Trane bespeaks the ways that numerous forms of contemporary popular culture wonder about whether America, given its petro-leum-based culture, pre-emptive militarism, and social fracturing, is sustainable. The postfeminist character of some such representation is revealed in a heavy emphasis on refuge lifestyling and female guardianship of the home.

In her book *To Hell with All That: Loving and Loathing Our Inner House-wife*, Caitlin Flanagan expresses a sense of the emotional poverty of "home" in contemporary American culture. She writes that "nowadays the home is foreign territory, a kind of very large household suite unintended for long-term habita-tion"[42] Flanagan longs for a prefeminist certitude about the pleasure and value of female custodianship of the home and offers descriptions of contemporary domestic chaos as a state of material and corporeal imbalance. She notes at one point, "In my mother's house, things—physical, actual things—were steadier. Objects could be relied on to stay put."[43]

In bestselling advice books such as Cheryl Mendelson's *Home Comforts: The Art and Science of Keeping House* one can glimpse the elaboration of new dom-estic regimes that will restore the stability of home. Touted as this generation's housekeeping bible, *Home Comforts* clearly differs from its predecessors in the perceived necessity for a personalized preface by the author in which she mounts a careful argument for the importance of housekeeping. A Harvard-educated lawyer, professor, and novelist, Mendelson rather surprisingly characterizes herself as "having been born too late." She praises the domestic artistry of her southern and northern European grandmothers, and opens the book with a quintessentially postfeminist gambit, characterizing her love for housekeeping as a secret she had kept rather than engender the suspicion and even animosity of her professional colleagues. Mendelson sees "American housekeeping and homelife in a state of decline"[44] and deplores the ad hoc nature of contemporary (and implicitly two-career) middle-class households. In her roughly eight-hundred page book she offers precise instruction in preparing and serving meals, laundering, cleaning, safety, and (drawing upon her expertise in the law) the legalities of such things as insurance and hiring household help. By taking up housework in a commit-ted fashion Mendelson believes we will restore a sense of dignity, security, privacy, and comfort in the home. Observing that "home life as a whole has contracted. Less happens at home; less time is spent there,"[45] Mendelson seems to suggest that this state of affairs can be redressed by a partial if not complete return to a culture in which women identify deeply with their homes. Praising the "traditional woman," she observes that such a woman "lived her life not only through her own body but through the house as an extension of her body."[46] Mendelson's striking formulation here gets at the heart of some of the ways that postfeminist femininity responds to postmodern crises over the definition of self and home. As I will explore shortly, new domestic sensualists (and postfeminist icons) like Nig-ella Lawson and Rachael Ray incarnate the complex embodiment of domesticity traded on/in by postfeminism. What I want to underscore here is how new rhetorics of domestic practice symbolically extend the female body to include the home, and as a result housekeeping and cooking become classified as embodied, sensual acts. In this way postfeminism redresses the crisis over the female body, subject as it is to intense, deeply anxious, and often conflicting discourses of man-agement, regulation, and surveillance. The postfeminist domestic body is relaxed, integrated, bountiful, connected to nature and to others. It is healthy and free from the stress of weight management as is suggested by the fact that both Law-son's and Ray's bodies are voluptuous in a way that television seldom sanctions.

I single out Nigella Lawson and Rachael Ray as domestic gurus because their personae sustain revealing commonalities and differences across the (short) spec-trum of postfeminist performativity. Ray, whose *30 Minute Meals* became a hit on the Food Network, has diversified her brand into a range of television programs and a magazine entitled *Every Day with Rachael Ray*. She has been conspicu-ously/commercially mentored by Oprah Winfrey, and her most recent television venture, a daytime talk show, appears through Winfrey's King World Produc-tions.[47] Ray's intensely cheerful demeanor (she tends to use diminutive, collo-quial phrasing including peppy abbreviations for standard ingredients [extra virgin olive oil becomes "EVOO"], to employ homey phrases such as "Oh, my gravy," and cheers herself on in the cooking process by commenting on how good the food tastes and smells) is her signature style. As she cooks, Ray maintains a steady patter about her family members, thereby reinforcing the sense that cooking is a care activity and an expression of nurturance. Although Ray's persona is primarily

Figure 5.1 New domestic sensualists like Rachael Ray mediate their commercial clout through safe stereotypes of female sexuality and domesticity. (© Eric Cahan/CORBIS OUTLINE)

sisterly, it is notable that in 2003 she appeared in a photo layout in "lad mag" *FHM* and has been repeatedly ranked in the magazine's annual list of "sexiest women." Ray appears to be attaining considerable success by updating domestic femininity in such a way that she embodies efficient managerial domesticity (her stock-in-trade *30 Minute Meals* accord well with the time-pressured postfeminist cultural landscape I detailed in Chapter 3) while remaining available as a non-threatening erotic fantasy figure in such a way that her significant multi-media commercial clout is occluded. In postfeminist terms, Ray is both affectively correct (coming across as artless and cheerful) and behaviorally correct (her interests are traditionally domestic yet occasional soft core imaging is not perceived as disruptive to her persona).

Like Ray, Nigella Lawson has expanded from a television cookery expert into a brand that sources cookbooks, kitchenware, and other culinary merchandise. However, the British Lawson is older, more aristocratic (a graduate of Oxford, her father is former Chancellor of the Exchequer Nigel Lawson), and deeply sensuous in her approach; if the sexual elements of Ray's persona are generally held in check, they are aggressively foregrounded in Lawson's who has published books with such sexually playful titles as *Nigella Bites* (2001). Lawson's sexuality is matched with a strong sense of decorous composure, a heavy emphasis on craft and a linkage to the implicit restoration of essential femininity in the home as is apparent in the title of her 2000 book *How to Be a Domestic Goddess: Baking and the Art of Comfort Cooking*. Notably, the performance styles of Rachael Ray and Nigella Lawson highlight the two primary affective registers of postfeminism: serenity and cheerfulness (as I shall elaborate below).

However, in addition to modeling exemplary female domesticity, both Ray and Lawson operate as what Sharon Zukin has referred to as "honest brokers," authority figures who "speak to our inner feelings about products. They guess what matters most to us, and they express our concern."[48] Such brokers may be seen to operate as crucial agents in converting consumerist conundrums (particularly at a time when the status of the middle class is uncertain and its purchasing power potentially in decline) into lifestyle scripts. As Zukin writes:

> The honest brokers have given us a powerful language—in which consumers seem to hold their own against producers . . . But this language also balances two primal motives of modern life—the desire for both rationality and pleasure. It applies the aesthetic judgments of high culture to products of mass culture. And it eases people who would otherwise suffer bloody conflicts over wages and power into a more peaceful, though still competitive, concern with consumer goods. Above all, the honest brokers' language transforms the conflict-prone struggle for a higher standard of living into a more ambiguous struggle for a better "lifestyle."[49]

The sensuousness and craft with which new domestic authorities are associated endow the home with a new power to idealize and eroticize femininity. This is in marked contrast to the hausfrau of the past whose close association with cleaning and the management of "dirt" (whether in the form of laundry, used dishes, or household garbage) often explicitly or implicitly made her abject. Suellen Hoy has examined the ways that campaigns for cleanliness (personal, domestic, urban, and national) historically came to underpin emergent American concepts of citizenship.[50] As her analysis shows, there are indeed deep historical roots that associate femininity with the imposition of cleanliness. Postfeminist domesticity emphatically reclaims this connection while freeing the homemaker from the tra-

Figure 5.2 Personalized stamps literalize the importance of family capital in postfeminist culture

ditional stigmas of her labor. At the same time, the homemaker role is updated and modified to respond to specific aspects of contemporary culture. While the ideal postfeminist homemaker's elaborate care and craft may seem excessive, it specifically conveys the reassurance that such intensive domesticity is a reflection of the time and care necessary to avoid the non-nutritious and low-status processed foods consumed by working-class (and often stereotypically nutritionally dysfunctional) families. In addition, the new postfeminist domestic is also a guardian of the household interests in a highly pragmatic way—she emerges from the broad awareness that someone needs to transact on behalf of the family in an era when paid work often demands long hours and extraordinary dedication to the workplace and when social, educational, and economic protections are scarce. Postfeminism's close association with managerial motherhood thus responds to specific felt needs. Furthermore, in a neoliberal political environment in which the family is increasingly charged with taking over the responsibilities of the state, the home increasingly feels like an administrative entity in its own right, arrogating a variety of functions once transacted externally and elsewhere (the penetration rate of the home computer has of course been key to this shift). One striking example of this transformation of the home and elevation of family capital is apparent in the emergence of US Postal Service-approved personalized stamps which enable the home computer user to generate their own stamps using favorite photos. (In a brochure advertising the PhotoStamps service, four of the six model stamps feature babies or children, one is a wedding photograph, and another is of pets.) The emergence of customized stamps that can be made at home and that use the image of the family as (both literal and symbolic) capital forcefully illustrates the convergence of neoliberal commerce and postfeminist family values.[51]

Another facet of this trend toward the re-sanctification of home has been the emergence of a set of reality television series which read failed domesticity as a manifestation of personal inadequacy. In *How Clean Is Your House?* (Lifetime), *Clean Sweep* (TLC), and *Room Raiders* (MTV) the morality of domestic hygiene is enforced through a set of aesthetic and narrative structures designed to disclose and indict untidiness and domestic sloth. The dating series *Room Raiders* is particularly noteworthy for the way that it calls upon potential dates to read domesticity as a statement of personal character; in it, a selected teen or 20-something is given the keys to the homes of three potential dates and is invited to look around at leisure while delivering interpretive commentary to camera about what they discover. Meanwhile the prospective dates are gathered together at a video monitor to watch and respond (often with chagrin) as their homes and rooms are analyzed. The episode concludes with a dating choice being made and explained in relation to the domestic investigation which has occurred.

The intense domesticity of postfeminism is not a historic or economic co-incidence. Rather, it appears as a manifestation of anxieties about atomization and dislocation at a time when social connections are thin on the ground, where long-haul moves for corporate careers are rather common and where as I have argued in Chapter 2, fantasies of being safely situated at home and in a hometown community proliferate widely. Some of these uncertainties are clearly transferred into an obsessive and fashionable houseproudness. They are also discernible in the darker conceptual shadings of homeownership that stress immense privilege and the defense of home as a display of citizenship. The shift in the nature of home to a luxurious preserve for a family life so morally entitled it conceives of itself as quasi-aristocratic (note the emergence in recent years of a popular home design element called a "great room") or so detached that it symbolically operates as its own country (note the terminological shift away from "breaking and entering" toward the conceptual primacy of "home invasion" in describing robberies) is often signaled through language.

In the American economy of the early millennium the surging real estate market and increasing concentration of wealth in homes stand alongside dwindling pensions and stagnant returns in the stock market. Indeed, as Randy Martin has observed "The redefinition of the family home as an object of speculation and credit, together with the infusion of its interior design with financial tastes, displaces domestic life in a number of ways."[52] Fluctuations in the real estate market have come to anxiously index the precarious financial health of Americans in an era in which the social provisions for healthcare and retirement are conspicuously declining. As we shall see, *InStyle* magazine and a variety of other popular culture sites compensate for this, vigorously and insistently demonstrating the need to overperform showplace domesticity. Such outlets are caught in a paradox however; in their anxious attempts to assert the separation of domesticity from the culture of the market, they most often substantiate the overlap of the two.

Thus, the sense that one is burnishing one's most reliable asset expressed through hyperdomesticity juxtaposes sharply with 100-year mortgages, reverse mortgages, and other highly speculative financial arrangements that have emerged to underwrite the fantasy of safe and comfortable domesticity. Such domestic overinvestment also helps to explain cinematic fictions in which the dreamhome operates as salvation as in *13 Going on 30* or as the glue between a romantic couple as in *Just Like Heaven* and *The Notebook*, and in inverse fashion the primacy of showplace homes in "home anxiety" films like *Panic Room* and *Mr. and Mrs. Smith* (2005) and "homewrecker" comedies like *You, Me and Dupree* (2006). (In the latter the dubiously matched couple of Matt Dillon and Kate Hudson is eclipsed by the tastefulness of their well-decorated bungalow.)

An interesting permutation of the postfeminist domestic logic displayed in the films above can be found in a set of recent texts which anxiously situate the couple in relation to economic downsizing, morally dubious enterprise, and criminality. In films like *Mr. and Mrs. Smith* (2005), *Red Eye* (2005), and *Fun with Dick and Jane* (2005) the couple/family is not an innocent ideological/ economic unit and the violent suppression of outsiders to coupledom and domesticity takes center stage. Notably in *Red Eye* a highly competent hotel manager, Lisa Reisert (Rachel McAdams), is held hostage by a terrorist who wants to kill the Head of Homeland Security and requires her involvement in ensuring that the man and his heavily idealized family are booked into a particular room in the hotel Lisa manages. Although Lisa copes with remarkable conditions of adversity, *Red Eye* contrives to conclude the long struggle between her and the terrorist in her own family home where it is her father who ultimately defeats the attacker. In this way, *Red Eye* forces an equivalence between the broader goals of homeland defense and the immediate defense of one's own affluent home and family. Films of this kind (which produce a particularly strained version of the postfeminist "coming home" story explored in Chapter 2) may be seen to adjust concepts of postfeminist domesticity, while working hard to hold in place notions of patriarchal legitimacy in a world in which it appears to be in danger of dissolving.

While films from *Fatal Attraction* to *Blast from the Past* to *Red Eye* posit the affluent family home as a bulwark, the impulse to stage and shelter family capital finds its fullest mode of expression in a recent real estate trend toward the marketing of "family compounds" for either full-time residential or vacation use. With its militaristic and separatist connotations, the term "compound" implies a ratcheting up of even the fortified and homogenous clustering of gated communities, and in upper-end real estate categories offers a potent means for attempts to set a scene of family affluence and intimacy on an enlarged scale. In an article reporting on the trend, Christina S. N. Lewis noted that such compounds

> are growing in popularity and can keep a clan together . . . Developers are putting a new spin on an old-money idea: Hailing nostalgia and togetherness, they're pushing planned compounds—properties with multiple dwellings that let extended families stay separately, yet together.[53]

One of the most successful romantic comedies of all time, 2002's *My Big Fat Greek Wedding*, an unheralded independent film which was an enormous hit with audiences, harmonizes notably with such trends in its conclusion. Though at the start of the film Toula Portokalos, a Greek-American woman who feels intensely trapped by her family's fervent and tribalistic closeness, seeks ways to change her life and in so doing, meets, falls in love with and marries a non-Greek man, her parents' wedding present to her is a house right next door to theirs, and at the film's conclusion Toula and her husband walk their daughter to Greek school under the watchful eyes of the senior Portokaloses.[54] While the film doesn't establish a family compound as such, the domestic arrangements that signal the film's "happy ending" (whether spectators experience it this way or not) are strongly in line with the family insularity promoted by such real estate trends.

The affective economy of postfeminism

When it comes to popular perceptions of gender, perhaps the most voluminous body of contemporary textual material is to be found in the various forms of self-help literature that have driven American publishing over the last 20 years.[55] Sandra K. Dolby has accurately observed that "Critics envision the typical reader of self-help literature as female rather than male" and she points out that this literature frequently centralizes a paradoxical conception of the self as simultaneously "simple" and abstruse.[56] In their exhortations to readers to free themselves from cultural conditioning, self-help books present themselves as free of such conditioning. Yet their advocacy of a return to a "simple self" unencumbered by cultural dogma often plays directly into postfeminist identity categories.

While it is beyond my scope to fully address the manifold forms of contemporary self-help material and their interrelationship with postfeminist culture, I would like to focus here on two particular types of self-help print bestsellers that may be specifically identified as intensively postfeminist: conduct literature in regard to dating and panic literature in regard to marriage and procreation. The former category is dominated by the blockbuster bestseller by Ellen Fein and Sherrie Schneider, *The Rules: Time-Tested Secrets for Capturing the Heart of Mr. Right* (1995), but has also been refreshed in recent years by the publication of such books as Greg Behrendt and Liz Tuccillo's 2004 *He's Just Not That into You.*[57] The commercial and ideological durability of this category speaks to the importance many women would seem to attach to the emotional governance of the self in a postfeminist culture.

The sensational impact of *The Rules*, which urges women to adhere to a set of directives limiting their availability (emotional and otherwise) to heighten men's interest has imprinted itself upon the dating culture in ways that still reverberate more than ten years after the book's publication. For my purposes I want to underscore a set of assumptions about affect and emotional performativity that are central to the logic of becoming a "rules girl." *The Rules* advises women not to initiate an encounter with a man they like, to be "hard to get but easy to be with," and to strive to be "honest but mysterious." The book's strict emphasis on its code of conduct is explained by its authors who note that "You may feel offended by these suggestions and argue that this will suppress your intelligence or vivacious personality. You may feel that you won't be able to be yourself, but men will love it!"[58]

The Rules' emphasis on a studied femininity associated with secret-keeping and the mysterious helps to define the emotional posture advocated by postfeminism. This posture is presented as necessary in a world in which gender roles have been distorted by feminism and masculinity thrown into crisis by such developments as women's improved access to paid labor. Where feminism held that men should/would adapt to changes/challenges to their traditionally authoritative status, postfeminist conduct literature presupposes that they will not or cannot. Consequently, the care skills and "intimacy work" that are presented as innately feminine are redirected toward the female self which is charged not only with rebuilding healthy relationships in an unhealthy culture but also with a new awareness of the importance of self-care as we go about relationship-building. This notion is even more bluntly reinforced in *He's Just Not That into You* which addresses itself to the variety of ways in which women incorrectly and over-optimistically interpret male behavior, urging them to pragmatically read the signs of male disinterest rather than investing in a relationship that is unlikely to progress. Central to Behrendt and Tuccillo's book and to the category as a whole is again the notion that modifying their expectations and behaviors in line with patriarchal ideological precepts gives women the best chance of achieving fulfillment and intimacy.

Postfeminist relationship literature is clearly shaped to respond to the emotional bruising many women seem to experience in a dating climate no longer governed by traditional moral strictures. Yet this literature is also strikingly unified in coaching women on how to adapt to such a climate rather than challenging or seeking to modify it. The postfeminist self, in the words of Lisa Blackman, must adapt by becoming "low needs" and learning to "minister to itself." As Blackman argues:

> It is not the case that postfeminist women are not waiting for men, but that, while they are waiting (for a man worth waiting for), they are encouraged to engage in emotional practices that produce them as feminine subjects who are capable of emotional detachment from others, but who are also capable of taking their own emotionality as an object of personal development and growth. What we might see as a retraditionalization is occurring in this process whereby women are encouraged to work on themselves so that they remain open to relationships and do not become "defensive."[59]

Another high-profile manifestation of postfeminist relationship culture has been the turn toward matchmaking, and a crop of films and television series of the early millennium have addressed this theme even while there has been a conspicuous escalation in the matchmaking services industry. On television *Miss Match* (NBC, 2003) starring Alicia Silverstone has featured the exploits of a Los Angeles attorney who develops a side business based on her flair for matchmaking while enduring romantic travails of her own. In cinema the trope of the matchmaking family member who posts a single woman's details in a personal ad arises with regularity in both high- and low-budget chick flicks (in *Next Stop Wonderland* [1998], a well-meaning mother runs an ad on her daughter's behalf, and though outraged the daughter does indeed meet with the ad's respondents; in *Because I Said So* [2007] Diane Keaton's frenetically overinvolved mother advertises on her unwitting daughter's behalf; while in *Must Love Dogs* a recently divorced woman's sister posts her profile on PerfectMatch.com, a real-world Internet dating site). Such representational emphasis has accompanied the rising cultural profile of online and traditional dating services in recent years. Perhaps the most well-known of these (partly because of its relentless broadcast and Internet advertising) has been the marriage-minded EHarmony founded by Neil Clark Warren, a former Dean of Fuller Theological Seminary and author of numerous Christian-themed self-help books who claims to have founded EHarmony out of a desire to reduce national divorce rates. Although it does not advertise as a Christian website, EHarmony practices policies of exclusion that are tied to conservative Christian beliefs and will not accept multiply divorced, gay, or severely depressed clients. Notably the service makes "match" choices on behalf of its registrants, operating as a matchmaking service rather than a clearinghouse for clients to exercise their own choices based on listed profiles. In such ways, the matchmaking industry reflects the limited personal agency so characteristic of postfeminist culture and a twist on the "destiny" theme characteristic of contemporary romantic comedies.

If marriage is the unquestioned goal for all women in the advice books on dating, motherhood is a deep and abiding quest in the body of panic literature directed to professional women that emerged in the early 2000s. The highest-profile example of such literature is Sylvia Ann Hewlett's *Creating a Life: What Every Woman Needs to Know About Having a Baby and a Career* which caused a sensation upon its publication in 2002, sparking a flurry of television, magazine, and radio coverage about the personal losses deemed attendant to professional success in the lives of many women. Hewlett advises women to find a male partner early in life and to have children before undertaking the commitments of a professional career which often demand so much time and energy that professional women are susceptible to what she terms a "creeping non choice" for which they pay a high emotional and financial price when they realize (often too late) the urgent priority of motherhood. Hewlett's detailed account of the (physical, financial, and emotional) lengths to which such women will go in their attempts to conceive strongly suggests there is something unnatural about later-in-life pregnancy. Thus, just as postfeminist dating literature urges women to be vigilant in their prioritization of mate-seeking, postfeminist conception primers dramatically reinforce the ticking of the "biological clock" and the time-beset mode of female identity I discussed in Chapter 3.

In tandem with a vast self-help industry that prompts women to re-calibrate their expectations and desires, other forms of postfeminist popular culture consistently model a femininity that stays emotionally within bounds. Indeed, one might suggest that the affective hallmark of postfeminism is composure—by contrast, feminist women or women whose lives are "off script" tend to be depicted as angry, melancholy, or paralyzed by ambivalence. Various forms of popular culture showcase this postfeminist emotional etiquette; most notably the contemporary chick flick heroine will always resolve her emotional dilemmas in conventional ways. In the contemporary romance, emotional distress certainly arises in the context of romantic disappointment but is significantly most often accompanied by the epiphany that the heroine must moderate her expectations and frequently be prepared to live without the man she loves. Accordingly, romantic resolution is often achieved via dramatic precipitating action by the male protagonist (as in *Two Weeks' Notice, How To Lose a Guy in Ten Days*, and *French Kiss*) or a stage managed resolution by friends or family (*In Her Shoes* and *Failure to Launch*). The conclusion of *While You Were Sleeping* manages to incorporate both conventions as Jack Callaghan (Bill Pullman) appears suddenly when Lucy Moderatz (Sandra Bullock) is at work in a Chicago tollbooth and in the company of his extended family offers a ring in place of a metallic subway token.

The point I want to underscore here is that many of the texts I analyze in this book act as "affect primers" for the mood management of postfeminist culture, reinforcing (at their most extreme) a culture of lockstep emotional lives. Post-feminism most often demands hyper-engagement with the needs and concerns of others while requiring (at least outwardly) a romanticized emotional passiv-ity in regard to one's own desires. Moreover, it tends to be squeamish about (if not openly repulsed by) aggressive displays of female agency and desire. Thus, the composure of the postfeminist heroine is often countermatched by a female foil for whom "rougher emotions" such as intense jealousy, anger, and resent-ment are reserved. *Maid in Manhattan*'s Caroline Lane (Natasha Richardson) exemplifies this figure in her zealous romantic pursuit of Senatorial candidate Chris Marshall (Ralph Fiennes) while the film's heroine Marisa Ventura (Jennifer Lopez) attracts his notice through her serene demeanor and understated style. In *You've Got Mail*, Joe Fox's (Tom Hanks) girlfriend Patricia Eden (Parker Posey), a woman of roiling emotions who is constantly calculating ways to get ahead in the publishing business, is (the film suggests rightfully) replaced by Kathleen Kelly (Meg Ryan), whose lively repartee with Joe is understood not to contradict her fundamentally tranquil nature.

Conceptualizing postfeminism as a form of affective tyranny helps to explain why a figure like domestic doyenne Martha Stewart is regarded so negatively by many; while utterly postfeminist in the ways that she models hyperdomestic-ity, Stewart is "off script" in affective terms. That is to say that the star's grim, controlling persona and icy demeanor make her cooking and crafts skills appear more as a display of virtuosity than a demonstration of labor in the service of others. In effect, Stewart gives away how much of the postfeminist affective pro-gram must be devoted to rigid self-control. The drama of repudiation around Martha Stewart when she was convicted and jailed for insider trading in 2004 spoke not only of public discomfort with a female corporate magnate whose degree of influence over public taste had grown worryingly high, but also of sat-isfaction is seeing a woman who was affectively transgressive put in her place.

The need to care for others and to maintain a kind of personal spiritual tran-quility drives the emotional characterization of postfeminist lifestyle gurus such as Oprah Winfrey and Nigella Lawson fully as much as it does the heroine of the contemporary romance. In the context of a postfeminist culture which has re-energized suspicion in regard to "working women," the need to represent female labor as simply an extension of innate femininity rather than an active response to the market structures of capitalism reverberates in a variety of ways. It is worth observing however that the issue of serenity is by no means an inci-dental one—indeed, postfeminist women are constantly working to fend off the neurosis and hysteria which is attributed to them; in chick flicks like *Bridget Jones' Diary* Bridget is fixated on acquiring "inner poise" while Andie in *How To Lose a Guy in Ten Days* works for *Composure* magazine. In the "serenity indus-tries" of the day spa and the nail salon, women clients may be seen to be com-plying with postfeminist strictures about health and appearance but also doing the kind of emotion work postfeminism values.

Figure 5.3 Fully installed as a cultural archetype, the chick flick spectator can now be appropriated to anchor other consumerist formations as in this advertisement for Bliss Cosmetics.

Indeed, self-care is far from unimportant within the postfeminist mindset and in fact as I hope to have shown, the prioritization of self-care is a prominent element (both economically and ideologically) within this system. Elliott Currie, Robert Dunn and David Fogarty have noted that "[t]he rise of the 'service society' has brought not greater leisure but, in many cases, the opposite; not increased freedom from toil but, often, an ever faster race to stay in one place."[60] The new "consolation commodities/services" such as candles, day spas, manicures, and massages intervene in this dynamic, symbolically soothing the awareness of intensified competition and inequity in America life.

In these ways postfeminism aligns itself with a sense of entitlement to rest and respite.

Self-care redresses not only the duress of contemporary life in an era of greater economic pressure and diminished social support and amidst the brutality of a society that leaves many of its members' most basic needs unfulfilled; we might also speculate that it helps to redress the national crisis of loneliness identified by some scholars. A variety of academic and popular press commentaries have observed the contemporary economic, geographical, and social conditions that heighten alienation and isolation in American life. Political scientist Robert D. Putnam and sociologist Laura Pappano have generated some of the most extensive and influential studies of this phenomenon while more specialized analyses have more recently emerged such as one by Douglas E. Morris examining the specific links between the segregated, compartmentalized environments of suburban sprawl and social isolation. Morris attributes the incivility, hostility, and violence of contemporary culture to a built environment in which

> The zoned segregation of sprawl has dramatically separated the functions of daily life so that even though we are constantly surrounded by swarms of people, the vast majority of them are strangers. Outside of work and other structured activities, we go through our days without being recognized by others.[61]

Pappano, meanwhile, asserts that "As a society, we face a collective loneliness, an empty feeling that comes not from lack of all human interaction, but from the loss of *meaningful* interaction."[62] In June, 2006 a flurry of news coverage attended a study in the *American Sociological Review* reporting a decline in friendship in American life (in a longitudinal study, respondents reported a declining number of close friends and confidants and fully one-fifth reported that they had only one confidant, their spouse).[63]

Design for living: postfeminist lifestyling in O: The Oprah Magazine

O: The Oprah Magazine exemplifies the fusion of celebrity emulation, luxury consumerism and self-care that anchor the program of postfeminist lifestyling. In tandem with Oprah Winfrey's daily talk show, the magazine deploys a highly unified rhetorical system, reliant on tropes such as the "Aha moment," the exhortation to be one's "best self," and the mantra of personal certitude "What I know for sure." Such sloganistic lifestyling is supported and extended through intermittent recourse to the wisdom of literary elites such as the sayings of Toni Morrison and Czeslaw Milosz. More frequently, it is enveloped in a discourse of "soft spiritualism" that reinforces the conceptual centrality of "your spirit" in a way that both connects with and yet strategically transcends/evades conventional religious views. As Trysh Travis has shown, the rhetorical system that pervades

Figure 5.4 *O: The Oprah Magazine* exemplifies the fusion of celebrity emulation, luxury consumerism, and self-care that mark postfeminist lifestyling. (*O: The Oprah Magazine*, November 2005)

the Oprah universe derives from "New Thought" principles that emphasize the power of thought to alter material reality. It is thus a system which glorifies individual self-making but is studiously inattentive to any context of social and/or economic inequality. In writing about the celebrated Oprah Winfrey book club, Travis notes that the club relies on a worldview that celebrates "the spirit for its ability to transcend the market—while simultaneously deploying the spirit, through the discourse of Brand Oprah, to serve the market's ends."[64]

In a related way *O* magazine continually endorses the value of a purposeful, highly managerial relationship to life. Its articles celebrate and elaborate (often through celebrity endorsement) such activities as reading, healthy eating, exercise, emotional connectedness to others, self-nurturance, and personal epiphanies (often framed as "listening to your inner voice"). *O* draws heavily from the knowledge of experts and cultivates a sense of expertise in the reader in regard to health, happiness, financial security, and rewarding/transformative consumerism.

The Oprah Winfrey franchise posits a self that quests for emotional knowledge and is also naturally acquisitive of commodities that are endowed with the signs of healthy emotion and care—in this way gift-giving to others is deemed important but gift-giving to the self is also valued and commodities work within an aestheticized lifestyle that is both backdrop for and proof of the questing self. In moderate contrast to the more bluntly commodity-oriented sloganizing of someone like Martha Stewart, whose endorsement of home products and painstaking craftwork is signaled in her signature phrase "It's a good thing," Oprah's totalizing epistemological system works to de-stigmatize blunt commercialism. Couched within a discourse of health, pleasure, relaxation, and social generosity the star can frankly endorse products without any taint of commercialization. Accordingly "The *O* List: A Few Things Oprah Thinks Are Great," included in each issue, singles out a half dozen stylish items each month ranging from clothing to jewelry to home décor items and gifts. Accompanying picture, price, and purchase details is a testimonial from Winfrey describing the appeal of the product and/or suggesting a use value for it. In these ways high-end commodities are reclassified as tokens/totems of the questing "best self;" they do not substitute for emotions but are expressive, wholly legitimate signs of emotional connectedness with oneself and with others.

While I do not intend a full analysis of the Oprah Winfrey phenomenon here, but rather some brief observations about the star's connectedness to postfeminist lifestyling, it bears noticing that this case is virtually the only one I have alluded to that deviates from postfeminism's customary default whiteness. The rhetoric, style, and tone of the Oprah brand is not only postfeminist, it also presents itself to a significant extent as post-racial. (This is of course not to suggest that the Oprah brand is not race-conscious, rather that it restricts its view of race to those questions/issues/concerns that can be ideologically held in check.) In this way we can see how among its other neutralizing political functions, postfeminism tends to want to push past the notion of racial inequality.

Celebrity style and how to get it: *InStyle* magazine and the uses of stardom

To close this chapter, I want to turn to the case of an exceptionally successful lifestyle magazine, *InStyle*, as a source par excellence for the culmination of all the discourses I have been analyzing of the postfeminist body, the postfeminist self, and the postfeminist home. *InStyle*'s primary purpose is to celebrate the "private lives" and consumerist habits of celebrities ("private lives" for the magazine's purposes are comprised of beauty and fashion choices, home décor and decoration, and entertaining). *InStyle*'s operations as a register for closer and closer scrutiny of celebrity bodies and ideologies are thoroughly in keeping with the ideological propensities of postfeminism.

This discussion takes as its context the foregoing intensification of material priorities and the regularization of luxury-oriented consumption that took shape in the boom years of the late 1990s and continues to flourish. As the only lifestyle magazine that lists its cover celebrity's name on the binderback of each issue, *InStyle* furnishes a useful site for understanding how star meanings have tended to be adapted into this new consumption context. I will discuss the configurations of celebrity in the pages of *InStyle* as a highly successful lifestyle magazine whose terms of address were established in the neo-conservative, family values-driven culture of affluence of the late 1990s. In so doing, I mean to gesture at some of the important and underexplored interconnections between the history of Hollywood representations and the history of consumer culture. Although the study of stardom has thoughtfully attended to the celebrity culture of fan magazines, it has not (with some notable exceptions) been equally attentive to lifestyle publications that also make prominent use of interviews, star photos, and pictorial layouts. It is through these forms that *InStyle* has undertaken an expansion of what counts as interesting/useful information about celebrities, promulgating new regimes of knowledge about star fashion, consumption, and domesticity.

Who counts as a star in the pages of *InStyle* and why? Among the most dramatic developments in the uses of stardom for the magazine are an intense reification of domesticity, an eroticization and aggressive new commodification of pregnancy and motherhood (of the kind discussed in Chapter 3), and a nomination to celebrityhood of marginal entertainment figures who are deemed style icons for conforming to the magazine's definitions of idealized femininity.[65] Stars who are best able to embody the idealization of lifestyle will draw heavy coverage by the magazine; unlike talk show appearances and feature articles in most magazines and newspapers which are driven by the promotional schedule of a film or other major project, *InStyle* doesn't make a particular effort to time its celebrity coverage in this manner. Here, celebrity endorsement of clothing, makeup, hair, and home decoration products trumps the normative promotional priorities of the entertainment industry. Indeed, *InStyle*'s approach to stardom can well be understood as a particularly post-studio system development, one which cultivates a generically habitual spectator, rather than one whose observation of stars is bound to their film vehicles.

InStyle and intensified domesticity

At a time of rapid change in the magazine industry that saw the demise of publications such as *Lear's* and *Ms* devoted to working, older, and/or feminist women, and the emergence of "simplicity" as a potent keyword in the lifestyling discourse propelling new titles like *Realsimple*, the dramatic success of *InStyle* upon its founding in 1995 bears noticing. The intense privileging of commodified domesticity in *InStyle* well reflects Jim Collins' observation that "within the past decade the home has become not just a site, but a form of popular culture unto itself."[66] In one sense, it is not surprising that equally intense public interests in celebrities and homes can be so easily brought together. In Marjorie Garber's discussion of the various psychological and emotional needs houses are currently being made to address, she suggests that the culture of celebrity and the culture of real estate in fact, bump up against each other. She maintains that

> In the twentieth-century culture of the celebrity, a new kind of "aristocracy" based on popular fame and even notoriety replaced an older, apparently "stable" image of hereditary privilege . . . And the twentieth-century culture of the house and home is in a way a chronicle of the house as star.[67]

It could arguably be asserted that these days home ownership is the key credential of US citizenship (a trend that I think was well underway before September 11 further invigorated the home-as-retreatist fortress mindset). Just as the American family now serves as the exclusively-recognized social unit, the affluent home is regularly presented as universally available. Certainly American popular culture has exploded with domestic dream narratives over the last five years and the popularity of *InStyle* should be placed adjacent to the high-profile success of series such as *Trading Spaces* (HGTV) and the emergence of a number of new shelter magazines. Among its other functions, *InStyle* speaks to/from a highly intensified cult of domesticity driven by "low interest rates and an inhospitable stock market" to redirect "money and attention back to real estate."[68] Notably, its celebration of celebrity homes insists on an expressive domesticity; the decorative and design choices we make *must* reflect who we are and communicate this to others.[69] In this respect celebrity domesticity in *InStyle* differs markedly from such coverage in the recent past which was just as likely to emphasize a fashionable undomesticity. It was not unusual, for instance, in the 1980s or early 1990s for a magazine article to highlight the vacant domestic space of a busy star (typically in such coverage the star is photographed in a barely furnished home or a home furnished by a decorator whose taste the star doesn't necessarily share). Coverage of this sort reflected an intensely minimalist aesthetic, visually emphasizing elements such as an empty refrigerator and verbally quoting the star as saying that he/she didn't even choose the furnishings to convey an image of a celebrity whose public status and devotion to work outweighed any need for domesticity. Now, however, domestic space must be shown as intensely personal and meaningful and decorators have become somewhat discredited (their contributions are seldom acknowledged and when they are the decorator is likely to be identified as a friend whose sympathy and understanding reflect care, not work, as they help to transform a house into a reflection of the star's personality).[70] One of the most notable features of *InStyle*'s coverage of celebrity domesticity is that while a number of profiled stars voice a fervent commitment to family values, the ability to live a personal expressive style is more important than any single model of the domestic. Notably, gay couples are recuperable under the new, hyperconsumptive paradigm, as the achievement of lifestyle and good taste are seen to overwhelm all other differences.

InStyle, the high-pop mindset, and counter-tabloidism

In a cultural context that inscribes an increasingly corrupt and/or threatening public sphere, the success of *InStyle* should certainly be set against a backdrop of widespread cultural retreatism and hometown fantasizing. With glamour photography in the beginning of the issue, selective celebrity endorsements of individual commodities in the middle section, and extensive layouts of star homes in the closing pages, the chronology of each *InStyle* issue is designed to reinforce the sense that a successful exterior is the result of an orderly, stylish, harmonious interior life (with interior defined as domestic). The domestic layouts at the end are meant to culminate an achievement of domesticity that catalyzes, rationalizes, and buttresses public success. Moreover, it is especially important that these layouts confirm the celebrity's (or celebrity couple's) personalized good taste. In this respect, the home as showplace theme in *InStyle* represents not just a new stage in the drama of possessions, but the cultivation of what Collins has identified as "popular connoisseurship." It well reflects Collins' characterization of a new "high-pop" cultural mindset that he describes as follows:

> Where the academy has abandoned taste as an antiquated concept, popular tastebrokers have repositioned it as a thoroughly contemporary value by conceiving of taste as the ability to make informed personalized choices out of a sea of consumer options. Within this new evaluative dynamic a higher education is judged essential but incomplete, in need of the finishing that only high-end popular culture authorities can now provide as they make taste into a process of converting one's stored cultural literacy into registers of personal preference articulated by the proper consumer choices.[71]

As celebrities model the new lifestyle priorities, the dynamic of exceptionalism and typicality that undergirds every star persona is forcefully played through the register of consumerism, with many stars now held to account for their ability to stage individuality through the codes of affluent good taste. While fan magazines have certainly done this before in individual articles, and publications like *Architectural Digest* and *Sunset* have periodically included lengthy article and photo layouts of celebrity homes, *InStyle*'s codified formula for celebrity-inspired consumerism is its raison d'etre and the magazine has attained a cultural prominence far in excess of those other publications. In the advertising industry,

InStyle is understood to be a huge success. When *Brandweek* compiled its 2001 "Hotlist" of the ten most successful magazines based on ad page, revenue, and circulation gains and interviews with media buyers and consultants, *InStyle* was second only to *Fortune*. "This all-access pass to celebrities' closets and cabinets has been a top circ performer three years in a row," notes the piece, citing a rise in revenue of 52.7% and a rise in circulation of 10.5%.[72] A further sign of the magazine's success is the fact that the *InStyle* brand name has proved strong enough to be adapted into broadcast formats and I will address some of the ways this has happened later in the chapter.

InStyle's emergence was also part of a wave of current cultural forms recuperating stardom from the intense tabloidization and scandalization trends of the mid-1990s. Like *Biography* (A & E) and *Inside the Actors Studio* (Bravo) which retrieve a more respectful approach to stardom by highlighting discourses of craft, *InStyle* does so through an emphasis on discourses of taste.[73] Indeed, *InStyle*'s rejection of tabloid concerns is exemplified in its "Truth or Tabloid" feature which details a recent celebrity rumor and then cites the star's representative to discredit it. Kevin Glynn's definition of tabloid news provides a good way of delineating everything that *InStyle* is not. Glynn defines the tabloid mindset as follows:

> It dwells on social and moral disorder. Among its favorite themes are the ubiquity of victimization and the loss of control over the outcomes of events, and of one's fate. Also typical are stories involving gender disturbances and ambiguities, troubled domestic and familial relationships, and paranormal phenomena that apparently outstrip the explanatory power of scientific rationalism. Tabloid media simultaneously defamiliarize the ordinary and banalize the exotic.[74]

InStyle, with its glamour photography of female stars in couture clothing and monthly profile of a male star as "Man of Style," underscores the stability of fixed gender positions. Meanwhile, its strong emphasis on motherhood and family reinforces the sanctity of domesticity. Finally, its representational strategies work to cultivate a sense of consumer enchantment which is the very opposite of the tabloid destabilizations Glynn chronicles. In contrast to tabloid stars who are vividly and exclusively public, stardom for *InStyle* tends to be couched in a discourse of domestic privacy even as the magazine "pulls back the curtain" to facilitate our interest, an interest that places us in the position of consumer peer rather than prurient film fan.[75] In raising stars from tabloid muck to the sanctity of domesticity, new representational forms such as *InStyle* work to assuage what David Brooks has referred to as "the anxieties of abundance."[76] Exalting consumerism and domesticity from the practical to the near-spiritual (and using stars to do it) frees us from an unflattering self-perception of crass materialism or callow interest in the behavior of celebrities.

Rather, the celebrity-driven hyper-commodified domesticity of *InStyle* removes the taint of gossip or prurience even while it reflects a closer and closer scrutiny of star bodies and lifestyles. The respectful coverage of stars and their possessions is intended to create a loop that confirms that their good taste is (or can be) our good taste too. In this way, the magazine acknowledges an identificatory element that has long existed in star/audience relations but brings it forward in accordance with a new assumption that purchasing power, good taste, and the achievement of a privatized domesticity are the key concerns of celebrities and non-celebrities alike. *InStyle* is not terribly interested in what stars think; it is interested in what they buy.

InStyle, luxury lifestyling, and retreatism

InStyle's glorification of the self and the home perpetuates a retreatist cultural mindset that deeply distrusts the public sphere. Reed Mercer Schuchardt has correlated road rage to the expanded use of the Internet and provocatively suggested that new forms of public anger arise at least in part from the frustration we feel when real space fails to provide us with the mobility of virtual space.[77] The broad cultural characterization of public sphere experiences as traumatic and corrupt is in many respects balanced by a parallel idealization of the private. As Laura Pappano has argued, "We may be lonelier than ever, more disappointed in the quality of our social interactions, but we are tireless in our pursuit of privacy and seclusion."[78] The intensified pursuit of a perfected domesticity is often accompanied by a deep dedication to fantasies of historical simplicity (in the form of heritage) and the family as a refuge (via family values) that enable us to steer clear of the dissatisfactions of the present and the public.

As a variety of social roles have come up for critical scrutiny, the one category that seems immune to this, and that increasingly correlates with fantasies of security and comfort, is the category of the consumer. *InStyle* is only one of a number of contemporary cultural forms that redefine shopping as an act of creativity, even an art form. The capacity to stage identity away from the public sphere becomes an act of private re-consolidation. As I have argued throughout this book, postfeminism has emerged in tandem with broad socioeconomic trends toward luxury lifestyling and retreatism and the manifestations of these trends are conspicuous not only in *InStyle* but throughout the mass media. *The New York Times*, for instance, has introduced a special "Nesting" section devoted to trends in home ownership and decoration. A February 2002 article in that section summarized broad trends in the American housing market as follows:

> As formality ebbs, luxury flows. Though the average family size is shrinking, square footage is growing. Average ceiling heights in new homes are rising from 8 to 9 feet, the latter once considered standard only in affluent homes. Homeowners are installing "his" and "her" sinks, even in relatively modest residences.[79]

The normalization of luxury expectations is part of a trend economist Juliet Schor has termed the "New Consumerism" whereby the declining importance of neighborhood peer groups and the growing importance of media representations skewed toward the wealthy have significantly re-crafted the mainstream horizon of expectations. Schor maintains that current economic and lifestyling trends reflect a new dynamic in which the top 20 percent of income earners "are approaching the status of cultural icons" with their lifestyles increasingly "looked to by those with far less income as increasingly necessary and worth having."[80] Robert H. Frank makes the point in slightly different terms when he observes in *Luxury Fever* that

> the spending of the superrich, though sharply higher than in decades past, still constitutes just a small fraction of total spending. Yet their purchases are far more significant than might appear, for they have been the leading edge of pervasive changes in the spending patterns of middle- and even low-income families.[81]

In a similar vein, economist Paul Krugman has demonstrated with devastating accuracy and scope the contemporary disappearance of the American middle class, a symptom of a broader climate that mimics the features of the Gilded Age in its reconcentration of income and wealth.[82] Publications such as *InStyle* devote themselves to repairing the evident and increasing gap between the wealthy and everyone else by promulgating a discourse of consumer parity and paying lip service to the democratization of glamour.

While it is common to bemoan the low thematic values of contemporary popular films, and to complain that they serve no legitimate cultural function, it may be more productive to observe that one of Hollywood's key functions at the moment is to generate an ongoing series of lifestyle commercials facilitated by both product placement and ever more lavish set dressing. Increasingly, such lifestyle commercials showcase the home and indeed, the compulsion to establish a pleasant, private identity-confirming space is illustrated across a variety of sites in current popular culture. Real estate themes have taken on an increasing prominence in recent popular film. In *Life as a House* (2001) Kevin Kline's George Munroe responds to being diagnosed with a terminal illness by symbolically making over his life when he and his son tear down an old vacation shack and build a sturdy house in its place. A year prior in *What Lies Beneath* we have the strong suggestion that Claire Spencer's (Michelle Pfeiffer) relationship with her beautiful home is more reliable and rewarding than that with her deceptive husband. In *Panic Room* (2002) a mother's purchase of an opulent Manhattan brownstone targeted by thieves provides her with the opportunity to work through the grief of her divorce as she puts the features of the house to work in her own vigorous defense. In the breakaway romantic hit of summer 2004, *The Notebook*, a young man expresses his love for his sweetheart by fulfilling his promise to renovate a mansion for her. The interest in celebrity homes, meanwhile, has become regularized in forms such as *Entertainment Weekly's* "Gimme Shelter" feature—a weekly spotlighting of a celebrity home on the market often with only distant glimpses of the property gleaned through telephoto lenses. This section never fails to include the name of the broker who has the listing, another symptom of the phenomenon *InStyle* represents more broadly, that suggests that what celebrities have you can have too.

Celebrity domesticity has become a theme of some prominence in contemporary television. MTV's *Cribs* was probably the first series to capitalize on this theme and it nicely illustrates how the rhetoric of home display can be productively attached to a wide variety of star personae, with a selected pop or rock performer taking us on a tour of their home each week. In its recuperation of a slang rap term as its title, *Cribs* suggests how transcendent and all-encompassing the theme of domesticity has become; yet unlike most of the numerous home shows that have proliferated on cable in the last five years, one of the pleasures of *Cribs* is that though it confirms wealth and the achievement of expressive domesticity it is just as likely to reveal spectacularly bad taste as good. A more recent related development has been the emergence of a reality show formula that takes celebrity domesticity as its starting point—notably in MTV's *The Osbournes*, which in Spring 2002 was drawing four million viewers a week and emerged as one of the most talked-about shows on television. The series began with middle-aged metal star Ozzy Osbourne, his manager wife Sharon, and two of their three children moving into a new home, and unfolded to become one of the most intimate views of celebrity homelife that have so far been broadcast. As the family settled in, we observed them engaging in everything from counseling sessions with an animal psychologist to cultivate better understanding of their pets, to Ozzy advising his daughter to practice safe sex as she went out for the evening, to comical disputes with their new neighbors that caused the Osbournes to fondly recall their previous neighbor Pat Boone. The success of *The Osbournes* was instrumental in the conceptualization of *Newlyweds*, the 2003–2005 hit MTV reality series that launched postfeminist pin-up Jessica Simpson (and to a far lesser extent her then-husband Nick Lachey) to stardom.

Co-promotional ventures between *InStyle* and media outlets such as NBC and CNN have also reinforced the importance of celebrity icons in the cultivation of lifestyle trends. Co-branding now takes place under a variety of rubrics as the *InStyle* brand name circulates widely in different broadcast formats, sometimes as an explicit point of departure for primetime specials such *InStyle Celebrities at Home* and *InStyle Celebrity Weddings*, sometimes merely as a discursive designation of sponsorship for the lifestyle segments within cable news formats. The celebrity-driven hyper-commodified domesticity promulgated by *InStyle* is potent enough to be adapted into a variety of new print and broadcast contexts. The brand name, linked as it is to an idealized, luxurious domesticity that does cultural work on a number of fronts, is increasingly activated not just as the name of a magazine but as a whole way of life.

Conclusion

In this chapter I have argued that postfeminism cooperates significantly with a shift toward the hyper-aestheticization of everyday life and that it is crucial to realize that aesthetic value is real value in the current cultural marketplace. As traditional discourses of moral caution around consumption have receded, American popular culture is now broadly characterized by a sense of material entitlement (we can all have everything), one which is leavened by a quasi-moral and distinctively feminized discourse of peaceful respite.

Toward this end, I have considered some of the forms of the domestic dream narrative that proliferated in the late 1990s/2000s. Two features are particularly of note here: firstly, a trend toward the regularization of luxury domesticity fostered by new kinds of style guides that celebrate celebrity home life and secondly, an intensified emphasis on expressive domesticity in which subjectivity is understood to be most fully and truthfully manifested at home. What makes this period distinctive is its emphasis on a perfectionistic domesticity and new discourses of "homemaker chic." Whether in the commodity empires of trans-mediated domestic gurus and postfeminist icons like Martha Stewart, Nigella Lawson, and Rachael Ray, on the pages of *InStyle* magazine, or in the sometimes rueful but nevertheless sincere calls to fortify domesticity sounded by commentators like Caitlin Flanagan, postfeminism is consistently associated with a design for living that is deeply traditionalist and that centralizes a female homemaker figure. In analyzing the frenzy of postfeminist domestic perfectionism I have sought to be mindful of the decisive role of class formations and of the economic conditions (neoliberalism, radical income inequality) that have helped to give rise to the new hyperdomesticities.

Postfeminism is marked by an idealization of traditionalist femininities, a habit of criminalizing the female professional, and powerful entrancing visions of perfected female bodies and sumptuous domestic scenes. A great number of fictional and non-fictional postfeminist texts embed the assumption that women remain uniquely responsible for the conditions of family life. In this chapter I have asked how/why the socially alienating conditions of contemporary life are counterbalanced by fantasies of privatized domestic sensuality through *InStyle* magazine and other outlets. Throughout this book I have argued that it is essential to consider postfeminism when analyzing what the new American "good life" feels and looks like. In some ways the passage from prefeminism to postfeminism may be glimpsed in the shift from enforced domesticity to an excessively celebrated elective domesticity in the lives of many women. And yet as Imelda Whelehan has cautioned, "Lifestyle politics leaves many victims in its wake—those who don't conform to its preferred images and those who are too poor to exercise 'control' over their lives through the 'liberation' of consumerism."[83] Postfeminism continually hypes empowerment but a closer examination of its affective registers reveals a sense of stern disapproval and judgment for any manifestations of "off-script" femininity. Indeed, postfeminism looks disapprovingly upon those forms of female agency unrelated to couple and family formation, preferring a self-surveilling subject whose concepts of body and behavior are driven by status anxiety. In this book I have sought to remind readers that there are social concerns and constituencies that cannot be addressed through the solipsism of self-care and the rectitude of family values. In tracking the characteristic preoccupations of postfeminism, what is perhaps most striking is the diversity of identities and social experiences it neglects.

Notes

I INTRODUCTION

1. Leonhardt, "Scant Progress on Closing Gap in Women's Pay," p. A1.
2. See Imogen Tyler's shrewd account of the emergence and functions of the cultural stereotype of the "selfish feminist." Tyler writes that "By the late 1970s, the mediation of feminist politics through the pejorative figure of the selfish feminist generated a mass dis-identification with feminism." "The Selfish Feminist: Public Images of Women's Liberation," p. 185.
3. Farhi, "Elizabeth Vargas, Exiting Stage Center."
4. See Projansky's *Watching Rape: Film and Television in Postfeminist Culture.*
5. See Levy's *Female Chauvinist Pigs: Women and the Rise of Raunch Culture.*
6. Banner, *American Beauty*, p. 286.
7. McCarty, Poole, and Rosenthal, *Polarized America: The Dance of Ideology and Unequal Riches*, p. 2.
8. See Leonhardt, "The College Dropout Boom," and Scott, "Life at the Top in America Isn't Just Better, It's Longer."
9. For an account of the former see Ann Burlein, *Lift High the Cross: Where White Supremacy and the Christian Right Converge*, and for the latter see Estella Tincknell's *Mediating the Family: Gender, Culture and Representation.*
10. Giroux, "The Conservative Assault on America: Cultural Politics, Education and the New Authoritarianism," pp. 140–141.
11. Brenner, *Women and the Politics of Class*, p. 209.
12. Whelehan, *Overloaded: Popular Culture and the Future of Feminism*, p. 119.
13. For instance, although postfeminist texts often appear to prioritize female sociality, many, in fact, replace substantive notions of collectivism with an ersatz vision of "bonding." Meanwhile, postfeminism also trades heavily in discourses of presumptive innate female competitiveness and an emphasis on female-to-female criticism as may be seen in two 2006 relationship texts: Deborah Tannen's *You're Wearing That?: Understanding Mothers and Daughters in Conversation* and Susan Shapiro Barash's *Tripping the Prom Queen: The Truth About Women and Rivalry* as well as numerous female-centered reality television competition series such as *America's Top Model* (2003–).
14. Preston, "Hanging on a Star: The Resurrection of the Romance Film in the 1990s," p. 229.
15. Negra, "Romance and/as Tourism: Heritage Whiteness and the (Inter)National Imaginary in the New Woman's Film."
16. No doubt in the process this study sacrifices attentiveness to individual media forms. I hope that the value of breadth will go some way toward alleviating the problem of neglecting to consistently and/or fully take stock of the specificities of individual media.

17. See Frank and Cook, *The Winner-Take-All Society*.
18. In her essay "Divas, Evil Black Bitches, and Bitter Black Women: African-American Women in Postfeminist and Post-Civil Rights Popular Culture," Kimberly Springer has observed that "The arrival of postfeminist discourse in popular culture, especially, needs to be interrogated about how race is always present." p. 249.

2 POSTFEMINISM, FAMILY VALUES, AND THE SOCIAL FANTASY OF THE HOMETOWN

1. Gross, "Forget the Career: My Parents Need Me at Home," p. A1.
2. Stewart, "Trauma Time: A Still Life," p. 326.
3. Morley, *Home Territories: Media, Mobility, and Identity*, p. 29.
4. Hage, "'Comes a Time We Are All Enthusiasm': Understanding Palestinian Suicide Bombers in Times of Exighophobia," p. 86.
5. The concept of home is an expedient one that can be bluntly disregarded as often as it is sentimentalized. One might argue that the national debate over the viability of New Orleans after Hurricane Katrina offers evidence of the former.
6. Such images are particularly prevalent in the recently expanded business travel sections of newspapers like *USA Today* and *The Wall Street Journal* and correspond with images of female hospitality in the aviation industry. For a discussion of the latter see "Popular Media, Postfeminism, and the Return of Flight Attendant Chic" in Chapter 4.
7. Iyer, "The New Business Class," p. 27.
8. Jeffords, "Breakdown: White Masculinity, Class, and US Action-Adventure Films," p. 224.
9. There are certainly male-centered variants of the going home story (though they are far more infrequent). These might include the films *The Family Man* (2000), *Garden State* (2004), *Jersey Girl* (2004), and *Just Friends* (2005) (all of which, strangely, return a protagonist to New Jersey) and the NBC television series *Ed*.
10. In this sense, the series focalizes a broader representational trend aptly discussed by Moya Luckett who writes that "Current television shows glorify marriage and motherhood in a variety of ways, presenting them as alternately hip, comforting, rare, and hard-to-find, under attack, and even a little rebellious." See "Marriage as the New Trend."
11. The trend looked set to continue with industry reports that David E. Kelley would spin off a character from *The Practice* (Camryn Manheim's Eleanor Frutt) in a series in which she returns to her hometown, teaching law at a local university. (The series has yet to appear.) In cinema the "small-town girl" has been mobilized as recently as *Win a Date with Tad Hamilton* (2004) which requires a jaded male Hollywood star to ideologically refresh himself through contact with an idealized West Virginia small town and the beautiful, disingenuous blonde girl who personifies it. I discuss this film more fully later in the chapter.
12. It will be clear, I hope, that this discussion analyzes conceptual hometowns rather than literal ones. A related yet methodologically distinct investigation might well be undertaken of the turn in architecture, town planning, etc. (frequently under the auspices of "New Urbanism") toward the design of simulated hometowns, ranging from such well-known cases as Disney's Celebration, Florida, to innumerable more prosaic examples.
13. I would not want to give the impression that the formula I am describing springs up out of nowhere and without precedent in the late 1990s. An earlier film such as *Baby Boom* (1987) for instance works in the same general terrain even if it finds a way to combine domesticated, rural motherhood with a new version of business success for its heroine.

14. Tasker and Negra, "Feminist Politics and Postfeminist Culture," p. 8.
15. See Negra, "Structural Integrity, Historical Reversion and the Post-9/11 Chick Flick."
16. Part of the film's (fond) critique of Hollywood culture rests on the casting of Sean Hayes (*Will & Grace*) and Nathan Lane (*The Birdcage*, etc.), two gay-identified actors who appear here as figures of knowing cosmopolitanism in contrast to the residents of Frazier's Bottom.
17. The scene enables *Win a Date with Tad Hamilton* to score a quick point about racial diversity in Frazier's Bottom, although everyone else we see in town throughout the film is white. It is also in keeping with a chick flick tendency to employ minority women to sponsor, validate, or root for the romantic success of a white female protagonist. This occurs in *Two Weeks' Notice* for instance and in a slight modification in *Maid in Manhattan* where the "white enough" Jennifer Lopez is contrasted with a group of dark-skinned black maids in the hotel where she works.
18. Bronfen, *Home in Hollywood: The Imaginary Geography of Cinema*, p. 21.
19. I have in mind here such hit songs as Paula Cole's "Where Have All the Cowboys Gone?" and Britney Spears' "Not a Girl, Not Yet a Woman" though there are doubtless many other examples.
20. A broader definition of the retreatist romance would encompass films such as *How to Lose a Guy in Ten Days* in which the heroine's retreat is to the hero's idealized working-class family home in Staten Island.
21. Martin, "Anti-Feminism in Recent Apocalyptic Film."
22. That these kinds of series have emerged as reliable sites for the congregation of female viewers is suggested in a recent news article on the rising DVD sales among women consumers. New Line's specialty campaign highlighting the strength and personality of the female characters in *The Lord of the Rings: The Two Towers* led to advertisements broadcast on the Lifetime network and on *Judging Amy*. See Thomas K. Arnold "Women Hot Target for DVD Sales."
23. Lotz, *Redesigning Women: Television after the Network Era*, p. 225. Although my focus here is on hour-long dramas, it is worth noting that, in the period in which these series flourished, the sitcom also registered some important changes in the performance of gender and family roles. Jennifer Reed has shrewdly analyzed a set of updated patriarchal sitcoms including *Everybody Loves Raymond*, *The King of Queens*, *Yes, Dear*, and *According to Jim* which showcase a breadwinning blue-collar male besieged by domestic life and emotionally tutored by his wife. As she argues, in the domestic sitcoms of the new millennium "We are not back in the 1950s, but we are close. These sitcoms are postfeminist plus, in that they are relentless in their pull back to traditional ideas of marriage, family, and the performance of gender, framed by the assumption that women choose these lives." See Read, "Beleaguered Husbands and Demanding Wives: The New Domestic Sitcom."
24. The long-running series *Frasier* also included some elements of this formula, as it focused on a divorced man who returns to his hometown of Seattle after a divorce and shares an apartment with his father.
25. Linda Hansen communicates this directly in an episode entitled "Home for the Holidays" where she tells her daughter, "Every family needs a leader, Syd. And whether you want it or not, for our family that person is you."
26. Interestingly, the star of that series, Jennifer Garner, had a hit film in *13 Going on 30* which plays in reverse motion many of the dilemmas of maturation that anchor the retreatist television series. In the series adult female protagonists are often wistful for their lost childhoods. In the film, Garner's character, Jenna Rake, is a 13-year-old who experiences instant maturation when she is doused with "wishing dust" and her life is instantly forwarded by 13 years. I should add that I am specifically limiting my view here and that a variety of other female-centered primetime series have conceptualized differing and complex relations between a protagonist and a hometown.

Series from *Ellen* to *Buffy the Vampire Slayer* have also negotiated the meanings and challenges of "home" in ways that deserve critical scrutiny.

27. The dialogue is from "Things That Go Bump in the Night," broadcast in the UK on February 4, 2004. *Gilmore Girls* offers a precisely similar character to David in Rachel, Luke's former girlfriend. While Lorelai characterizes Rachel as "Wonder Woman" for her accomplishments as an international press photographer, Lorelai's friend Sookie says the reason Rachel and Luke split up was because "Stars Hollow was too small for her" whereas Luke's (sometimes cantankerous) sense of loyalty to his hometown is his defining feature.

28. The choice of this black woman to leave Rhode Island for her Georgia hometown inevitably picks up historical racial overtones.

29. They may also be enacted through tourism. In the case of *Providence* the series had a palpable effect on tourism in that city, becoming one of the factors most cited for the way that Providence has seen its economy flourish in recent years.

30. Hollows, "Can I Go Home Yet? Feminism, Postfeminism, and Domesticity," p. 7.

31. Ibid., p. 6.

32. Burlein, *Lift High the Cross: Where White Supremacy and the Christian Right Converge*, p. 158.

33. One of the commonalities between *Judging Amy* and *Providence* is that the female protagonist in each series has a subordinate black character (in the former a court services officer and in the latter a nurse) who shadows them in their day-to-day professional experiences. It is a measure of the differences between the two series that in the former Bruce Van Exel challenges as often as he confirms Amy's views while black characters such as Helen in *Providence* seem to exist mostly to draw from a stock set of validations of Syd's medical prowess. Indeed, Helen's signature phrase is "Nice work, Syd."

34. Brenneman commented to this effect in a Museum of Television and Radio William S. Paley seminar devoted to the series on March 3, 2001. In "Meanwhile, Back in the Emergency Room . . . Feminism, Aesthetic Form, and Narrative Politics in *Judging Amy*," Mimi White has observed further that Brenneman's mother is a paid consultant to the series.

35. Lotz, *Redesigning Women*, p. 122.

36. Fantasies of social health in the series work in a manner reminiscent of Hillary Clinton's popularization of the "It takes a village to raise a child" mantra in the mid-1990s. Rory Gilmore is fussed over and catered to by all the residents of Stars Hollow and Lorelai takes evident pride in the care and interest focused by the community on her beautiful and intelligent daughter. At one stage, Lorelai warns Rory's first boyfriend Dean, that should he hurt her, he will have to answer to the entire town.

37. Lotz, *Redesigning Women*, p. 123.

38. See Oake, "*Reality Bites* and Generation X as Spectator."

39. Bagby, *Rational Exuberance: The Influence of Generation X on the New American Economy*, p. 3.

40. Gates, "There's No Place Like Home," p. 59.

41. Karlyn, "*Scream*, Popular Culture, and Feminism's Third Wave: 'I'm Not My Mother.'"

42. Katz, "The State Goes Home: Local Hypervigilance of Children and the Global Retreat from Social Reproduction," p. 49.

43. Masius offered this description in a Museum of Television and Radio seminar devoted to *Providence* (date unknown).

44. Later in the series Robbie and his new wife Tina live in a small building outside the main Hansen house.

45. In this way it resembles *Gilmore Girls*, where virtually all the residents of Stars

Hollow are proprietors of a local business, notably Luke who has converted his father's hardware store into a diner. To emphasize the heritage connection a sign marking it as a hardware store still appears above the building in the series pilot.

46. By contrast *Providence* concludes with Syd quitting her job because a professional opportunity for Owen requires that they move to Chicago. The series sanctions this departure by suggesting that Syd's work in healing and restoring her family has been accomplished and she can now transfer her allegiance to her relationship with Owen.

47. I have in mind here the distinct category of celebrity profile (in both print and television) in which a female celebrity testifies to the transformative effect of motherhood. Another example would be Céline Dion's hit pop song "A New Day Has Come" (the title of which is also the creative concept name for her Las Vegas revue) that linked the star's return to the stage to the rejuvenating effects of motherhood after the birth of her son René-Charles. More recently, celebrity mother Angelina Jolie has attested in interviews that parenting her adopted son "made [her] a woman." I discuss these dynamics in greater detail in Chapter 3.

48. The Family Friendly Programming Forum is made up of more than 40 corporations who collectively represent about one-third of the spending in US television advertising. It seeks to support and promote content deemed family friendly, offering development grants and giving awards to the series that meet its ideological criteria.

49. The girl-centered teen film has been particularly conspicuous in its habit of erasing mothers in narratives of female teens coming of age. Films from *Clueless* (1995) to *Ten Things I Hate About You* (1999) to *Win a Date with Tad Hamilton* (which doesn't even bother to explain why its female protagonist is being raised by a single father) all have participated in this trend.

50. Douglas and Michaels, *The Mommy Myth: The Idealization of Motherhood and How It Has Undermined Women*, pp. 4–5.

51. Ibid., p. 24.

52. "American Dreamers," p. 131.

53. In this respect these series are regionally unified in a manner reminiscent of early 1990s television which seemed to gravitate to the northwest and far west in its settings. Series such as *Twin Peaks* and *Northern Exposure* seemed to be in dialogue with a recession culture's search for "frontier" locales. Professional dramas in the 1980s, such as *LA Law* and *Moonlighting*, tended to emphasize Southern California.

54. Brooks, "Our Way: Root and Hoot."

55. Putnam, *Bowling Alone: The Collapse and Revival of American Community*, p. 19.

56. This data is available at http://national.unitedway.org/stateofcaring. In *Bowling Alone* Robert D. Putnam assesses the geographical dispersion of "social capital" in the US (as measured through such things as community volunteerism, social trust, engagement in public affairs, etc.) and finds the upper midwest the highest ranked region. However, New England is quite close behind.

57. Though it must be acknowledged that *Gilmore Girls* deviates in some respects from the other series I am discussing, in part because of the rather open way in which it shows its hand in "inventing" a hometown setting for its protagonist. Not only is Stars Hollow not the town Lorelai grew up in, the series regularly draws attention to the commercialization of hometown rhetoric and conceptualization. The town's residents are highly conscious of invented traditions and rituals and many of them operate businesses that rely on tourist trade. A town troubadour and contrived regular "town meetings" also work to de-naturalize the image of the hometown displayed in other series.

58. In this respect it is worth noting how the highly detailed forensic penetrations of these series operate in relation to the codes of pornography. For Susan Willis "*CSI* is pornography displaced into forensics." *Portents of the Real: A Primer for Post-9/11 America*, p. 134.

59. Glynn, *Tabloid Culture: Trash Taste, Popular Power and the Transformation of American Television*, p. 19.
60. See *Headline Hollywood: A Century of Film Scandal*.
61. In doing, so, incidentally, they were implicitly asserting their own innocence of any crime—of course when women are murdered, it is male partners and family members who are the most ready suspects given the statistical realities of such crime. At the time that Jennifer Wilbanks resurfaced, John Mason had passed one polygraph test but police wanted him to take another.
62. McElroy, "Runaway Bride Lost in Junk Journalism." Notably, when Wilbanks was filmed at an airport traveling home to Georgia the spectacle complied with familiar codes of criminal performativity as she appeared hunched under a blanket and led along by two police officers.
63. See Otnes and Pleck's co-edited *Cinderella Dreams: The Allure of the Lavish Wedding*.
64. See Allison McCracken's "Lost" in *Flow: A Critical Forum on Television and Media*. For an analysis of the phenomenon of uncanny female vanishings in popular culture, see Karen Beckman's *Vanishing Women: Magic, Film, and Feminism*.
65. Just as Jennifer Wilbanks' behavior would come to be viewed as a lapse in her middle-classness, so too would Nichols'. Some of the shock and trauma of the Nichols case might have been based on his difference from the social profile of the violent black male criminal. At the time of his arrest for rape, Nichols, who had grown up in a middle-class home, and attended college where he played on the football team, was earning a six-figure salary as a computer engineer at Hewlett-Packard and attended church regularly.
66. Smith subsequently revealed in a memoir published in autumn 2005 that her encounter with Nichols included not just prayer and conversation, but that the two also took methamphetamines together (from her own supply). In making promotional rounds for the book, Smith stressed her honesty in bringing this information to light and testified that her involvement in the hostage drama catalyzed her re-dedication to her faith and to living drug-free.
67. "Nichols to Make Court Appearance Today," CNN.com
68. Applebome, *Dixie Rising: How the South Is Shaping American Values, Politics, and Culture*, p. 11.
69. Southernness is indeed really the only consistently intelligible regional identity on *American Idol*. In the case of southern finalists it is seldom an incidental feature but one that is regularly and emphatically underscored.
70. Cobb, *Away Down South: A History of Southern Identity*, p. 237.
71. Applebome, *Reconstructing Dixie: Race, Gender, and Nostalgia in the Imagined South*, p. 39.
72. At least one news article would unfavorably compare Wilbanks with Smith, approvingly noting that Smith's deal for a book detailing her experiences included plans to donate some of the profits to a memorial fund for shooting victims, while excoriating Wilbanks as selfish and insensitive toward her community. See Rick Badie, "Making the Most of Fame's 15 Minutes."
73. Ibid., p. JJ3.
74. Michelle Meyers, "Runaway Bride Toast Attracts Auction Bread."
75. Richard P. Carpenter, "For the Betrothed or Runaway Brides: Packages That Are Expensive, or Not?" p. M4.
76. Roberts, "A Heady Apex, but Is a Dead End Just up Ahead?" p. D1.
77. The fact that she drifted to the outskirts of anonymous Sunbelt cities only further feeds the problem by referencing the opposite of hometown stability and sharpening the distinction between hometown sociality and urban anonymity at work in accounts of Wilbanks' flight.

78. Though observant viewers may note that in many ways the film validates Maggie's desire to avoid marriage in a hometown that though superficially idyllic is full of people who are rather viciously unkind about her Runaway Bride status. In this sense, it is important that closure is achieved when Maggie seeks out Ike in Manhattan and their wedding happens elsewhere and privately, with most of Maggie's neighbors and friends having to rely on phone calls to establish that she has finally been married.
79. Jefferson, "The Return of the Shrew, and Other TV Woes," p. E5.

3 TIME CRISIS AND THE NEW POSTFEMINIST LIFECYCLE

1. In 2004 a *USA Today* article took note of a trend toward young celebrity brides noting "a recent spate of nearly child brides" among film, television, and popular music stars. See Barker, "The Young and the Wed List."
2. Sennett, *The Culture of the New Capitalism*, p. 49.
3. Christian self-help author Stephen R. Covey elaborates strategies in his book *The 7 Habits of Highly Effective Families* in *How to Develop a Family Mission Statement* (2001). In April, 2006 after George W. Bush characterized himself as "the decider" in speaking to the press about his unwillingness to dismiss Defense Secretary Donald Rumsfeld, the news media briefly latched onto the phrase applying it in various other contexts. The term inspired *The New York Times* to run a front-page article exploring the decision-making habits of married couples and found that "in practice it seems that many contemporary marriages hew to a corporate management template" (A16) with couples using terms like "core competencies" in relation to their roles. See Steinhauer, "Never Mind Mars and Venus: Who Is 'The Decider?'"
4. Tasker and Negra, "Feminist Politics and Postfeminist Culture," in *Interrogating Postfeminism: Gender and the Politics of Popular Culture*, p. 10.
5. See Kelly, "Princess for the Post-Feminist Generation."
6. For a fuller discussion of nepotism and contemporary media culture see my "Celebrity Television, Family Values and E Television."
7. Strauss, "Princesses Rule the Hearts of Little Girls," Lifestyle section, p. 1.
8. In his "Consumed" column, *The New York Times Magazine*'s Rob Walker has mused on the significance of Club Libby Lu. See "Girls Just Want to Belong."
9. As I briefly noted in Chapter 1, such a conclusion occurs rather regularly in the contemporary chick flick. Other romances which emphasize that the couple has been destined since childhood include *Bridget Jones' Diary* and *Sweet Home Alabama*. The very concept of "destiny," so potent in the contemporary chick flick, is itself (among other things) a fantasy of temporal continuity and an evasion of postmodern ambiguities.
10. Flanagan's book is *To Hell with All That: Loving and Loathing Our Inner Housewife*.
11. Warner, *Perfect Madness: Motherhood in the Age of Anxiety*, p. 55.
12. Ibid., pp. 56–57.
13. Specifically in *Portents of the Real: A Primer for Post-9/11 America*, Willis writes, "We, the denizens of the world's superpower state, experience ourselves as powerless," p. 100.
14. Currie, Dunn, and Fogarty, The Fading Dream: Economic Crisis and the New Inequality," p. 325.
15. Drieben and Pomilio, "Sweet 16 Party: Pricey."
16. I'm paraphrasing here the series formula as sketched in Ogunnaike, "Taking a Sour Pleasure as the Rich Turn Sweet 16," p. B8.
17. Luckett, "Life's So Good When You Have a Credit Card."
18. Ingraham, *White Weddings: Romancing Heterosexuality in Popular Culture*.
19. Rebecca Mead cites the latter figure in *One Perfect Day: The Selling of the American Wedding*, p. 10.

20. Ibid., p. 8.
21. This would include books by Jaclyn Geller (*Here Comes the Bride: Women, Weddings, and the Marriage Mystique*), Elizabeth Freeman (*The Wedding Complex: Forms of Belonging in Modern American Culture*), Sharon Boden (*Consumerism, Romance and the Wedding Experience*), Carol Wallace (*All Dressed in White: The Irresistible Rise of the American Wedding*), and Cele C. Otnes and Elizabeth H. Pleck (*Cinderella Dreams: The Allure of the Lavish Wedding*), as well as Mead.
22. Montemurro, *Something Old, Something Bold: Bridal Showers and Bachelorette Parties*, p. 147.
23. Mendelsohn, "The Bride Wore Blue."
24. Boo, "The Marriage Cure."
25. Ali and Scelfo, "Choosing Virginity."
26. See Siroto, "When Two Is Not Enough."
27. For two accounts of the rise in midlife female eating disorders see Bellafante, "When Midlife Seems Just an Empty Plate" and Newsome, "Not Just for Kids." In the former, Bellafante interviews clinicians who attribute the rise of eating disorders and overexercise among midlife women to "not just anxiety about aging, but a fear of aging in a culture that is 20 years into a fitness obsession" (4) and a culture where "the cultural pressure to look 23 at 45 has never been so palpable" (9).
28. Saul, "Record Sales of Sleep Pills Cause Worry," p. A1.
29. See Garrett, *Postmodern Chick Flicks*, pp. 312–313.
30. A critique of fiftiesness is attempted in the 2004 remake of *The Stepford Wives* though the film fails to achieve much clarity in its efforts.
31. It is worth noting also the ubiquity of time-travel themes in popular print fiction as well, as exemplified, for instance, in the bestselling *The Time Traveler's Wife*, which is set to appear as a film adaptation in 2008 starring Eric Bana and Rachel McAdams.
32. Movies.com lists *50 First Dates* as the fifteenth-highest-grossing film of the year, a predictably strong result for a comedy starring Sandler and Barrymore. *The Notebook* is ranked thirty-second, a noteworthy success given that the film's young leads were essentially unknown and its senior stars Gena Rowlands and James Garner would not have had top-tier box office clout. *The Notebook* was a breakaway hit whose theatrical success was extended in DVD/video release and a film that found particular favor among young female audiences. It significantly boosted the career of (already critically regarded) young actor Ryan Gosling and was career-making for Rachel McAdams, the stars who play the couple in young adulthood.
33. In an unusually penetrating dialogue exchange in this scene Kate tells her ex-boyfriend that she wasted the "best years of her life" on her relationship with him. His caustic response "Those were your best?" drew gasps from the audience when I saw the film in a multiplex.
34. She also implicitly gets to rest—Kate's exhaustion and weary cynicism are important features of the film's affective script and *Kate & Leopold*'s frenetic style and emphasis on urban chaos and confrontation are slowed only in the scenes where the couple have a romantic rooftop dinner and then he carries her to bed.
35. Forging a link to the postfeminist virtue of retreatism, the film establishes that the house was built as a tribute to Mary, the ideal mother as recalled by Alex, who was "smart and funny and could have done anything," but who chose instead to stay home and mother her children.
36. Garrett, *Postmodern Chick Flicks*, p. 329.
37. DePaulo, *Singled Out: How Singles Are Stereotyped, Stigmatized, and Ignored, and Still Live Happily Ever After*, p. 29.
38. Ibid., p. 72.
39. Boteach, author of a number of dating and relationship books such as *Kosher Sex: A Recipe for Passion and Intimacy* and *Dating Secrets of the Ten Commandments* and

host of *Shalom in the Home*, a Learning Channel show dedicated to analyzing family dynamics, exemplifies the commercialization of conservative relationship rhetoric in the postfeminist era.

40. La Ferla, "Sexy Singles, Make Way for Glamour Moms."
41. See Shinseki, "Maternity Photography: A Growing Pregnancy Trend."
42. On this transition see William Safire's column "On Language: Swelling Toward Motherhood" in which he notes "Needless embarrassment has been replaced by pride in pregnancy, and the unmistakable sign of impending childbirth is called a *bump*." p. 22.
43. Traister notes the degree to which celebrity pregnancies now drive coverage of female stars (leading not only to "baby watches" when a star is expected to give birth but to breathless speculation about when a star will become pregnant). She also explores the ambivalent emotions that accrue to readers/viewers of such coverage who may feel more intimately linked to stars subject to human biological processes but also derive pleasure when relentlessly trained and sculpted celebrity bodies grow bigger. See "Pregnancy Porn."
44. Tahmincioglu, "Pregnant Workers Filing More Complaints of Bias," p. 1. See also Armour, "Pregnant Workers Report Growing Discrimination."
45. See Siroto, "More Companies Downsize Family-Friendly Programs."
46. See Flanagan, "More Respect for Mothers Staying Home."
47. Ozment, "Sexy Singles, Make Way for Glamour Moms."
48. See "When Two Is Not Enough."
49. *To Hell With All That: Loving and Loathing Our Inner Housewife*, p. 106.
50. "A Winter of Discontent, Then Along Comes Baby," p. 9.
51. "Baby Battle," p. 40. Cheever's account gains greater depth than the others I cite here as she reflects on the hostility she experienced toward other people's public selfishness as parents, her complete disregard for such feelings when she herself became a mother, and her subsequent regaining of such resentments as her children grew toward adulthood.
52. Walker, *Baby Love: Choosing Motherhood after a Lifetime of Ambivalence*, p. 8.
53. Ibid., pp. 6–7.
54. Ibid., p. 168.
55. http://www.britneyspears.com (accessed May 15, 2006).
56. See Sales, "Sex and the Single Mom," p. 83.
57. See Kiley, "Chrysler Bets Big on Dion's Auto Endorsement Deal."
58. Yagoda, "My Heart Belongs to 'Mother.'"
59. Ibid.
60. Garrett, *Postmodern Chick Flicks*, p. 167.
61. Flanagan, *To Hell with All That: Loving and Loathing Our Inner Housewife*, p. 239.
62. Jayson, "Autism Shouts in This Family," p. 9B.
63. Douglas and Michaels, *The Mommy Myth: The Idealization of Motherhood and How It Has Undermined Women*, p. 24.
64. See Caitlin Flanagan's well-known 2004 *New Yorker* article "Bringing Up Baby," in which she notes that "Americans spend six billion dollars a year on gear for their babies" (p. 46) and chronicles a variety of high-end strollers, baby monitors, cribs, and even baby wipe warmers.
65. Chura, "Here Comes the Baby, and an Itch to Overbuy," p. 6.
66. Barker, "Mommie Hottest." That the postfeminist maternalization of femininity rests upon race and class privilege is suggested by the urban slang term "baby mama" which points toward the kind of mothering experience of which postfeminist culture is strikingly unaware—black single motherhood. The term has also found crossover usage particularly in tabloid coverage of entertainment celebrities.
67. The song's longevity and popularity was sufficient to draw notice in *USA Today* in an

article that told how the song had inspired a "hot mom contest" in Fresno and served as a soundtrack to a Dr. Pepper ad in which a minivan-driving mom fueled the fantasies of a group of teen boys. See Barker, "Fountains of Wayne Has One Splashy Mama."

68. They certainly did not do so in strictly uniform ways, although (not surprisingly) a threat of Oedipal anxiety runs through the majority of such films. In *8 Mile* Eminem's Rabbit is deeply troubled by his mother Stephanie's (Kim Basinger) sexual relationship with a man his own age and one of his rap lines refers to sleeping with a competitor's mother. Basinger was similarly placed as an older woman involved with a younger man in such films as *The Door in the Floor* and *LA Confidential.*

69. Katz and Marshall, "New Sex for Old: Lifestyle, Consumerism, and the Ethics of Aging Well," p. 3.

70. Holahan, "Actresses Inspire All Women to Sail Past 40 With Confidence."

71. Leonard, "Prematurely Gray," p. 3.

72. Levy, *Female Chauvinist Pigs: Women and the Rise of Raunch Culture,* p. 195.

73. See, for instance, Judy Dutton, "The New Housewife Wanna-Bes," in which a series of young professional women related to Dutton their desire to leave their jobs and stay at home.

74. Smith, "Post-Salad-Days Women Agree: They Want 'What She's Having,'" p. B35.

75. Wearing, "Subjects of Rejuvenation: Aging in Postfeminist Culture and Feminist Critique," p. 373.

76. Tally, "'She Doesn't Let Age Define Her': Sexuality and Motherhood in Recent 'Middle-Aged Chick Flicks,'" p. 51.

77. On this subject see my "Romance and/as Tourism: Heritage Whiteness and the (Inter)National Imaginary in the New Woman's Film."

78. Such portrayals are, of course, not wholly new. For instance, as Mandy Merck has pointed out, "Male sexual initiation by a maternally inflected older girl or woman is a venerable feature of teen comedies." "American Pie," p. 263.

79. Seymour has herself been cited as an icon of late-in-life postfeminist motherhood, having had twins in her 40s, and then writing an advice book about meeting the challenges of motherhood while maintaining a slim figure.

80. Leonard, "Prematurely Gray," p. 5.

81. Karlyn, "'Too Close for Comfort': *American Beauty* and the Incest Motif," p. 71.

82. See "These Serial Dads Have Full Houses," which notes the late in life fatherhood of Larry King, Rod Stewart, and Donald Trump, all of whom in 2005 were parents of five or six children and had either very young families or babies on the way. In this context it is also worth noting a high-profile Hollywood film currently in pre-production entitled *Father Knows Less* starring Dustin Hoffman as a man whose trophy second wife leaves him, forcing him to call upon the children of his first marriage for help in raising the children from his second.

83. While my focus here is on postfeminist conceptualizations of normative femininity, there would be much to say as well in regard to new conditions of normative masculinity and the heightening and de-stigmatizing of social discourse regarding male sexual capacity. In her study of the social and economic impact of Viagra, Meika Loe provocatively contends that "since Viagra's debut, 'normal sex' in America is more and more narrowly defined and difficult to achieve. Then again, normal sex is a seeming requirement for normal personhood." *The Rise of Viagra: How the Little Blue Pill Changed Sex in America,* p. 19.

84. The recurrence of stories about female teacher/male student sexual involvement in the press drew the attention recently of Ariel Levy who wrote about the phenomenon in an article for *New York* entitled "Dirty Old Women."

85. In a review essay dealing with *Birth,* Denby wrote "What's going on out there? This is the third Hollywood movie in the past six months in which a beautiful woman falls in love with a boy who reminds her of someone else." "Night and Day," p. 147.

86. *White Noise*, a 2005 film starring Michael Keaton, varies the formula, providing an example of a failed reincarnation romance. In that film, Keaton's deceased wife communicates from beyond the grave and he seeks to interpret her signals to prevent further deaths in an ongoing supernatural conspiracy. Other proximate films would include *The Good Girl* (2002) and *Lovely and Amazing* (2001) in which female characters played by Jennifer Aniston and Catherine Keener carry out affairs with teenage boys, although without any sort of reincarnation plot in effect.

87. Specifically Basinger was 51, Linney 40, and Kidman 37 at the time of these three films' releases in 2004.

88. In deeming *P.S.* a conservative film, I want to stress that I do so largely because of the film's need to attribute female melancholy to unfulfilled maternal desire. In another context, such as the one provided by Susan Felleman in her book *Art in the Cinematic Imagination*, the film seems more progressive. Felleman is concerned with the long trajectory of Hollywood's depiction of male necrophilic desire and she charts a spectrum of films including *Pandora and the Flying Dutchman* (1951), *Vertigo* (1958), and *Obsession* (1976) in which a male protagonist obsessively focused on a dead love object has an uncanny encounter with a female revenant. For Felleman, *P.S.* breaks this narrative mold, and she hails the film as "a welcome answer in this echo chamber of love and death." She notes that *P.S.* treats "a male object [revenant?] of female desire with almost exactly the same type of morbid and erotic fascination that his female equivalents have received, and situates him in the glare of the desiring female gaze" (p. 52).

89. The malignancy of family ties is further suggested by the presence of an unnamed aunt who takes it on herself to ruin the moment in which Anna had planned to tell her mother about setting a wedding date by blurting out the news first. This same woman is identified by Sean as the person who spoiled Anna's happiness as a child by telling her the truth about the fictional identity of Santa Claus.

90. One of the few representational precedents for linking a concluding wedding with ambivalence, uncertainty, and despair is Nancy Savoca's 1989 film *True Love* in which a young Italian-American couple realize at their wedding reception that they have sharply different views of marriage and commitment.

91. *Rosemary's Baby* is a significant intertext for *Birth*. Kidman's pixie haircut causes her to resemble Mia Farrow while the emphasis on interior space in a grand New York apartment building calls to mind the earlier film's setting.

92. *Girls Gone Wild* is so conspicuous a manifestation of postfeminist exploitation culture that Ariel Levy begins her book *Female Chauvinist Pigs: Women and the Rise of Raunch Culture* with a discussion of the soft-core video empire and the expansion of the brand into clothing, music, and restaurants.

4 POSTFEMINIST WORKING GIRLS: NEW ARCHETYPES OF THE FEMALE LABOR MARKET

1. Leonard, "'I Hate My Job, I Hate Everybody Here.'"
2. Brenner, *Women and the Politics of Class*, p. 173.
3. Kristof, "Health Care? Ask Cuba," p. 9.
4. See Leonhardt, "More Americans Were Uninsured and Poor in 2003, Census Finds."
5. See correspondents of *The New York Times*, *Class Matters*.
6. See Armour, "Your Appearance Can Affect Size of Your Paycheck."
7. See Armour, "Pregnant Workers Face Growing Discrimination." In its broadcast of May 14, 2006, the CBS Evening News also reported on the rise in pregnancy bias complaints over the last ten years.
8. Taken from the website.

9. Porter, "Stretched to Limit, Women Stall March to Work." Corroborating and particularizing these developments, a 2005 *USA Today* article documenting a rise in mothers working part-time from home noted that the labor force participation of women aged between 25 and 54 with at least four years of college declined from 84.7% in 1994–1995 to 81.8% in 2003–2004. See Armour, "Job Opening? Work-at-home Moms Fill Bill." In an article sketching the appointment of external male candidates to top jobs at media companies where strong internal female candidates were passed over, David Carr suggests that the "glass ceiling" metaphor so often used to describe the limits of women's promotability should be updated. He writes "as some women in the media business found last week, once you get through the ceiling, you find a secret glass treehouse suspended far above your head. That's where the men sit." See "To Reach the Heights, First Be Male," p. C1. In a somewhat more anecdotal opinion piece in which Maureen Dowd contends that ABC's dramatic reversal of ratings fortune in recent years has largely to do with its appeal to a postfeminist female viewing audience, Dowd notes that Susan Lyne, the former president of ABC, had advanced shows like *Desperate Housewives* and *Grey's Anatomy* but was fired even as those shows became hits. See "From McBeal to McDreamy."

10. Simon, *Governing through Crime: The War on Crime and the Transformation of America, 1960–2000*, p. 24.

11. See their book *The Winner-Take-All Society.*

12. Storper, "Lived Effects of the Contemporary Economy: Globalization, Inequality, and Consumer Equality," p. 97.

13. Ames, *Going Postal: Rage, Murder, and Rebellion from Reagan's Workplaces to Clinton's Columbine and Beyond*, p. 110.

14. Ehrenreich, *Bait and Switch: The (Futile) Pursuit of the American Dream.*, p. 3.

15. Fraser, *White-Collar Sweatshop: The Deterioration of Work and Its Rewards in Corporate America*, p. 182.

16. Ibid., pp. 184–185.

17. Sennett, *The Culture of the New Capitalism*, pp. 9–10.

18. The frequency with which the film's female characters reiterate the inadequacy of Elizabeth's pre-coma life is startling. Abby, Elizabeth's mentor at the hospital, her neighbors, and even her young niece all testify at various times to her status as a problem subject who needed to "get a life." When David claims to have been dating Elizabeth before the accident, her mentor is conspicuously relieved, saying "It would have been so awful if she'd gone through her whole life not knowing what it's all about." After repeatedly hearing such comments, Elizabeth herself concludes that "It's like I was a ghost before I was dead." These presumptions about the insufficiency of Elizabeth's life register all the more forcefully given that she appears to have attained the rank of attending physician while in her late 20s and has done so in a climate the film openly acknowledges to be marked by sexist discrimination.

19. In generating a "garden in the city" as a testament to the power of nature and nurture in an urban milieu, *Just Like Heaven* resembles several 1990s romantic comedies including *Green Card* and particularly *Bed of Roses* in which former stockbroker turned florist Lewis (Christian Slater) woos workaholic businesswoman Lisa (Mary Stuart Masterson) in part through his elaborate Manhattan roof garden. In that film as in *Just Like Heaven* the implication is that the heroine is being restored through romance to her "natural" state.

20. See Negra, "Structural Integrity, Historical Reversion and the Post-9/11 Chick Flick."

21. Kate's costuming (particularly a succession of plunge-front minidresses) in a film that makes much of her need to "dress for the job she wants" (a mandate delivered by her boss in an unfavorable comment on her wardrobe) reveals an underlying concern that urban corporate culture is making Kate a whore.

22. One of the film's signs cuing us to await the next stage of the "miswanting" plot comes when Nick diagnoses the telltale symptoms of dysfunctional female decisiveness. He tells Kate very soberly that "I never met anyone in my life who knew what they wanted more than you do." The catalyst for Kate's epiphany is Nick's gift to her of a pink Cinderella watch identical to one she had once been given by her father. The watch clearly conveys the promise that Kate will gain back through romance the sense of protection and care associated with childhood.

23. The adaptation of romantic comedy formulae for the stardom of Will Smith requires an adjustment of Smith's self-willed military hero persona that is apparent in some of the film's moments of comedy, such as Hitch's use of a walkie-talkie to make an unconventional request to Sara for a date and when he coaches Albert to achieve his objective of "shock and awe" in impressing Allegra. These moments reinforce the fundamental male agency involved in Hitch's conceptualization and direction of worthy romantic "campaigns" and work to negotiate any potential risk of feminization that arises from placing this star in this genre.

24. Casting supports these characterizations, with James recognizable from his role on the CBS sitcom *The King of Queens* where he plays a sympathetic working-class schlub, and Valetta, a well-known supermodel, transitioning to acting roles.

25. The film's broad suspicion of and dislike for professional women is suggested by a deleted scene in which Hitch re-meets the woman who had broken his heart and is repelled by her name-dropping and efforts to tout her importance as an executive for Sotheby's.

26. "Stupid Girl" exemplifies a conspicuous trend in contemporary postfeminist rock and pop performance for female singer/songwriters to generate hits whose lyrics chastise other women. Artists including Avril Lavigne, Gwen Stefan, and Pink have all produced songs in this vein; the song in question here is by a female-fronted rock band. Its lyrics "You pretend you're high, pretend you're bored, pretend you're anything, just to be adored" underscore early on the inauthenticity of Rose's professional identity.

27. Keveney, "Hollywood Gets in Bed with Porn."

28. Rothman, *Neon Metropolis: How Las Vegas Started the Twenty-First Century*, p. 99. While I identify this as a national phenomenon, it is worth noting that it is also being internationalized to some extent as well. In London the promotion of such clubs touts their import status and they are deemed "American-style gentlemen's clubs."

29. For one account of [straight] women patronizing a strip club see Kitty Bean Yancey, "Stripping's New Side," in which Yancey contends that "stripping itself, once a forbidden topic in polite circles, is now strutting into the mainstream, propelled by pop culture and the loosening of societal taboos." http://www.usatoday.com/life/2003-10-27-strip-clubs_x.htm

30. Levy, *Female Chauvinist Pigs: Women and the Rise of Raunch Culture*, pp. 26–27.

31. Paul, *Pornified: How Pornography Is Transforming Our Lives, Our Relationships and Our Families*, p. 10.

32. Ibid., p. 64.

33. Ibid., p. 53.

34. Luckett, "Playboy Feminism? Hugh Hefner and *The Girls Next Door*."

35. Whelehan, *Overloaded: Popular Culture and the Future of Feminism*, p. 110.

36. Denizet-Lewis, "Whatever Happened to Teen Romance?" p. 30.

37. Flanagan, *To Hell with All That: Loving and Loathing Our Inner Housewife*, p. 74.

38. Ibid., p. 201.

39. See Ehrenreich and Hochschild, *Global Woman: Nannies, Maids, and Sex Workers in the New Economy*.

40. Flanagan, *To Hell with All That: Loving and Loathing Our Inner Housewife*, p. 76.

41. Ibid., p. 150.

42. Ibid., p. 143. Here and elsewhere Flanagan writes in a tone of moderate ambivalence, vacillating between an ironic awareness of the traditionalism of her position as mother, wife, and domestic staff-employer and an enchantment with that very position. *To Hell with All That* is deeply frustrating in its postfeminist evasiveness as Flanagan repeatedly identifies a concern or anxiety about current ideals of motherhood, family life, or consumer culture but then represses that concern through sentimentalization. Flanagan means to "score points" with her reader for her honesty and ambivalence while essentially never deviating from a highly conformist script in which women's only truly meaningful rewards are achieved in making a home, emotionally supporting a husband, and nurturing children.

43. Ibid., pp. 48–49.

44. Public condemnation of Deborah Eappen may have also, for some, carried a racist tint given that her husband Sunil Eappen was from India and theirs was a conspicuously "mixed-race" marriage.

45. Eisenberg, "Childlessness Equals Accountability?" p. 1.

46. See Grant, "Rich and Strange: The Yuppie Horror Film."

47. Hale, "Long-Suffering Professional Females: The Case of Nanny Lit," pp. 114–117.

48. Kline, *White House Nannies: True Tales from the Other Department of Homeland Security*, p. 7.

49. For an account of "underling lit" see Alessandra Stanley, "Revenge of the Underling Becomes a Literary Genre."

50. This phrase is used in the jacket copy of Hansen's *You'll Never Nanny in This Town Again?* Although Hansen's nannying career took place in the late 1980s the implication is that her observations of 15 years ago bear in a timely way on current Hollywood culture.

51. Ibid., p. 133.

52. For a history of flight attendant labor, activism, and changing industrial and cultural status see Kathleen M. Barry's scrupulously researched *Femininity in Flight: A History of Flight Attendants*.

53. Court, "'Coffee, Tea or Me?' Back from Blue Yonder of '67," *USA Today*, June 3, 2003.

54. In this series authored by Helen Wells and Julie Tatham, Vicki even learns to pilot a small plane in her spare time. I thank Yvonne Tasker for bringing the series to my attention.

55. This image of sexual availability was centralized in 1960s and 1970s airline advertising campaigns such as National Airlines' "Fly Me" and Continental's "We Really Move Our Tail for You."

56. In this respect the stereotype was often internationalized so that the flight attendant was no longer automatically cast by popular culture as an American woman. Indeed nationalized/ethnicized fantasies of female sexuality tended to color such depictions, producing, for example, the stereotype of the Scandinavian stewardess whose casual attitudes towards sex and new international mobility were defining attributes of her fantasy figuration.

57. She was also decidedly de-glamorized. Where once the figure of the purposeful, precise stewardess dominated popular understanding of the aviation industry, by the 1990s this narrative of flight attendant exceptionalism seemed to have thoroughly broken down and she had become merely another kind of service worker in an industry where passenger experience had broadly moved from "special" to "casual."

58. For perceptive discussion of the recent reality television series in which a nanny comes to the rescue of a beleaguered American family, see "Elevating Servants, Elevating American Families" by L. S. Kim and "Nanny TV" by Laurie Ouellette. Both appear on the electronic forum *Flow: A Critical Forum on Television and Media* Vol. 1 Issues 12 and 11 respectively.

59. Thurlow and Jaworski, "The Alchemy of the Upwardly Mobile: Symbolic Capital and the Stylization of Elites in Frequent-Flyer Programmes," p. 102.

60. Ibid., p. 122.

61. See "New Retro Look for BA Staff," CNNInternational.com.

62. The image of the entitled male business traveler is peculiarly and distinctively embodied by CNN Europe's Richard Qwest who hosts a program called *Business International* for the network. Quest's robustly self-satisfied persona is put to use exploring new airports, travel amenities, and the business lifestyle in general. His hearty style of delivery, hyperbolic Britishness, and gushing embrace of service expansions for the privileged as forms of innovation help to reify the gendered/classed dynamics of business travel.

63. For a discussion of the segmentation of the aviation industry into "mass transit" services, business class, and private executive travel, as well as the trend toward business-only flights, see Roger Collis, "What the Future Holds in Worldwide Air Travel."

64. In their shrewd analysis of the rhetoric of frequent-flyer programs, Thurlow and Jaworski have observed that the materials related to such programs represent women only as accompanying partners or flight attendants. They contend that "the world according to frequent-flyer programs is a patently masculine, heterosexual one." "The Alchemy of the Upwardly Mobile: Symbolic Capital and the Stylization of Elites in Frequent-Flyer Programmes," p. 123.

65. Two separate female callers to Britain's Radio One on July 10, 2004 identified themselves as Virgin Airlines employees paid to massage first-class passengers and who had worked on flights taken by members of Busted. Each caller reported proudly that she believed herself to be the inspiration for "Air Hostess."

66. See Craig Wilson, "Hooters and Those Wings to Take Wing," *USA Today*, February 27, 2003.

67. See Ben Mutzabaugh, "Today in the Sky," *USA Today*, December 8, 2004. An August, 2003 *New York Times* article by Elizabeth Olson placed the reporter as a passenger on one of Hooters Air's early flights. Olsen observed "The Hooters Air concept might be politically incorrect," but noted that for male travelers "being fussed over by two scantily clad females on loan from the Hooters restaurant can be a diversion from the usual problems of flying. And if conversations with Hooters passengers last week were any guide their wives or girlfriends just take the whole thing in stride."

68. See "Flight Attendant Unions Dislike Foster Movie," *St. Petersburg Times*. Online October 2, 2005, http://www.sptimes.com/2005/10/02/Floridian/Film_briefs_Flight_ashtml. *Flightplan* was part of a renewed Hollywood interest (five years after 9/11) in the airplane thriller. In films like *Redeye* (2005), *Flight 93* (2006), and *Snakes on a Plane* (2006) as well as the ABC television drama *Lost* (whose cast is made up of a disparate group who find themselves on a mysterious island after a plane crash), this theme engaged, according to one critic, a widespread American fear of strangers and the question of who might be sitting next to you in the vulnerable environment of an airplane. See Breznican, "Fear in Flight."

69. This is not to suggest that television has been inattentive to the remaking of air travel. Series such as *Seconds to Disaster*, *Air Crash Investigation*, and *When Planes Crash* for instance elaborately reconstruct aviation disasters.

70. John Leland, "The Airport as a Laboratory," *International Herald Tribune*, July 13, 2004, p. 20.

71. Dowd, "Wanted: Powerful Male Looking for Maid to Marry," p. 7.

5 HYPERDOMESTICITY, SELF-CARE, AND THE WELL-LIVED LIFE IN POSTFEMINISM

1. Whelehan, *Overloaded: Popular Culture and the Future of Feminism*, p. 4.
2. King, *Pink Ribbons, Inc.: Breast Cancer and the Politics of Philanthropy*, p. 99.
3. Scott, "Life at the Top in America Isn't Just Better, It's Longer," p. 29.
4. On the spa industry's cultivation of young clients, see Deborah Schwabe, "Teen Spa Trends: Day Spas Are Becoming Teen Territory." Schwabe writes that "More than ever teens are getting their eyebrow waxes and even bikini lines. What was once a more requested service with the adult crowd, teens are seeing how quick and easy an eyebrow wax can be. Clean lines in the summer time make a bikini wax a popular choice." Implicit in Schwabe's language (for instance her use of the phrase "clean lines") is the notion that to choose to go without such depilatory functions is to be unhygienic.
5. Newman, "Depilatory Market Moves Far Beyond the Short-Shorts Wearers," p. C3.
6. Steinhauer, "When the Joneses Wear Jeans," pp. 144–145.
7. Singer, "Not to Be Outdone: The New Urban Spa."
8. Kang, "The Managed Hand: The Commercialization of Bodies and Emotions in Korean Immigrant-Owned Nail Salons," p. 836.
9. Ibid., p. 823.
10. Brooks, "'Under the Knife and Proud of It': An Analysis of the Normalization of Cosmetic Surgery," p. 24.
11. Rubin, "Buoyed by Bigger Breasts."
12. Singer, "Is the 'Mom Job' Really Necessary?"
13. Lasertreatments.com home page.
14. "Pole Dancing Shows up in Health Clubs."
15. Ibid.
16. Goodman, "Trend Alert: Strip Aerobics."
17. Cardoze, "Teaching People to Take It Off—Pounds, Too"
18. Goodman, "Trend Alert: Strip Aerobics."
19. "Mom of the Month," http://iparenting.com/moms/3912.php.
20. http://www.partypop.com/vendors/4059235.htm
21. Kipnis, *The Female Thing: Dirt, Sex, Envy, Vulnerability*, p. 67.
22. Barker, "Makeovers Change Lives, Not Just Looks."
23. See for instance Elizabeth A. Ford and Deborah C. Mitchell's *The Makeover in Movies: Before and After in Hollywood Films, 1941–2002*, as well as Angela Dancey, "Before and After: The Makeover in Film and Culture," PhD dissertation, Department of Women's Studies, Ohio State University, 2005.
24. Weber, "Beauty, Desire and Anxiety: The Economy of Sameness in ABC's *Extreme Makeover*."
25. Ibid.
26. Tasker and Negra, "Feminist Politics and Postfeminist Culture," in *Interrogating Postfeminism: Gender and the Politics of Popular Culture*, p. 13.
27. Schor, "The New Politics of Consumption: Why Americans Want So Much More Than They Need," p. 194.
28. *The Substance of Style: How the Rise of Aesthetic Value Is Remaking Commerce, Culture, and Consciousness*, p. 21.
29. Thurlow and Jaworski, "The Alchemy of the Upwardly Mobile: Symbolic Capital and the Stylization of Elites in Frequent-Flyer Programmes," pp. 115 and 117 respectively.
30. Ibid., p. 127.
31. *The Substance of Style: How the Rise of Aesthetic Value Is Remaking Commerce, Culture, and Consciousness*, p. 186.

32. King, *Pink Ribbons, Inc.: Breast Cancer and the Politics of Philanthropy*, p. 45.
33. David Campbell uses this phrase in his article "The Biopolitics of Security: Oil, Empire, and the Sports Utility Vehicle," p. 945.
34. Ibid., p. 938.
35. Ibid., p. 967.
36. Schor, "The New Politics of Consumption: Why Americans Want So Much More Than They Need," p. 185.
37. Kendall, "Twenty-Four Karat Gold Frames: Lifestyles of the Rich and Famous," p. 53.
38. Steinhauer, "When the Joneses Wear Jeans," p. 135.
39. Wegenstein, *Getting Under the Skin: The Body and Media Theory*, p. 89.
40. Roseberry, "The Rise of Yuppie Coffees and the Reimagination of Class in the United States," p. 123.
41. http://www.destination.kohler.com/spa
42. Flanagan, *To Hell With All That: Loving and Loathing Our Inner Housewife*, p. 192.
43. Ibid., p. 200.
44. *Home Comforts: The Art and Science of Keeping House*, p. 7.
45. Ibid., p. 8.
46. Ibid., p. 9.
47. Ray is not Winfrey's first postfeminist spinoff figure. That would be the authoritarian Texan psychologist "Dr. Phil" (Phil McGraw) whose own daytime talkshow/book success came after a long series of appearances as a featured guest on *The Oprah Winfrey Show*. To watch Phil McGraw practicing his form of "tough love," berating and hectoring female guests for their emotional misconduct, is to experience a deep sense of squeamishness.
48. "Consumer Guides and the Invention of Lifestyle," in *Point of Purchase: How Shopping Changed American Culture*, p. 172.
49. Ibid., p. 173.
50. See Hoy, *Chasing Dirt: The American Pursuit of Cleanliness*.
51. This is not to say that such services cannot be used transgressively. Indeed wikipedia. org reports that the Smoking Gun informational website managed to use the service to produce stamps featuring Jimmy Hoffa, Ted Kaczynski, and Monica Lewinsky's infamous stained dress.
52. Martin, *Financialization of Daily Life*, p. 195.
53. Lewis, "Family Compounds: Haven or Hassle?"
54. Although the film repeatedly tells us that the family name "Portokalos" means "orange" in Greek, to an English speaker the word sounds like nothing so much as the term portcullis, the fortified entrance of medieval castles. Its use adds a suggestive resonance to the film's hyperfamilial and retreatist thematics. This point was made by Oliver Gruner, a graduate student in my class when we studied the film.
55. Of course the American self-help industry encompasses much more than print material and when this is borne in mind the scope of the industry is truly remarkable. Wikipedia reports that "research firm Marketdata estimates the 'self-improvement' market as worth $8.5 billion in 2003—including infomercials, mail-order catalogues, holistic institutes, books, audio cassettes, motivational speaker seminars, the personal coaching market, weight-loss, and stress-management programs.
56. Blackman, *Self-Help Books: Why Americans Keep Reading Them*, p. 64. Dolby discusses the concept of the "simple self" in self-help books on pp. 66–68.
57. Books such as *The Rules* modify some of the formulae presented in earlier primers, including notably Helen Gurley Brown's 1962 *Sex and the Single Girl* although Brown's book underscored the importance of career and financial autonomy in a way that the postfeminist advice literature generally does not. In a consummate display of postfeminist media synergy *He's Just Not That into You* has been adapted into a

film with a high-profile cast including Ben Affleck, Jennifer Aniston, and Drew Barrymore which will be released in 2008.

58. Fein and Schneider, *The Rules: Time-Tested Secrets for Capturing the Heart of Mr. Right*, pp. 19–20.
59. Blackman, "Self-Help, Media Cultures and the Production of Female Psychopathology," p. 228.
60. Currie, Dunn, and Fogarty, "The Fading Dream: Economic Crisis and New Inequality," p. 331.
61. Morris, *It's A Sprawl World after All: The Human Cost of Unplanned Growth and Visions of a Better Future*, p. 47.
62. Pappano, *The Connection Gap: Why Americans Feel So Alone*, p. 8 (original emphasis).
63. "Isolated Americans Trying to Connect," *USA Today*, August 5, 2006.
64. Travis, "'It Will Change the World if Everybody Reads This Book': New Thought Religion in Oprah's Book Club," p. 1037.
65. Dylan McDermott's wife, Shiva Rose, who receives regular attention in the magazine is a useful example in this regard. Also among *InStyle*'s most regularly featured figures is Kelly Preston, the actress wife of John Travolta, and the object of devoted coverage for her clothing, home, pregnancy, and fitness tips.
66. Collins, "No (Popular) Place Like Home?" in *High-Pop: Making Culture into Popular Entertainment*, p. 182.
67. Garber, *Sex and Real Estate: Why We Love Houses*, p. 148.
68. Saporito, "Inside the New American Home," pp. 65–66.
69. Certainly one of *InStyle*'s most striking features is the sheer comprehensiveness of the magazine's tips for social conduct. A regular feature profiling a celebrity party is accompanied by detailed tips for re-enacting the event. Readers are told, for instance, what music to (buy and) play, what food to prepare, how to arrange the table, and what schedule to keep to. Implicitly, of course, these layouts also instruct on what occasions are worth celebrating and how.
70. This occurs for instance in the April 2002 issue where a profile of Melanie Griffith and Antonio Banderas' palatial 1926 villa in Los Angeles emphasizes Griffith's oversight of the renovation and decoration project they commissioned before moving in. The article notes "the actress called on an old friend, Mela Eventoff, an interior designer based in Bellingham, Wash., who helped her combine Old World drama with modern comfort" (p. 404).
71. Collins, *High-Pop: Making Culture into Popular Entertainment*, p. 18.
72. Brunell, "The Adweek Top 10 Hot List."
73. Other manifestations of this phenomenon would include the highly successful *Rosie O'Donnell Show* (1996–2002) and its successor *The Ellen DeGeneres Show* (2003–), as well as the long-running *Larry King Live* on CNN, all of which exhibit a warm, adulatory approach to the celebrity interview.
74. Glynn, *Tabloid Culture: Trash Taste, Popular Power, and the Transformation of American Television*, p. 7.
75. In what I would see as a related development, major film and television stars now increasingly do voicework for television ads (see "Flashes," *Entertainment Weekly*, 682, November 15, 2002, p. 18). While not compromising their identity capital visually, this new acceptability of celebrity sponsorship marks a change in the previously established boundaries of upper-end stardom, and suggests another way in which stardom now migrates into other consumer categories. When a star's domestic privacy and family values are constructed as "impeccable" she becomes free to openly shill product in television ads—witness Catherine Zeta-Jones' work on behalf of T-Mobile cellular phone service.
76. See Brooks' effort at "comic sociology" *Bobos in Paradise: The New Upper Class and How They Got There*, p. 40.

77. See Read Mercer Schuchardt, "Understanding Road Rage."
78. Pappano, *The Connection Gap: Why Americans Feel So Alone*, p. 16.
79. Ivry, "More Homeowners, More Luxury, More Moving," p. D6.
80. Schor, "What's Wrong with Consumer Society?: Competitive Spending and the 'New Consumerism,'" p. 45.
81. Frank, *Luxury Fever: Money and Happiness in an Era of Excess*, p. 3.
82. See Krugman, "For Richer: How the Permissive Capitalism of the Boom Destroyed American Equality."
83. Whelehan, *Overloaded: Popular Culture and the Future of Feminism*, p. 178.

Bibliography

Ali, Lorraine and Julie Scelfo. "Choosing Virginity." *Newsweek* December 9, 2002, pp. 61–62.

Ames, Mark. *Going Postal: Rage, Murder, and Rebellion from Reagan's Workplaces to Clinton's Columbine and Beyond*. Brooklyn, NY: Soft Skull Press, 2005.

Applebome, Peter. *Dixie Rising: How the South Is Shaping American Values, Politics, and Culture*. New York: Random House, 1996.

Armour, Stephanie. "More Companies Downsize Family-Friendly Programs." *USA Today* October 19, 2003.

Armour, Stephanie. "Pregnant Workers Report Growing Discrimination." *USA Today* February 16, 2005, http://www.usatoday.com/money/workplace/2005-02-16-pregnancy-bias-usat_x.htm

Armour, Stephanie. "Job Opening? Work-at-Home Moms Fill Bill." *USA Today* July 20, 2005, http://www.usatoday.com/money/jobcenter/2005-07-19-call-center-moms-usat_x.htm

Armour, Stephanie. "Your Appearance Can Affect Size of Your Paycheck." *USA Today* July 20, 2005, http://www.usatoday.com/money/workplace/2005-07-19-bias-usat_x.htm

Arnold, Thomas K. "Women Hot Target for DVD Sales." *USA Today* May 10, 2004.

Arthurs, Jane. "Sex Workers Incorporated." In *Feminism in Popular Culture*, eds Joanne Hollows and Rachel Moseley. Oxford and New York: Berg, 2006, pp. 119–139.

Badie, Rick. "Making the Most of Fame's 15 Minutes." *Atlanta Journal-Constitution* June 19, 2005, p. JJ3.

Bagby, Meredith. *Rational Exuberance: The Influence of Generation X on the New American Economy*. New York: Penguin, 1998.

Banner, Lois W. *American Beauty*. Chicago: University of Chicago Press, 1984.

Barash, Susan Shapiro. *Tripping the Prom Queen: The Truth about Women and Rivalry*. New York: St. Martin's Griggin, 2007.

Barker, Olivia. "Makeovers Change Lives, Not Just Looks." *USA Today* July 30, 2003, http://www.usatoday.com/life/2003-07-30-makeover.main_x.htm

Barker, Olivia. "The Young and the Wed List." *USA Today* April 6, 2004, p. 9B.

Barker, Olivia. "Fountains of Wayne Has One Splashy Mama." *USA Today* January 27, 2005.

Barker, Olivia. "Mommie Hottest." *USA Today* January 27, 2005.

Barry, Kathleen M. *Femininity in Flight: A History of Flight Attendants*. Durham: Duke University Press, 2007.

Beckman, Karen. *Vanishing Women: Magic, Film, and Feminism*. Durham: Duke University Press, 2003.

Behrendt, Greg and Liz Tuccillo. *He's Just Not That into You: The No-Excuses Truth to Understanding Guys*. New York: Simon Spotlight Entertainment, 2004.

Belkin, Lisa. "The Opt-Out Revolution." *The New York Times Magazine* October 26, 2003, pp. 42–47, 58, 85–86.

Bellafante, Ginia. "When Midlife Seems Just an Empty Plate." *The New York Times* March 9, 2003, section 9, pp. 1, 4.

Blackman, Lisa. "Self-Help, Media Cultures and the Production of Female Psychopathology." *European Journal of Cultural Studies* 7(2) (2004), pp. 219–236.

Blum, Virginia L. *Flesh Wounds: The Culture of Cosmetic Surgery*. Berkeley: University of California Press, 2003.

Boden, Sharon. *Consumerism, Romance, and the Wedding Experience*. New York: Palgrave Macmillan, 2003.

Boo, Katherine. "The Marriage Cure." *The New Yorker* August 18 and 25, 2003, pp. 104–120.

Boteach, Shmuley. *Kosher Sex: A Recipe for Passion and Intimacy*. New York: Main Street Books, 2000.

Boteach, Shmuley. *Hating Women: America's Hostile Campaign against the Fairer Sex*. New York: Regan Books, 2005.

Brenner, Johanna. *Women and the Politics of Class*. New York: Monthly Review Press, 2000.

Breznican, Anthony. "Fear in Flight." *USA Today* August 22, 2005, http://www.usatoday.com/life/movies/news/2005-08-18-plane-movies-cover_x.htm

Bronfen, Elisabeth. *Home in Hollywood: The Imaginary Geography of Cinema*. New York: Columbia University Press, 2004.

Brooks, Abigail. "'Under the Knife and Proud of It': An Analysis of the Normalization of Cosmetic Surgery." In *Culture, Power, and History: Studies in Critical Sociology*, eds Stephen Pfohl, Aimee Van Wagenen, Patricia Arend, Abigail Brooks, and Denise Leckenby. Boston: Brill, 2006, pp. 23–58.

Brooks, David. *Bobos in Paradise: The New Upper Class and How They Got There*. New York: Simon and Schuster, 2001.

Brooks, David. "Our Way: Root and Hoot." *The New York Times* October 14, 2003.

Brown, Helen Gurley. *Sex and the Single Girl*. New York: Giant Cardinal, 1962.

Brunell, Richard. "The AdWeek Top 10 Hot List." *Brandweek* March 5, 2001.

Burlein, Ann. *Lift High the Cross: Where White Supremacy and the Christian Right Converge*. Durham: Duke University Press, 2002.

Campbell, David. "The Biopolitics of Security: Oil, Empire, and the Sports Utility Vehicle." *American Quarterly* 57(3) (September 2005), pp. 943–972.

Cardoze, Christina. "Teaching People to Take It Off—Pounds, Too." Columbia News Service, February 22, 2002, http://www.jrn.columbia.edu/studentwork/cns/2002-02-22/224.asp

Carpenter, Richard P. "For the Betrothed or Runaway Brides: Packages That Are Expensive, or Not?" *Boston Globe* June 5, 2005, p. M4.

Carr, David. "To Reach the Heights, First Be Male." *The New York Times* January 9, 2006, pp. C1, C3.

Charles, Maria and David B. Grusky. "The Past, Present, and Future of Occupational Ghettos." In *Occupational Ghettos: The Worldwide Segregation of Women and Men*. Stanford: Stanford University Press, 2005.

Cheever, Susan. "Baby Battle." In *Mommy Wars: Stay-at-Home and Career Moms Face Off on Their Choices, Their Lives, Their Families*, ed. Leslie Morgan Steiner. New York: Random House, 2006, pp. 37–43.

Chura, Hillary. "Here Comes the Baby, and an Itch to Overbuy." *The New York Times* January 8, 2006, p. 6.

Cobb, James C. *Away Down South: A History of Southern Identity*. Oxford: Oxford University Press, 2005.

Collins, Jim, ed. "No (Popular) Place Like Home?" In *High-Pop: Making Culture into Popular Entertainment*. Malden, MA: Blackwell, 2002.

Collis, Roger. "What the Future Holds in Worldwide Air Travel." *International Herald Tribune* March 25, 2005, p. 10.

Correspondents of *The New York Times, Class Matters*. New York: Henry Holt & Co., 2005.

Court, Ayesha. "'Coffee, Tea or Me?': Back From Wild Blue Yonder of '67." *USA Today* June 3, 2003.

Covey, Stephen R. *How to Develop a Family Mission Statement*. Provo, UT: Covey Leadership Center, 1996.

Currie, Elliott, Robert Dunn, and David Fogarty. "The Fading Dream: Economic Crisis and New Inequality." In *Women, Class, and the Feminist Imagination: A Socialist-Feminist Reader*, eds Karen V. Hansen and Ilene J. Philipson. Philadelphia: Temple University Press, 1990, pp. 319–337.

Damon-Moore, Helen. *Magazines for the Millions: Gender and Commerce in the Ladies' Home Journal and the Saturday Evening Post 1880–1910*. Albany: SUNY Press, 1994.

Dancey, Angela. "Before and After: The Makeover in Film and Culture." PhD dissertation, Department of Women's Studies, Ohio State University, 2005.

Danziger, Pamela. *Let Them Eat Cake: Marketing Luxury to the Masses*. New York: Kaplan Business, 2004.

Denby, David. "American Dreamers." *The New Yorker* September 1, 2003, p. 131.

Denby, David. "Night and Day." *The New Yorker* November 8, 2004, pp. 145–147.

Denizet-Lewis, Benoit. "Whatever Happened to Teen Romance?" *The New York Times Magazine* May 30, 2004, pp. 29–35, 54, 56, 58.

DePaulo, Bella. *Singled Out: How Singles Are Stereotyped, Stigmatized, and Ignored, and Still Live Happily Ever After*. New York: St. Martin's Press, 2006.

Dixon, Simon. "Ambiguous Ecologies: Stardom's Domestic Mise-en-Scene." *Cinema Journal* 42(2) (Winter 2003), pp. 81–100.

Dolby, Sandra K. *Self-Help Books: Why Americans Keep Reading Them*. Urbana: University of Illinois Press, 2005.

Douglas, Susan and Meredith W. Michaels. *The Mommy Myth: The Idealization of Motherhood and How It Has Undermined Women*. New York: Free Press, 2004.

Dowd, Maureen. "Wanted: Powerful Male Looking for Maid to Marry." *The International Herald Tribune* January 14, 2005, p. 7.

Dowd, Maureen. "From McBeal to McDreamy." *The New York Times* May 17, 2006, p. A23.

Dribben, Melissa and Natalie Pompilio. "Sweet 16 Party: Pricey." *The Philadelphia Inquirer* March 12, 2006.

Dutton, Judy. "Meet the New Housewife Wanna-Bes." *Cosmopolitan* June 2000, pp. 164–167.

Ehrenreich, Barbara and Arlie Russell Hochschild. *Global Woman: Nannies, Maids and Sex Workers in the New Economy*. London: Granta, 2002.

Ehrenreich, Barbara. *Bait and Switch: The (Futile) Pursuit of the American Dream*. New York: Metropolitan Books, 2005.

Eisenberg, Rebecca. "Childlessness Equals Accountability?" reprinted from *The Harvard Law Record* February 26, 1993, http://www.omino.com/~dom/clips/zoe.html

El Nasser, Haya. "For More Parents, 3 Kids Are a Charm." *USA Today* March 9, 2004.

Elliott, Chris. "Looking for Friendly Skies?: Stay on the Ground." *The New York Times* August 23, 2005, p. C8.

Epstein, Rebecca. "Sharon Stone in a Gap Turtleneck." In *Hollywood Goes Shopping*. Minneapolis: University of Minnesota Press, 2000, pp. 179–204.

Farhi, Paul. "Elizabeth Vargas, Exiting Stage Center." *The Washington Post* May 29, 2006, p. C07.

Farkas, Carol-Ann. "Bodies at Rest, Bodies in Motion: Physical Competence, Women's Fitness and Feminism" *Genders* 45 (Spring 2007).

Fein, Ellen and Sherrie Schneider, *The Rules: Time-Tested Secrets for Capturing the Heart of Mr. Right*. New York: Warner Books, 1995.

Felleman, Susan. *Art in the Cinematic Imagination*. Austin: University of Texas Press, 2005.

Fisher, Melissa S. and Greg Downey, eds. *Frontiers of Capital: Ethnographic Reflections on the New Economy*. Durham: Duke University Press, 2006.

Flanagan, Caitlin. "Bringing up Baby." *The New Yorker* November 15, 2004, pp. 46–48, 50, 52.

Flanagan, Caitlin. *To Hell with All That: Loving and Loathing Our Inner Housewife*. New York: Little, Brown & Co., 2006.

"Flashes." *Entertainment Weekly* 682 November 15, 2002, p. 18.

"Flight Attendant Unions Dislike Foster Movie." *St. Petersburg Times*. Online October 2, 2005, http://www.sptimes.com/2005/10/02/Floridian/Film_briefs_Flight_ashtml

Ford, Elizabeth A. and Deborah C. Mitchell. *The Makeover in Movies: Before and After in Hollywood Films, 1941–2002*. Jefferson, NC: McFarland & Co., 2004.

Fraiman, Susan. *Cool Men and the Second Sex*. New York: Columbia University Press, 2003.

Frank, Katherine. *G-Strings and Sympathy: Strip Club Regulars and Male Desire*. Durham: Duke University Press, 2002.

Frank, Robert H. *Luxury Fever: Why Money Fails to Satisfy in an Era of Excess*. New York: Free Press, 1999.

Frank, Robert H. and Phillip J. Cook. *The Winner-Take-All Society*. New York: Free Press, 2005.

Fraser, Jill Andresky. *White-Collar Sweatshop: The Deterioration of Work and Its Rewards in Corporate America*. New York: W. W. Norton & Co., 2001.

Freeman, Elizabeth. *The Wedding Complex: Forms of Belonging in Modern American Culture*. Durham: Duke University Press, 2002.

Freydkin, Donna. "Flight Attendants Are Really Taking Off." *USA Today* March 21, 2003.

Freydkin, Donna. "These Serial Dads Have Full Houses." *USA Today* September 28, 2005.

Garber, Marjorie. *Sex and Real Estate: Why We Love Houses*. New York: Pantheon, 2000.

Garrett, Roberta. *Postmodern Chick Flicks: The Return of the Woman's Film*. Basingstoke: Palgrave Macmillan, 2007.

Gates, Anita. "There's No Place Like Home." *TV Guide* October 14–20, 2000, pp. 7–21, 59.

Geller, Jaclyn. *Here Comes the Bride: Women, Weddings, and the Marriage Mystique*. New York: Four Walls Eight Windows, 2001.

Ghirardini, John. "Jittery Bride-to-Be Spells Green for Retailers." *Atlanta Journal Constitution* June 4, 2005, p. E2.

Giroux, Henry A. "The Conservative Assault on America: Cultural Politics, Education and the New Authoritarianism." *Cultural Politics* 1(2) (2005), pp. 139–164.

Glynn, Kevin. *Tabloid Culture: Trash Taste, Popular Power, and the Transformation of American Television*. Durham: Duke University Press, 2000.

Goodman, Abbey. "Trend Alert: Strip Aerobics." IVillage Diet and Fitness, http://diet. ivillage.com/workouts/0,,79rwbc87-p,00.html

Grant, Barry Keith. "Rich and Strange: The Yuppie Horror Film." *Journal of Film and Video* 48(1/2) (Spring–Summer 1996), pp. 4–16.

Gross, Daniel. "Northeast of Eden." http://slate.msn.com/id/2089990/

Gross, Jane. "Forget the Career: My Parents Need Me at Home." *The New York Times* November 24, 2005, pp. A1, A28.

Hage, Ghassan. "'Comes a Time We Are All Enthusiasm': Understanding Palestinian Suicide Bombers in Times of Exighophobia." *Public Culture* 15(1) (2003), pp. 65–89.

Hale, Elizabeth. "Long-Suffering Female Professionals: The Case of Nanny Lit." In *Chick Lit: The New Woman's Fiction*, eds Suzanne Ferriss and Mallory Young. New York: Routledge, 2006, pp. 103–118.

Hansen, Suzanne. *You'll Never Nanny in This Town Again*. 2nd edition. New York: Crown Publishers, 2005.

Heller, Agnes. "Where We Are at Home." *Thesis Eleven* 41 (1995).

Hewett, Heather. "You Are Not Alone: The Personal, the Political, and the 'New' Mommy Lit." In *Chick Lit: The New Woman's Fiction*, eds Suzanne Ferriss and Mallory Young. New York: Routledge, 2006, pp. 119–139.

Hewlett, Sylvia Ann. *Creating a Life: Professional Women and the Quest for Children*. New York: Talk Miramax, 2002.

Hochschild, Arlie Russell. *The Managed Heart: Commercialization of Human Feeling*. Berkeley: University of California Press.

Holahan, Catherine. "Actresses Inspire All Women to Sail Past 40 with Confidence." *The Providence Journal* June 28, 2006, p. H9.

Hollows, Joanne. "Can I Go Home Yet?: Feminism, Postfeminism and Domesticity." Paper delivered at Interrogating Postfeminism: Gender and the Politics of Popular Culture conference, University of East Anglia, April, 2004.

Horovitz, Bruce. "Middle Class Buys into Lap of Luxury." *USA Today* January 31–February 2, 2003, pp. 1A–2A.

Horowitz, Daniel. *The Anxieties of Affluence: Critiques of American Consumer Culture, 1939–1979*. Amherst: University of Massachusetts Press, 2004.

Howell, Jeremy and Alan Ingham. "From Social Problem to Personal Issue: The Language of Lifestyle." *Cultural Studies* 15 (2001), pp. 326–351.

Hoy, Suellen. *Chasing Dirt: The American Pursuit of Cleanliness*. New York and Oxford: Oxford University Press, 1995.

Ingraham, Chrys. *White Weddings: Romancing Heterosexuality in Popular Culture*. New York: Routledge, 1999.

"Isolated Americans Trying to Connect." *USA Today* August 5, 2006, http://www.usa-today.com/news/nation/2006-08-05-lonely-americans_x.htm

Ivry, Sara. "More Homeowners, More Luxury, More Moving." *The New York Times* February 15, 2002, Nesting: a special section, p. D6.

Iyer, Pico. "The New Business Class." *The New York Times Magazine* March 8, 1998, p 27.

Jacobs, Jerry A. and Kathleen Gerson. *The Time Divide: Work, Family, and Gender Inequality.* Cambridge, MA: Harvard University Press, 2004.

Jayson, Sharon. "Autism Shouts in this Family." *USA Today* March 29, 2005, pp. 8B, 9B.

Jefferson, Margo. "The Return of the Shrew, and Other TV Woes." *The New York Times* September 5, 2005, p. E5.

Jeffords, Susan. "Breakdown: White Masculinity, Class, and US Action-Adventure Films." In *Action and Adventure Cinema*, ed. Yvonne Tasker. London: Routledge, 2004, pp. 219–234.

Kang, Milliann. "The Managed Hand: The Commercialization of Bodies and Emotions in Korean Immigrant-Owned Nail Salons." *Gender & Society* 17(6) (December 2003), pp. 820–839.

Karlyn, Kathleen. "*Scream*, Popular Culture, and Feminism's Third Wave: 'I'm Not My Mother.'" *Genders* 38 (2003).

Karlyn, Kathleen. "'Too Close for Comfort': *American Beauty* and the Incest Motif." *Cinema Journal* 44(1) (Fall 2004), pp. 69–93.

Katz, Cindi. "The State Goes Home: Local Hypervigilance of Children and the Global Retreat from Social Reproduction." *Social Justice* 28(3) (2001), pp. 47–55.

Katz, Stephen and Barbara Marshall. "New Sex for Old: Lifestyle, Consumerism, and the Ethics of Aging Well." *Journal of Aging Studies* 17 (2003), pp. 3–16.

Kelly, Katy. "Princess for the Post-Feminist Generation." *USA Today* September 2, 1997, p. A20.

Kendall, Diana. "Twenty-Four Karat Gold Frames: Lifestyles of the Rich and Famous." In *Framing Class: Media Representations of Wealth and Poverty in America.* Lanham, MD: Rowman & Littlefield, 2005, pp. 21–57.

Keveney, Bill. "Hollywood Gets in Bed with Porn." *USA Today* October 16, 2003, http://www.usatoday.com/life/2003-10-16-porn_x.htm.

Kiley, David. "Chrysler Bets Big on Dion's Auto Endorsement Deal." *USA Today* June 8, 2003.

Kim, L. S. "Elevating Servants, Elevating American Families." *Flow: A Critical Forum on Television and Media* 1(12) (2005).

King, Samantha. *Pink Ribbons, Inc.: Breast Cancer and the Politics of Philanthropy.* Minneapolis: University of Minnesota Press, 2006.

Kipnis, Laura. *The Female Thing: Dirt, Sex, Envy, Vulnerability.* New York: Pantheon Books, 2006.

Klaver, Elizabeth. *Sites of Autopsy in Contemporary Culture.* Albany: SUNY Press, 2005.

Klein, Joe. "The Strip Is Back!" *Time* 164(4) (August 2, 2004), pp. 48–56.

Klein, Naomi. *No Logo: No Space, No Choice, No Jobs.* New York: Harper Collins, 2000.

Kline, Barbara. *White House Nannies: True Tales from the Other Department of Homeland Security.* New York: Penguin, 2005.

Kobrin, Sandy. "More Women Seek Vaginal Plastic Surgery." *Women's ENews* November 14, 2004.

Kord, Susanne and Elisabeth Krimmer. "Is This as Good as It Gets?" In *Hollywood Divas, Indie Queens and TV Heroines: Contemporary Screen Images of Women.* Lanham: Rowman & Littlefield, 2005, pp. 161–168.

Kristof, Nicholas D. "Health Care? Ask Cuba." *The New York Times* January 12, 2005.

Krugman, Paul. "For Richer: How the Permissive Capitalism of the Boom Destroyed

American Equality." *The New York Times Magazine* October 20, 2002, pp. 62–68, 76, 78, 141–142.

La Ferla, Ruth. "Sexy Singles, Make Way for Glamour Moms." *The New York Times* November 10, 2002, section 9, p. 13.

Lasoff, Melanie and Manuel Roig-Franzia. "On Eve of Wedding, Ga. Bride-to-Be Still Missing." *The Washington Post* April 30, 2005, p. A2.

Leland, John. "The Airport as a Laboratory." *International Herald Tribune* July 7, 2004, p. 20.

Leonard, Suzanne. "Prematurely Gray: The 'Post-Sexual' Married Thirtysomething of Recent Cinema." Paper presented at 2006 Society for Cinema and Media Studies conference, Vancouver, Canada.

Leonard, Suzanne. "'I Hate My Job, I Hate Everybody Here': Adultery, Boredom, and the 'Working Girl' in Twenty-First Century American Cinema." In *Interrogating Postfeminism: Gender and the Politics of Popular Culture*, eds Yvonne Tasker and Diane Negra. Durham: Duke University Press, 2007, pp. 101–131.

Leonhardt, David. "More Americans Were Uninsured and Poor in 2003, Census Finds." *The New York Times* August 27, 2004, pp. A1, A18.

Leonhardt, David. "The College Dropout Boom." In *Class Matters*, correspondents of *The New York Times*. New York: Henry Holt & Co., 2005, pp. 87–104.

Leonhardt, David. "Scant Progress on Closing Gap in Women's Pay." *The New York Times* December 24, 2006, pp. A1, A16.

Levine, Elana. "Fractured Fairy Tales and Fragmented Markets: Disney's *Weddings of a Lifetime* and the Cultural Politics of Media Conglomeration." *Television & New Media* 6(1) (February, 2005), pp. 71–88.

Levy, Ariel. *Female Chauvinist Pigs: Women and the Rise of Raunch Culture*. New York: Free Press, 2005.

Levy, Ariel. "Dirty Old Women." *New York* May 29, 2006, pp. 28–33.

Lewis, Christina S. N. "Family Compounds: Haven or Hassle?" http://www.realestate. msn.com/Buying/Article_wsj.aspx?cp-documentid=4874513&GT1=1

Loe, Meika. *The Rise of Viagra: How the Little Blue Pill Changed Sex in America*. New York: New York University Press, 2004.

Lotz, Amanda. "Postfeminist Television Criticism: Rehabilitating Critical Terms and Identifying Postfeminist Attributes." *Feminist Media Studies* 1(1) (2001).

Lotz, Amanda. *Redesigning Women: Television after the Network Era*. Urbana: University of Illinois Press, 2006.

Low, Setha. *Behind the Gates: Life, Security, and the Pursuit of Happiness in Fortress America*. New York and London: Routledge, 2003.

Low, Setha and Neil Smith. *The Politics of Public Space*. New York: Routledge, 2005.

Luckett, Moya. "Marriage as the New Trend." *Flow: A Critical Forum on Television and Media* 3(4) (October 2005).

Luckett, Moya. "Playboy Feminism?: Hugh Hefner and *The Girls Next Door*." *Flow: A Critical Forum on Television and Media* 3(8) (January 2006).

Luckett, Moya. "Life's So Good When You Have a Credit Card." *Flow: A Critical Forum on Television and Media* 4(6) (May 2006).

Lyman, Rick. "Missing Woman's Case Spurs Discussion of News Coverage." *The New York Times* August 7, 2005, p. A16.

Lyons, James. *Selling Seattle: Representing Contemporary Urban America*. London: Wallflower, 2004.

Martin, Joel W. "Anti-Feminism in Recent Apocalyptic Film." *The Journal of Religion and Film* 4(1) (April 2000).

Martin, Randy. *Financialization of Daily Life*. Philadelphia: Temple University Press, 2002.

McCarty, Nolan, Keith T. Poole, and Howard Rosenthal. *Polarized America: The Dance of Ideology and Unequal Riches*. Cambridge, MA: MIT Press, 2006.

McCracken, Allison. "Lost." *Flow: A Critical Forum on Television and Media* 1(4) (November 19, 2004).

McCracken, Ellen. *Decoding Women's Magazines: From Mademoiselle to Ms*. New York: St. Martin's Press, 1993.

McElroy, Wendy. "Runaway Bride Lost in Junk Journalism." FoxNews.com May 11, 2005.

McGee, Micki. *Self-Help Inc.: Makeover Culture in American Life*. Oxford: Oxford University Press, 2005.

McGoldrick, Monica. *You Can Go Home Again: Reconnecting with Your Family*. New York: W. W. Norton & Co., 1995.

McHugh, Kathleen. *American Domesticity: From How-to Manual to Hollywood Melodrama*. New York and Oxford: Oxford University Press, 1999.

McKenzie, Evan. *Privatopia: Homeowner Associations and the Rise of Residential Private Government*. New Haven: Yale University Press, 1994.

McLaughlin, Emma and Nicola Kraus. *The Nanny Diaries: A Novel*. New York: St. Martin's Press, 2003.

McLean, Adrienne and David Cook, eds. *Headline Hollywood: A Century of Film Scandal*. New Brunswick, NJ: Rutgers University Press, 2001.

McNair, Brian. *Striptease Culture: Sex, Media and the Democratisation of Desire*. London and New York: Routledge, 2002.

McPherson, Tara. *Reconstructing Dixie: Race, Gender, and Nostalgia in the Imagined South*. Durham: Duke University Press, 2003.

McRobbie, Angela. "Postfeminism and Popular Culture." *Feminist Media Studies* 4(3) (2004).

Mead, Rebecca. *One Perfect Day: The Selling of the American Wedding*. New York: Penguin Press, 2007.

Mendelsohn, Jennifer. "The Bride Wore Blue." *The Washington Post* January 13, 2003, p. C10.

Mendelson, Cheryl. *Home Comforts: The Art and Science of Keeping House*. New York: Scribner, 1999.

Merck, Mandy. "American Pie." In *America First: Naming the Nation in US Film*, ed. Mandy Merck. London: Routledge, 2007, pp. 259–276.

Meyers, Michelle. "Runaway Bride Toast Attracts Auction Bread." CNET.com, May 7, 2005.

"Mom of the Month" http//iparenting/com/moms/3912.php, November 16, 2006.

Montemurro, Beth. *Something Old, Something Bold: Bridal Showers and Bachelorette Parties*. New Brunswick: Rutgers University Press, 2006.

Morley, David. *Home Territories: Media, Mobility and Identity*. London and New York: Routledge, 2000.

Morris, Douglas E. *It's A Sprawl World after All: The Human Cost of Unplanned Growth and Visions of a Better Future*. New York: New Society Publishers, 2005.

Morrison, Mark. "Estate of Their Union." *InStyle* April 2002, pp. 400–409.

Moseley, Rachel. "Having It *Ally*: Popular Television (Post)Feminism." *Feminist Media Studies* 2(2) (2002).

Mutzabaugh, Ben. "Today in the Sky." *USA Today* December 8, 2004.

Negra, Diane. "Romance and/as Tourism: Heritage Whiteness and the (Inter)National Imaginary in the New Woman's Film." In *Keyframes: Popular Cinema and Cultural Studies*, eds Amy Villarejo and Matthew Tinkcom. London: Routledge, 2001, pp. 82–97.

Negra, Diane. "Celebrity Nepotism, Family Values and E Television." *Flow: A Critical Forum on Television and Media* 3(1) (September 2005).

Negra, Diane. "Where the Boys Are: Postfeminism and the New Single Man." *Flow: A Critical Forum on Television and Media* 4(3) (April 2006).

Negra, Diane. "Structural Integrity, Historical Reversion and the Post-9/11 Chick Flick." *Feminist Media Studies* 8(1) (March 2008), pp. 51–68.

Newman, Andrew Adam. "Depilatory Market Moves Far Beyond the Short-Shorts Wearers." *The New York Times* September 14, 2007, p. C3.

Newman, Katherine S. *Falling from Grace: Downward Mobility in the Age of Affluence*. Berkeley: University of California Press, 1999.

"New Retro Look for BA Staff." CNN.International.com, http://edition.cnn.com/2004/TRAVEL/04/05/ba.uniforms.ap/index.html

Newsome, Melba. "Not Just for Kids." *Time* 166(10) (September 5, 2005), pp. W11, W12.

"Nichols to Make Court Appearance Today." March 15, 2005, CNN.com

Nissenbaum, Stephen. "New England as Region and Nation." In *All over the Map: Rethinking American Regions*, eds Edward L. Ayers, Patricia Nelson Limerick, Stephen Nissenbaum, and Peter S. Onuf. Baltimore: Johns Hopkins University Press, 1996.

Nourie, Alan and Barbara, eds. *American Mass-Market Magazines*. New York: Greenwood Press, 1990.

Oake, Jonathan I. "*Reality Bites* and Generation X as Spectator." *The Velvet Light Trap* 53(2004), pp. 83–97.

O'Dell, Tom. "Meditation, Magic and Spiritual Regeneration: Spas and the Mass Production of Serenity." In *Magic, Culture and the New Economy*, eds Orvar Lofgren and Robert Willim. Oxford and New York: Berg, 2005, pp. 19–36.

Ogunnaike, Lola. "Taking a Sour Pleasure as the Rich Turn Sweet 16." *The New York Times* April 26, 2006, pp. B1, B8.

Ohmann, Richard M. *Selling Culture: Magazines, Markets, and Class at the Turn of the Century*. London: Verso, 1996.

Olson, Elizabeth. "Hostesses in Shorts? This Is No Ordinary Flight." *The New York Times* August 19, 2003.

Otnes, Cele C. and Elizabeth H. Pleck. *Cinderella Dreams: The Allure of the Lavish Wedding*. Berkeley: University of California Press, 2003.

Ouellette, Laurie. "Nanny TV." *Flow: A Critical Forum on Television and Media* 1(11) (2005).

Ozment, Katherine. "A Winter of Discontent, then along Comes Baby." *The New York Times* May 14, 2006, p. 9.

Pappano, Laura. *The Connection Gap: Why Americans Feel So Alone*. New Brunswick: Rutgers University Press, 2001.

Park, Peter Yoonsuk. "Smart Bomb, Serial Killing and the Rapture: The Vanishing Bodies of Imperial Apocalypticism." *Postmodern Culture* 15(1) (2003).

Paul, Pamela. *Pornified: How Pornography Is Transforming Our Lives, Our Relationships, and Our Families.* New York: Henry Holt & Co., 2005.

Pearson, Allison. *I Don't Know How She Does It.* New York: Knopf, 2002.

"Pole Dancing Shows up in Health Clubs." *USA Today* February 22, 2004.

Porter, Eduardo. "Stretched to Limit, Women Stall March to Work." NYTimes.com. March 2, 2006.

Postrel, Virginia. *The Substance of Style: How the Rise of Aesthetic Value Is Remaking Commerce, Culture and Consciousness.* New York: Harper Perennial, 2007.

Preston, Catherine L. "Hanging on a Star: The Resurrection of the Romance Film in the 1990s." In *Film Genre 2000: New Critical Essays*, ed. Wheeler Winston Dixon. Albany: SUNY Press, 2000, pp. 227–243.

Projansky, Sarah. *Watching Rape: Film and Television in Postfeminist Culture.* New York: New York University Press, 2001.

Putnam, Robert D. *Bowling Alone: The Collapse and Revival of American Community.* New York: Simon & Schuster, 2000.

Radner, Hilary. "Introduction: Queering the Girl." In *Swinging Single: Representing Sexuality in the 1960s.* Minneapolis: University of Minnesota Press, 1999, pp. 1–35.

Rakoff, David. *Don't Get Too Comfortable.* New York: Doubleday & Co., 2005.

Redmond, Sean. "Intimate Fame Everywhere." In *Framing Celebrity: New Directions in Celebrity Culture*, eds Su Holmes and Sean Redmond. London: Routledge, 2006, pp. 27–43.

Reed, Jennifer. "Beleaguered Husbands and Demanding Wives: The New Domestic Sitcom." *Americana: The American Popular Culture Online Magazine* (October 2003).

Rhode, Deborah L. *Speaking of Sex: The Denial of Gender Inequality.* Cambridge, MA: Harvard University Press, 1997.

Roberts, Selena. "A Heady Apex, but Is a Dead End Just up Ahead?" *The New York Times* May 30, 2005, p. D1.

Robinson, Eugene. "(White) Women We Love." *The Washington Post* June 10, 2005, p. A23.

Roseberry, William. "The Rise of Yuppie Coffees and the Reimagination of Class in the United States." In *The Cultural Politics of Food and Eating: A Reader*, eds James L. Watson and Melissa L. Caldwell. Malden, MA: Blackwell Publishing, 2005, pp. 122–143.

Rothman, Hal. *Neon Metropolis: How Las Vegas Started the Twenty-First Century.* New York: Routledge, 2003.

Rubin, Rita. "Buoyed by Bigger Breasts." *USA Today* December 18, 2006, http://www.usatoday.com/news/health/2006-12-18-breast-implants_x.htm

Safire, William. "On Language: Swelling Toward Motherhood." *The New York Times Magazine* May 14, 2006, p. 22.

Sales, Nancy Jo. "Sex and the Single Mom." *Vanity Fair* 538 (June 2005), pp. 80–88, 145–148.

Santino, Jack. *New Old-Fashioned Ways: Holidays and Popular Culture.* Knoxville: University of Tennessee Press, 1996.

Saporito, Bill. "Inside the New American Home." *Time* 160(16) (October 14, 2002), pp. 64–71, 74–75.

Satterthwaite, Ann. "Shopping: A Public Concern." In *Going Shopping: Consumer Choices and Community Consequences.* New Haven: Yale University Press, 2001, pp. 306–345.

Saul, Stephanie. "Record Sales of Sleep Pills Cause Worry." *The New York Times* February 7, 2006, pp. A1, C4.

Schor, Juliet B. *The Overspent American: Upscaling, Downshifting, and the New Consumer.* New York: Basic Books, 1998.

Schor, Juliet. "What's Wrong with Consumer Society?: Competitive Spending and the 'New Consumerism.'" In *Consuming Desires: Consumption, Culture, and the Pursuit of Happiness*, ed. Roger Rosenblatt. Washington, DC: Island Press, 1999, pp. 37–50.

Schor, Juliet. "The New Politics of Consumption: Why Americans Want So Much More Than They Need." In *Gender, Race, and Class in Media: A Text-Reader.* 2nd edition, eds Gail Dines and Jean M. Humez. Thousand Oaks: Sage, 2003, pp. 183–195.

Schuchardt, Read Mercer. "Understanding Road Rage." *Counterblast: The E-Journal of Culture and Communication* 1(1) November 2001.

Schwabe, Deborah. "Teen Spa Trends: Day Spas Are Becoming Teen Territory." *Associated Content* June 15, 2006.

Scott, Janny. "Life at the Top in America Isn't Just Better, It's Longer." In *Class Matters*, correspondents of *The New York Times.* New York: Henry Holt & Co., 2005, pp. 27–50.

Sennett, Richard. *The Culture of the New Capitalism.* New Haven: Yale University Press, 2006.

Shinseki, Michelle T. "Maternity Photography: A Growing Pregnancy Trend." *Better Homes and Gardens* July 26, 2004.

Sidler, Michelle. "Living in McJobdom: Third Wave Feminism and Class Inequity." In *Third Wave Agenda*, eds Leslie Howard and Jennifer Drake. Minneapolis: University of Minnesota Press, 1997, pp. 25–39.

Silverstein, Michael, Neil Fiske and John Butman. *Trading Up: Why Consumers Want New Luxury Goods . . . and How Companies Create Them.* New York: Portfolio, 2004.

Simon, Jonathan. *Governing through Crime: The War on Crime and the Transformation of America, 1960–2000.* Oxford: Oxford University Press, 2007.

Singer, Natasha. "Not to Be Outdone: The New Urban Spa." *The New York Times* August 11, 2005, p. G3.

Singer, Natasha. "Is the 'Mom Job' Really Necessary?" *The New York Times* October 4, 2007.

Siroto, Janet. "When Two Is Not Enough." *Redbook* October 1998, pp. 168–173.

Sivulka, Juliann. *Soap, Sex, and Cigarettes: A Cultural History of American Advertising.* Belmont, CA: Wadsworth, 1998.

Smith, Dinitia. "Post-Salad-Days Women Agree: They Want 'What She's Having.'" *The New York Times* January 13, 2006, pp. B35, B41.

Smith, Larry. "Hear That Wedding March Often Enough, You Fall in Step." *The New York Times* December 26, 2004, Style section, p. 7.

Spigel, Lynn. "Designing the Smart House: Posthuman Domesticity and Conspicuous Production." *European Journal of Cultural Studies* 8(4) (2005), pp. 403–426.

Springer, Kimberly. "Divas, Evil Black Bitches, and Bitter Black Women: African-American Women in Postfeminist and Post-Civil Rights Popular Culture." In *Interrogating Postfeminism: Gender and the Politics of Popular Culture*, eds Yvonne Tasker and Diane Negra. Durham: Duke University Press, 2007, pp. 249–276.

Stanley, Alessandra. "Revenge of the Underling Becomes a Literary Genre." *The New York Times* June 12, 2002, p. A1.

Steinhauer, Jennifer. "Never Mind Mars and Venus: Who Is 'The Decider?'" *The New York Times* April 26, 2006, pp. A1, A16.

Steinhauer, Jennifer. "When the Joneses Wear Jeans." In *Class Matters*, correspondents of *The New York Times*. New York: Henry Holt & Co., 2005, pp. 134–145.

Stewart, Kathleen. "Trauma Time: A Still Life." In *Histories of the Future*, eds Daniel Rosenberg and Susan Harding. Durham: Duke University Press, 2005, pp. 323–339.

Storper, Michael. "Lived Effects of the Contemporary Economy: Globalization, Inequality, and Consumer Society." In *Millennial Capitalism and the Culture of Neoliberalism*, eds Jean Comaroff and John L. Comaroff. Durham: Duke University Press, 2001.

Strasser, Susan. *Never Done: A History of American Housework*. New York: Owl Books (Henry Holt & Co.), 2000.

Strauss, Gary. "Princesses Rule the Hearts of Little Girls." *USA Today* March 2, 2004, Lifestyle section, pp. 1–2.

Studlar, Gaylyn. "The Perils of Pleasure? Fan Magazine Discourse as Women's Commodified Culture in the 1920s." *Wide Angle* 13(1) (1991), pp. 6–33.

Tahmincioglu, Eve. "Pregnant Workers Filing More Complaints of Bias." *USA Today* September 14, 2003, section 10, pp. 1, 3.

Tally, Margaret. "'She Doesn't Let Age Define Her' Sexuality and Motherhood in Recent 'Middle-Aged Chick Flicks'" *Sexuality & Culture* 10(2) (Spring 2006), pp. 33–55.

Tannen, Deborah. *You're Wearing That?: Understanding Mothers and Daughters in Conversation*. New York: Ballantine Books, 2006.

Tasker, Yvonne and Diane Negra. "Feminist Politics and Postfeminist Culture." In *Interrogating Postfeminism: Gender and the Politics of Popular Culture*, eds Yvonne Tasker and Diane Negra. Durham: Duke University Press, 2007, pp. 1–25.

Thurlow, Crispin and Adam Jaworski. "The Alchemy of the Upwardly Mobile: Symbolic Capital and the Stylization of Elites in Frequent-Flyer Programmes." *Discourse & Society* 17(1) (2006), pp. 99–135.

Tierney, John. "More Respect for Mothers Staying Home." *The New York Times* April 30, 2002, p. A26.

Tincknell, Estella. *Mediating the Family: Gender, Culture and Representation*. London: Hodder Arnold, 2005.

Traister, Rebecca. "Pregnancy Porn." Salon.com July 31, 2004.

Travis, Trysh. "'It Will Change the World if Everybody Reads This Book': New Thought Religion in Oprah's Book Club." *American Quarterly* 59(3) (Autumn 2007), pp. 1017–1041.

Twitchell, James B. *Living It Up: Our Love Affair with Luxury*. New York: Columbia University Press, 2002.

Tyler, Imogen. "The Selfish Feminist: Public Images of Women's Liberation." *Australian Feminist Studies* 22(53) (July 2007), pp. 173–190.

Walker, Rebecca. *Baby Love: Choosing Motherhood after a Lifetime of Ambivalence*. New York: Riverhead Books, 2007.

Walker, Rob. "Girls Just Want to Belong." *The New York Times Magazine* August 21, 2005, p. 22.

Wall, Angela. "Mothers, Monsters and Family Values: Assisted Reproduction and the Aging Natural Body." In *Wild Science: Reading Feminism, Medicine and the Media*, eds Janine Marchessault and Kim Sawchuk. London: Routledge, 2000, pp. 167–181.

Wallis, Claudia. "The Case for Staying Home." *Time* 163(19) May 10, 2004, pp. 46–53.

Warner, Judith. *Perfect Madness: Motherhood in the Age of Anxiety*. New York: Riverhead, 2005.

Wearing, Sadie. "Subjects of Rejuvenation: Aging in Postfeminist Culture and Feminist Critique." In *Interrogating Postfeminism: Gender and the Politics of Popular Culture*, eds Yvonne Tasker and Diane Negra. Durham: Duke University Press, 2007.

Weber, Brenda. "Beauty, Desire and Anxiety: The Economy of Sameness in ABC's *Extreme Makeover*." *Genders* 41 (2005).

Wegenstein, Bernadette. *Getting under the Skin: The Body and Media Theory*. Cambridge, MA: MIT Press, 2006.

Weisberger, Lauren. *The Devil Wears Prada*. New York: Doubleday, 2003.

Weise, Elizabeth. "Traditional Living Takes Modern Spin." *USA Today* October 4, 2006, http://www.usatoday.com/news/religion/22006-10-04-covering_x.htm

Whelehan, Imelda. *Overloaded: Popular Culture and the Future of Feminism*. London: The Woman's Press, 2000.

White, Mimi. "Meanwhile, Back in the Emergency Room . . . Feminism, Aesthetic Form, and Narrative Politics in *Judging Amy*." Paper delivered at Console-ing Passions conference on Television, Video, New Media and Feminism, New Orleans, Louisiana, May 2004.

Willis, Susan. *Portents of the Real: A Primer for Post-9/11 America*. London and New York: Verso, 2005.

Wilson, Craig. "Hooters Is Ready to Say It: 'Fly Me.'" *USA Today* February 27, 2003, p. 11B.

Woodward, Kathleen. *Aging and Its Discontents: Freud and Other Fictions*. Bloomington: Indiana University Press, 1991.

Yagoda, Ben. "My Heart Belongs to 'Mother.'" *The New York Times* May 14, 2006, p. 14.

Yancey, Kitty Bean. "Stripping's New Side." *USA Today* October 27, 2003.

Yee, Daniel. "New Engagement: Runaway Bride Cuts Grass." *Boston Globe* August 10, 2005, p. A3.

Zuckerman, Mary Ellen. *A History of Popular Women's Magazines in the United States, 1792–1995*. Westport, CT: Greenwood Press, 1998.

Zukin, Sharon. *Point of Purchase: How Shopping Changed American Culture*. New York and London: Routledge, 2004.

Index